Library of
Davidson College

U.S. Policy Toward Eastern Europe
and the Soviet Union

U.S. Policy Toward Eastern Europe and the Soviet Union

Selected Essays, 1956–1988

Robert F. Byrnes

Westview Press
BOULDER, SAN FRANCISCO, & LONDON

In Memory of
Stephen D. Kertesz,
Wise Diplomat and Scholar

All rights reserved. No part of this publication may be reproduced or transmitted in any form or by any means, electronic or mechanical, including photocopy, recording, or any information storage and retrieval system, without permission in writing from the publisher.

Copyright © 1989 by Westview Press, Inc.

Published in 1989 in the United States of America by Westview Press, Inc., 5500 Central Avenue, Boulder, Colorado 80301, and in the United Kingdom by Westview Press, Inc., 13 Brunswick Centre, London WC1N 1AF, England

Library of Congress Cataloging-in-Publication Data
Byrnes, Robert Francis.
  U.S. policy toward Eastern Europe and the Soviet Union: Selected Essays, 1956–1988/by Robert F. Byrnes.
    p. cm.
  Includes index.
  ISBN 0-8133-0952-2
  1. Europe, Eastern—Foreign relations—1945–   2. United States—Foreign relations—Soviet Union. 3. Soviet Union—Foreign relations—United States. 4. Soviet Union—Foreign relations—Europe, Eastern. 5. Europe, Eastern—Foreign relations—Soviet Union. 6. United States—Foreign relations—Europe, Eastern. 7. Europe, Eastern—Foreign relations—United States. 8. United States—Foreign relations—1945–   9. Soviet Union—Foreign relations—1945–   I. Title. II. Title: United States policy toward Eastern Europe and the Soviet Union.
DJK50.B97 1989
327.73047—dc20   89-36183
                                                              CIP

Printed and bound in the United States of America

 The paper used in this publication meets the requirements of the American National Standard for Permanence of Paper for Printed Library Materials Z39.48-1984.

Preface

In this volume I have collected for the first time essays of mine published between 1956 and 1988 describing and analyzing American policy toward Eastern Europe and the Soviet Union. Eastern Europe takes precedence over the Soviet Union in the book's title because most Americans define Europe as Western Europe. We fail to appreciate the European character of the peoples and states of Eastern Europe, overlooking the significant role Eastern Europe has played in European history and in international politics, and especially do not recognize the critical role Eastern Europe occupies in Soviet-American relations.

The essays presented here demonstrate how Soviet actions in the last months of World War II and in the years that followed became the immediate and most important cause of tensions between the Soviet Union and the West. I believe that the relationship between the Soviet Union and the West will remain one of fear and distrust until the Soviet Union acquires confidence in itself, withdraws its forces from Eastern European states, and allows the peoples of those nations independence and the right to govern themselves.

George Kennan, who provided the intellectual framework for the policy of containment, and Walter Lippmann, who was a fervent critic of that policy from its first appearance more than forty years ago, agreed with this belief, as do most observers of European history and the Soviet-American relationship. In brief, the essays in this volume are representative of a strand of Western academic thought on one of the central issues of our time.

I have dedicated this volume to Stephen D. Kertesz, a distinguished diplomat who chose a scholarly career in the United States when his country lost its independence. His deep knowledge and good judgment concerning the political character of the Soviet-Western struggle have exercised a profound influence on many Americans.

Robert F. Byrnes
Indiana University, Bloomington

Contents

Introduction: Looking Back ... 1

PART ONE
U.S. AND SOVIET POLICY TOWARD EASTERN EUROPE

1 The Triumph of Containment:
  The Problems of Prosperity ... 15

2 Soviet and Chinese Communist Relations
  with Yugoslavia ... 31

3 Russia in Eastern Europe:
  Hegemony Without Security ... 53

4 United States Policy Toward Eastern Europe:
  Before and After Helsinki ... 65

5 East Central Europe:
  Present Situation and Principal Trends ... 87

PART TWO
THE SOVIET UNION AND THE WEST

6 Russian and Soviet Attitudes Toward the West ... 109

7 Soviet Policy Toward Western Europe Since Stalin ... 133

8 Exchanges of Scholars with the Soviet Union:
  Advantages and Dilemmas ... 149

9 Cultural Exchange and Competition
  Between Societies: An American View ... 169

10 Influencing Soviet Policy
   by Western Trade Restrictions: Some Reflections ... 185

11 The USSR in the 1980s and Beyond ... 195

  Conclusion: Looking Ahead ... 211

Index ... 215

Introduction: Looking Back

As lively members of an open, democratic country, schooled in a critical approach to their society and its shortcomings, Americans are particularly censorious when they consider United States policies toward the outside world. They see only problems and disasters. They conclude that American leaders and diplomats are ill-informed, incompetent defenders of American national interests. They believe that United States behavior in the international area is especially vivid proof of the correctness of one of de Tocqueville's best-known observations:

> It is especially in the conduct of their foreign relations that democracies appear to me decidedly inferior to other governments. ... A democracy can only with great difficulty regulate the details of an important undertaking, persevere in a fixed design, and work out its execution in spite of serious obstacles. It cannot combine its measures with secrecy or await their consequences with patience.

Georges Clemenceau, another great Frenchman, endorsed de Tocqueville, but added that the head of a democratic government allied with other states faced even greater limitations in international relations than de Tocqueville had described. The longer the First World War lasted, the more Clemenceau's admiration for Napoleon declined, as he appreciated the advantages Napoleon had enjoyed as an emperor competing with a shifting series of alliances.

In short, democracy, especially a member of an alliance system that brings together for a common purpose a number of states whose national interests inevitably diverge on occasion, faces excruciating difficulties when it confronts a state whose leader can persevere in his design without regard for his fellow citizens or the interests of associated states.

In spite of the admitted wisdom of these two great French observers of democracy in action and of the criticism and complaining that constitute some of the benign hallmarks of democratic government, any even-handed review of the policy of the United States and its allies toward the Soviet Union and the states of the Eastern half of Europe over the past forty years would have to agree that they have achieved remarkable consistency in purpose, skill in execution, and success in performance against a formidable and determined foe. The United States and its associates have not only avoided nuclear war in the struggle with the USSR, but have so conducted themselves that Soviet leaders have not considered war a wise or necessary choice. We can appreciate this especially if we ponder Adlai Stevenson's observation at the UN Security Council on October 23, 1962:

> I have often wondered what the world would be like today if the situation at the end of the war had been reversed - if the United States had been ravaged and shattered by war, and if the Soviet Union had emerged intact, in exclusive possession of the atomic bomb and overwhelming military and economic might. Would it have followed the same path [as the United States] and devoted itself to realizing the world of the Charter?

Containment has been successful in the main theater. Communism has not advanced in Europe. Indeed, it has slipped in every way. Once powerful communist parties in Western Europe barely remain alive. The peoples of Eastern Europe since the mid-1950s have slowly and gradually reduced the Soviet grip upon their institutions and minds, in spite of the setbacks of 1956 and 1968 and the continued crises and repressions in Poland. The continued "unbinding" of Eastern Europe toward ever greater freedoms, pluralisms, and independence is of course not inevitable, but the pace has quickened each year and seems irreversible.

Within the Soviet Union, the mellowing and moderation that George Kennan thought containment would one day produce is proceeding, to the surprise of foreign observers and that of millions of Soviet citizens as well. Marxism-Leninism has faded even from the vocabulary of Soviet leaders, who now allow more freedoms than previously, encourage Western economic practices, and preach of economic interdependency and the need for cooperation with the former capitalist imperialists. Moreover, the communist wave has receded in Latin America, Africa, and Southwest Asia as the Soviet model of economic growth and Soviet capacity to provide economic assistance have both declined.

The People's Republic of China is further advanced toward a more open society and economy than is the Soviet Union. These powerful states will almost certainly remain authoritarian or despotic, but the changes of the past two decades have turned against what many considered "the wave of the future" only forty years ago.

Ambassador Charles Bohlen, an important contributor to the design and execution of American policy, at the end of his life wrote that "the only hope, and this is a fairly thin one, is that at some point the Soviet Union will begin to act like a country rather than a cause." The transformations Kennan and Bohlen planned and for which millions of others have fought are beginning to occur. Current Soviet domestic policies may fail or be reversed, but successive changes in the Soviet Union and Eastern Europe have left deposits that prevent the systems from reverting to the depths of 1949. Why would any person or any government turn to communism seventy years after the revolution? Who, comparing the recovery of Germany, Japan, and the Soviet Union from the devastations of the Second World War, would choose the Soviet Union as a model?

The fundamentals of American policy toward the Soviet Union and Eastern Europe have been simple. They rest first of all on the maintenance and improvement of the American system of government and of United States spiritual, economic, and military strengths. Its existence as a healthy and strong society has always been at the heart of the American program. Second has been the vision of a peaceful and secure world order, one in which each people should determine its own form of government and cooperate with other peoples in improving the conditions of life of all. The United States and its allies have then joined to restrict the advance of communism, with the highest priority to Western Europe and Japan, by creating such counterforces as to enforce prudence upon Soviet leaders. At great economic and political cost, they have therefore built and maintained military services, including nuclear missile forces, and have been resolute in using these resources whenever necessary. The military assistance provided Greece and Turkey, the Berlin Airlift, and the United Nations response to the invasion of South Korea were early illustrations of that resolution: separated greatly by distance, these actions contributed enormously to the success of American policy in the crucial early days.

Behind these defensive barricades, the United States has assisted in the economic, political, and spiritual recovery of Western Europe and Japan, the twin towers of the containment system, and provided economic assistance, military equipment and political advice to other threatened states, such as Greece and Turkey, and peoples establishing new states. The United States and its allies "held an umbrella" over Yugoslavia in the years after 1948, assisting that communist state to remain independent, inspire leaders of other communist states to give national concerns highest priority, and begin the unraveling of the international communist movement. Ultimately, the Americans recognized the Sino-Soviet rift, established relations with the People's Republic of China, and contributed in another way to reducing Soviet influence in the world.

For forty years, Radio Free Europe and Radio Liberty, the Deutsche Welle, the British Broadcasting Corporation, the Vatican radio services, and other Western government communications facilities have weakened communist state control over information by providing honest accounts and analyses of developments throughout the world. In an age in which knowledge is the most important product, these persistent information programs have maintained a constant link between the peoples under communist rule and the outside world. In fact, the great increase in the level of knowledge about affairs in their own countries and throughout the world from the depths of 1949 to the present peak in 1989 may constitute the most fundamental change that has occurred in these countries.

Above all, the United States and its allies have used the strengths of their political systems and their diplomatic skills to press the Soviet and other communist rulers toward Western political and judicial practices and toward honoring the agreements on human rights they have signed, especially that in Helsinki in 1975. Constant diplomatic pressure over the years, sometimes private and quiet and sometimes public, has gradually edged these governments into adopting more civilized procedures. In this program, the West has used its economic resources shrewdly, not only as a magnet demonstrating to communist governments and the peoples they govern the material advantages of an open society, but also as an instrument of diplomacy. Under the policy of building bridges and of treating each state differently as it advanced toward or moved away from democratic practices, the West has strengthened the liberalizing forces in these governments. The increased access to Western resources that the more liberal governments have received has led to greater openness and receptivity to change in these states, demonstrating to the more laggardly ones the high cost of remaining isolated and Stalinist, and gradually edging all but Rumania toward more responsible and civilized behavior.

Finally, American successes reflect quiet strengths that no communist state possesses; the resources and initiatives of individuals, religious organizations, universities, churches, foundations, and private business concerns. Christian churches and Jewish communities have maintained contact with believers through even the most difficult periods. They have provided spiritual and material assistance to threatened religious organizations, sustaining their spirit and aiding them quietly to retain ties with the outside world. The Ford Foundation in the 1950s began to provide fellowships enabling highly qualified scholars to continue their study in Western libraries and laboratories, especially in the United States. The Rockefeller Foundation and similar private organizations established programs that have assisted hospitals, research organizations, universities, and even private farms. American universities have invited graduate students and established scholars for long periods of research, refurbished libraries and laboratories, and helped establish centers for American studies and for business administration. Academic exchange programs begun in 1958 with the Soviet Union and extended into Eastern Europe in 1962 have enlarged American knowledge and understanding, established a visible Western presence in central intellectual institutions, and opened a door to the outside world for a significant part of the future elite. The principal consequences of their ventures have been the almost invisible advances that education contributes but that become increasingly powerful as years pass. The most visible fruits appeared in the Czechoslovak Government in 1968 and in the Gorbachev administration, because alumni of these programs helped change the entire climate of opinion in the ruling class and even occupied prominent state positions.

In short, over the years the United States has relied increasingly upon the vigor of American economic and cultural life to bring about beneficial changes in Eastern Europe and the Soviet Union. In 1949, the West could use only radios and balloons to communicate with the East. Modern science and technology and the exuberance of the West, especially compared with "the silence of Russian culture," have added another dimension to containment. The West has thus moved the competition from the military field to an economic and cultural rivalry in which it possesses and uses overwhelming superiority. In this test of strengths, the Soviet Union simply lacks resources: jazz and jeans, hamburgers and computers, movies and higher education, miniature electronics and hybrid corn, and the freedoms that produce this cornucopia have triumphed over Soviet military strengths.

Since the Truman Plan in 1947 and the Marshall Plan in 1948, American policy toward the Soviet Union has been remarkably consistent. The rhetoric of American statesmen has gone through great gyrations, to the discomfiture of American friends and the alarm of its enemies, because at various times American leaders have advocated containment, liberation, rollback, building bridges, detente, and a crusade against an evil empire. Respected Americans have on occasion urged that the United States withdraw its troops from Western Europe. Mr. Kennan has been especially mercurial. In the spring of 1956, he was so pessimistic that he wrote that "there is a finality, for better or worse, about what has happened in Eastern Europe." Six months later, he saw an "extensive disintegration of Moscow's authority within the Soviet orbit." In 1958, in a celebrated series of lectures in England, he declared the principal cause of tensions the presence of large armed forces confronting each other in Central Europe. Withdrawing these forces, or "disengagement," therefore became the solution. More recently, his savage criticisms of American life, institutions, and values have suggested that the United States possessed no qualities that justify an important role in international affairs.

Most observers devote more attention to the dramatic incidents and the failures that mark Soviet-American relations than to the economic, political, cultural, and military measures that lie at the heart of American policy and achievements. The failure of the European states to form a political union and united military forces in the first half of the 1950s was a vivid loss, although almost invincible historical forces guaranteed that defeat then. Western inability to help when revolts broke out in 1956 in Eastern Germany, Poland, and Hungary, similar inaction when the Berlin Wall was constructed in 1961, and passive observation of the brutal crushing of the Prague Spring suggested that containment was a failure and that the peoples of Eastern Europe were doomed. Presumably, that area would remain a Soviet pistol pointed at the head of Western Europe, which would sooner or later, somehow or other, fall into Soviet hands. Moreover, the West has not been able to provide significant help to the Polish people in their continued efforts to obtain a more free, civilized, and prosperous life.

In addition, while American policy has been coherent and on balance successful, the United States has erred and bungled on many occasions, as de Tocqueville recognized democracies would. Most Americans have recognized that the Soviet-American struggle is a political one between two greatly different societies and political philosophies. However, the United States has drifted in and out of an overemphasis upon military forces and expenditures that has strained its resources, often alarmed its friends, and increased a Soviet fear already powerful in 1945. Americans have underestimated the significance of the nationalist component of communist movements. Some of its leaders and especially of its intellectuals have lost their will and their faith in their country and even in democracy under the strain of the long confrontation. The skill and charm with which various Soviet leaders have suggested that the tensions had no fundamental cause have produced a number of "summer soldiers and sunshine patriots.

"McCarthyism disfigured the American life and image at one period, as so-called revisionist scholars and "the culture of appeasement" have at other longer times. The rhetoric of American leaders has often alarmed United States allies, who have had cause to worry also because of the constitutional crisis during the Nixon presidency, the serious spiritual and social problems that afflict American society in the 1980s, and, in recent years, budget and trade deficits. The Bay of Pigs was only the first of a series of disasters in Central America. American actions in Viet Nam over a tortured fifteen years not only divided the American public and embittered public life, but also created fissures between the United States and its friends. Some of the actions of the Central Intelligence Agency have raised doubts about American reliability, integrity, and even basic decency. These incidents have led millions around the world to conclude that no difference exists between communist and democratic systems and that the contest is only a meaningless and destructive great power rivalry. Indeed, by the 1980s anti-Americanism was a powerful force in many parts of the world - but not in Eastern Europe or the Soviet Union.

On the other hand, this troubled democratic state at the head of an alliance system has probably committed fewer errors than have the Soviet leaders. In 1989, the Soviet system and empire have proved far less capable than the United States and its allies in maintaining internal cohesion and strength. Soviet policies toward the economy, the national groups, and the distribution of resources among various sectors of the economy and social classes have visibly failed, as Mr. Gorbachev and his supporters loudly acknowledge. Briefly, Soviet domestic problems are even greater than those of the United States.

Soviet leaders, from Stalin through Gorbachev, have erred as Hitler did in misunderstanding the strengths and weaknesses of democracy and of American policy. Indeed, their failures have been even greater than the mistakes Americans have made in comprehending the Soviet system. Stalin had only to delay his attempt to absorb Eastern Europe for two or three years before the United States would have withdrawn its forces from Europe, as Mr. Roosevelt had told Stalin we would, and allowed Soviet access to all of Europe.

Soviet control over Eastern Europe has proved a colossal and costly error in many ways, turning peoples grateful for liberation from the Nazis into bitter and expensive opponents of the Soviet Union and of their communist rulers, and awakening the world to the nature and ambitions of the Soviet system. Engaging in a world-wide competition with the United States and the states that joined it in self-defense was folly for a country as backward economically as the Soviet Union: the Soviet leaders, at great human cost and deprivation, have themselves created the exhaustion that weakens their system today. The effort of this military giant but economic pygmy to expand its empire into Central America, Africa, and Southeast Asia has created colossal over-expansion and acute indigestion. Soviet policies toward Yugoslavia, the People's Republic of China, Israel, Egypt, and Australia at different times represent only a few of the disastrous moves the authoritarian leaders have taken. Some Soviet statesmen must wonder on occasion why they did not establish a commonwealth, as they announced they would in 1956, why they did not estimate correctly the capacities for growth of the Soviet and other economies, and why they misunderstood the power of nationalism.

The achievements of the United States since 1945 have been impressive, especially when one recognizes that the United States was inexperienced, ignorant, and totally unprepared for the responsibilities that fell upon it. It had only twelve professors of Russian history in 1940, and the Secretary of State negotiating the Italian peace treaty did not know the location of the Tyrol. Neither its leaders nor its informed public understood the nature of the Soviet system. The United States throughout the war had appeased the Soviet Union in the hope that repeated demonstrations of generosity and good will would ward off disagreements. Moreover, it entrusted the United Nations with the resolution of any troubles that should arise.

The situation the United States faced in 1945 was desperate. In the words of Raymond J. Sontag, Europe was "a broken world," barely alive after a murderous civil war, its economic structures smashed, its populations dislocated, its civil and international relations poisoned by hatreds, its empires gone or melting, and its self-confidence and will to survive almost destroyed. Communist parties were large, enthusiastic, and well-organized, and intellectuals such as Sartre provided support and respectability. Violence and tragedy dominated the public mind. Changes of every kind were succeeding each other in a world that seemed confused and meaningless. The atomic bomb hung over everyone, threatening the survival of human life. Some American leaders, with some justification, concluded that Europe was beyond repair and that the United States should withdraw to the Western hemisphere. One of these men was the father of the president who fifteen years later declared, "let every nation know, whether it wishes us well or ill, that we shall pay any price, bear any burden, meet any hardship, support any friend, oppose any foe, to assure the survival and success of liberty."

In Europe, the center of the world until 1939, the Soviet Union violated its various agreements with its allies concerning Eastern Europe, seized full authority over the governments and peoples of that part of the world, and began to transform those societies into satellites. The "iron curtain" was such a complete shield that the United States and its European associates could communicate with the peoples of Eastern Europe only by radio and by floating balloons into that area on prevailing westerly winds. The Soviet leaders, in part because of the grip Marxism-Leninism exercised upon their minds, believed that the iron law of history meant inevitable conflict with the capitalist world. This conviction that war was inevitable had roots as well in history and in Soviet fear of American economic and military power, the attractive opportunities for communism that the broken world offered, and Stalin's paranoia and ambition. The Soviet Government therefore manipulated communist parties in Western Europe, probed in the Middle East and Far East when it recognized opportunities, and created chaos and instability everywhere to advance its interests. Each effort of the United States, and then of the allied states, to restrict the spread of the communist system, to build containing walls, and to eliminate the economic and social ills on which radicalisms grew increased fear and uncertainty in Stalin's mind. This led to an arms race and tense tests of will in such parts of the world as Greece and Turkey, Berlin, Yugoslavia, Korea, Taiwan, and Cuba.

In 1989, the United States Government confronts serious domestic problems, ranging from the apparent permanency of a large group unable to break free from poverty, the ravages of widespread use of drugs, the collapse of old moral standards, a large budget deficit, and some inability to compete effectively on the world market. The American people, like those in all democracies at all times, are confused and divided concerning the policies the government should adopt to resolve these problems. In the international arena, the United States and its allies in Europe and in Northeast Asia disagree over trade policies, contributions to mutual defense, the nature of the changes taking place in the Soviet Union, and the likelihood that Gorbachev will survive and succeed. In the larger world, Central America, the Middle East, South Africa, terrorism, ecology, the ozone, and of course control of nuclear, chemical, and other weapons constitute only the major issues on which disagreements fester. Those dismayed by these problems and the fumbling efforts to face and resolve them should keep in perspective that issues such as these, like poverty, will presumably always be with us. Basically, the United States and the West are in sound condition. Above all, the past forty years, with all their advances and retreats, triumphs and tragedies, have produced significant progress toward the goal upon which the supporters and the critics agreed in 1947, the gradual reduction of Soviet authority over the peoples of Eastern Europe and, ultimately, the withdrawal of Soviet military forces from that area.

All observers, Soviet and foreign as well, would agree that the Soviet Government faces critical domestic problems and may not succeed in resolving them. Marxism-Leninism and Soviet nationalism have together lost the grip they once exercised over the Soviet mind. The young in particular have turned away from the old faiths. The economy is so stagnant and ineffective in meeting national needs that the government has turned against the command approach it venerated for half a century and turned toward Western models and practices to rejuvenate it. In addition, the scientific and technological revolutions that have transformed Western economies in the last two decades, and that have given South Korea and other small countries enormous growth rates, have widened the gap between the Soviet Union and its rivals and even "new" states. The Soviet Union cannot hope to attain the new level in this wave of the industrial revolution without substantial aid from the outside world. Moreover, there is no certainty that even full access to the wealth of the West would enable the Soviet economy to achieve the great transformation, because Gorbachev's restructuring does not touch the political system at the heart of Soviet backwardness.

In addition, Gorbachev's efforts to rejuvenate the economy by allowing openness and encouraging initiative have created a host of dangerous new difficulties. They have let loose a torrent of revelations about the Soviet past that raise increasing popular doubts about the state's legitimacy. Encouraging intellectual curiosity and independence constitutes a serious hazard in a society based on faith and discipline. The new thaw has also led to pressure from national and religious groups, often combined, in cooperation with intellectuals, consumers, and those opposed to pollution, to take political advantage of the limited popular participation in national government that the government has granted. These domestic policies, the announced reductions in Soviet armed forces, and the diplomatic initiatives designed to conceal basic Soviet weaknesses indicate that the Soviet Union has been forced to direct its attention inward, to divert resources from the empire and the outside world to critical domestic problems. They have also encouraged a process that could easily grow out of control. On one hand, they have excited appetites that were dormant. On the other hand, they have aroused conservatives who conclude that these changes, any changes, are hazardous, even suicidal. In short, they have indicated the validity of another de Tocqueville thesis: the most perilous situation for a despotic government is when it seeks to reform.

The skill and charm with which the Gorbachev administration conducts its foreign policy help conceal the character of Soviet domestic problems. They also distract the world to some degree from the slow, gradual disintegration of Soviet authority over the governments and peoples of Eastern Europe, where almost unbelievable changes are taking place daily, especially in Poland and Hungary. These transformations are more advanced in some countries than others, but they are growing everywhere. Indeed, the different rates of change and the varieties of policy indicate that the Soviet effort to transform the peoples of Eastern Europe upon the Soviet model have failed dismally and that the diversities that have marked this area of the world are returning. Even in Albania, some pressures have risen to modify the economy and the political system and to rejoin Europe and the world.

Fundamentally, the East European peoples are pressing for ever greater freedom to worship, to speak, to travel, and to govern themselves. Freer expression has produced solid evidence of Soviet actions in 1939 and at Katyn in 1940 that undermine Soviet credibility and destroy the legitimacy of the Soviet position in the Baltic states and throughout Eastern Europe. The same kind of openness that has produced revelations about Stalin and Stalinism began earlier in Poland and in Hungary than in the Soviet Union, has proceeded further, and has weakened the hegemony of the local communist rulers as well as of the Soviet Union. In Hungary and Poland in particular, powerful pressures from workers, peasants, intellectuals, churches, and students have combined with these governments' recognition of their inability to resolve massive economic problems without popular support to produce formal acceptance of non-communist political groups and the election of parliaments. The ruling groups are assured at least temporary dominance, the elections are indirect and weighted, and the authority of the parliaments is limited. However, these advances are part of a continuing process, one in which the balance of strength is gradually moving away from the communists.

Gorbachev's concentration upon the Soviet Union and his toleration of increased freedoms have contributed to the recent advances, as has the recognition by East European rulers that they too need popular support to rescue their economies from forty years of misrule. However, the internal changes taking place within these states and their increasing turn toward the West rest upon hard-fought advances achieved in earlier years, even by the apparent failures of 1956 and 1968. These peoples themselves have been most responsible for their progress, turning to national traditions, values, and religions in their keen determination to regain their independence. They have benefited from the modernized economies the communists have promoted, the rapid expansion of education, especially higher education, and the creation of new classes. They have also shown good sense and remarkable moderation, destroying the American myth that they were romantic and unsuccessful revolutionaries. The determination of these peoples to rule themselves, the moderation that Solidarity has demonstrated for more than two decades, the emphasis upon peaceful change that one finds in Charter 77, and the willingness of the Hungarians to cooperate with their rulers in the peaceful and slow dismantling of the system all have contributed to impressive progress over a tragic three decades.

But one should also recognize the Western contribution to this series of changes. The simple existence of Western Europe and the United States has given these peoples hope that they too would one day enjoy independence and liberties. The unsuccessful struggle the United States fought during the years Stalin was consolidating Soviet control did not discourage, but encouraged these peoples. The remarkable economic, political, and spiritual recovery of Western Europe was a stimulant. The transformations of Spain, Portugal, Greece, and Turkey from dictatorships to democracies persuaded East Europeans that they might effect similar change and also join the Common Market. The friendship and alliance between Germany and France, the establishment and achievements of NATO and other European and international institutions, and above all the Common Market have made Western Europe a sunflower, a magnet for the Europeans to the east. The 1992 target for the Common Market excites East Europeans as it does West Europeans. Communist leaders recognize that they must quickly revise their political systems, improve their economies, and establish close relations with the Common Market if they are to retain any hope of becoming modern states.

The American role has been critical. If the United States had returned to isolation, Europeans would have considered themselves doomed sooner or later to communist rule. With all its lurches and shortcomings, over the years since 1945 United States policy has combined firmness, generosity, and tact in its European policy. Its existence, its resolution, and its vitality in every field of activity have kept the winds of freedom blowing into the Soviet Union and Eastern Europe.

American emphasis upon freedom, science, and growth has been an essential component in the scientific and technological revolutions that have changed every aspect of human life, beginning with the economic base. The enormous advances in health care, architecture, clothing design, transportation, agricultural production, food distribution, miniature electronics, telecommunications, computer technology, and every other aspect of economic life have put the United States, Western Europe, and

Japan upon a totally different economic base. They have also placed pressure on the Soviet Union to follow. They have created the same stimulation to "catch up" or overtake and surpass that drove Peter the Great and Stalin. Finally, the technetronic age or the age of information in which the West thrives has penetrated and essentially destroyed the controls over information and peoples' minds at the heart of the Soviet system. The various cultural exchange programs, now more than thirty years old, and the opening of the Soviet world to increased information through academic exchange programs, radio, television, VCRs, telephone communications, summits, tourists, roundtables - all these instruments and many others - have helped slowly to melt the controls and to bring the Soviet world closer to its neighbors, into the world from which its rulers have tried to isolate it.

Looking back four decades, one finds that great changes have occurred within each East European country and in the relations between each of them and the Soviet Union. They are reversible, but the price of restricting present arrangements would be high: it would raise the high likelihood of revolts and would demolish the good will that Gorbachev's program and style have created: not even the most insensate ruler is likely to undertake such a step. The collapse of Marxism-Leninism as a philosophical base, the irrelevance of the Soviet system as an economic and political model, the "unbinding" of the Soviet Union and its controls, the increasing Westernization of these peoples in a shrinking world, and the rising level of knowledge suggest that the East European peoples, and probably the Soviet peoples as well, are entering a new stage, dismantling the shackles, and slowly returning to Europe. American policy and resolution have contributed greatly to this peaceful achievement.

PART ONE

U.S. and Soviet Policy Toward Eastern Europe

1

The Triumph of Containment: The Problems of Prosperity

American policy toward East Central Europe has undergone a number of revolutions since the beginning of the twentieth century, when the tensions between the great powers and among the various nationalities there first attracted the attention of informed Americans. In 1914, when the First World War erupted in Eastern Europe, Americans were almost totally ignorant of that part of the world and lacked a clear and coherent policy toward it. United States policy during the last years of the First World War and at the Congress of Versailles in 1919 was shaped by this remarkable ignorance. Indeed, one of the principal reasons for the failure of the Versailles Treaty was that some of its provisions reflected the gross lack of knowledge of American representatives at Versailles and of leaders in Washington. After the First World War, this part of the world dropped back into darkness as far as the United States was concerned, and Americans became interested again only during the late 1930s, when Hitler directed the attention of the Nazi state to that area and when war ultimately broke out there in September 1939.

Throughout the course of the Second World War, the American Government and the American people operated on the assumption that the Grand Alliance needed only to defeat the Germans and the Japanese and their allies in order to remove the causes of the Second World War and to insure some kind of durable peace to the world. America, therefore, concentrated on winning the war, paying very little attention to the political causes of the war or to the political problems which would appear at its end. Indeed, during the last year or two of the war, President Roosevelt and other American leaders assumed that the Soviet Union and England would emerge from the war as rival contenders and that the United States should seek to serve as a middleman or honest broker between the two. The United States, therefore, even refused to take part in some of the discussions concerning the postwar future of Eastern Europe. The principal exception to the policy of aloofness toward what was considered the conflict between England and the Soviet Union was the emphasis upon the United Nations, the new league of states designed to study and to resolve any problems which could not be resolved immediately after the war was over.

Reprinted with permission from *New Horizons for the United States in World Affairs,* Sydney N. Fisher, ed. (Columbus, Ohio: Ohio State University Press, 1966), 57-79.

During the first year or two after the war, the American Government and the American people followed a policy which one can properly call appeasement. Basically, the United States was determined to demonstrate to the Soviet Government that she had nothing but friendship for it, that she thoroughly appreciated the magnificent contributions of the Russian people to victory over the Nazis, and that she understood that they had a legitimate interest concerning the areas on their western borders across which the Nazis had attacked. Therefore, the United States protested only mildly and feebly over the Soviet violations of the various agreements and peace treaties which were made after the war.

Appeasement was finally replaced in the spring of 1947 by a policy which has since that time been called containment. Secretary of State George C. Marshall and George Kennan, who were the architects of that policy, both realized by the spring of 1947 that Soviet power had spread into Eastern Europe and was threatening Western Europe and the eastern edges of the Mediterranean Sea. To meet this oppressive threat, Kennan outlined a program for containing Soviet expansive tendencies "with unalterable counterforce at every point where they [the Russians] show signs of encroaching on the interests of a peaceful and stable world." He believed that the policy of containing the Soviet Union within the territories then under her control, particularly when carried out by an alert, healthy, civilized, and united group of Western states, would "increase enormously the strains under which Soviet policy must operate, to force upon the Kremlin a far greater degree of moderation and circumspection than it has had to observe in recent years, and in this way to promote tendencies which must eventually find their outlet in either the breakup or the gradual mellowing of Soviet power."

The policy enunciated by Kennan and put into effect by Secretary Marshall and President Truman has been the basic program for the United States toward the Soviet Union and Eastern Europe since 1947. It has been maintained by massive increases of American and West European military and economic strength, by a splendid program under which Western Europe has recovered first its economic and then its political and spiritual vitality, and by various treaties and agreements which have introduced a considerable amount of unity into the policies of the principal states of the Free World. The principal organization reflecting this new-found unity is the North Atlantic Treaty Organization, or NATO, which has become the armed umbrella under which Western Europe has been freed from the Soviet threat and from which in fact there now emanates a magnetic attraction for the countries in Eastern Europe under Soviet control.

The West's growing strength and unity have enabled it to make more effective use of diplomacy than it had exercised in its earlier efforts to cope with the Soviet Union. Probably the principal area in which Western diplomacy has been effective has been Yugoslavia, which was ousted from the Cominform in June 1948, and where the Western states have showed extraordinary skill in treating the "successful heretic," Marshal Tito. In other words, Western economic and military assistance has enabled Tito to maintain the unity and coherence of Yugoslavia and to defend his independence against the various pressures which the Soviet Union and her agents have been able to exert upon him. Western relations with Tito have not been uniformly friendly, but Western diplomacy has been exercised with such skill and restraint that Yugoslavia has been able to emerge as an independent state, serving therefore as an example to other communist states of what vigorous national leadership can achieve and of the probable American and Western reaction toward states which do break away from Soviet rule. The very existence of Tito's Yugoslavia has created serious problems for the Soviet Union in Eastern Europe and among communist parties elsewhere as well.

The emergence of Yugoslavia as an independent communist state has been one of the principal achievements of the policy of containment. The survival of Greece, which was almost overwhelmed in 1947 by civil war fanned from the outside, is another principal achievement. Indeed, the occasional agreements among Greece, Yugoslavia, and Turkey and the relative stability of that part of the world have been among the principal gains from the containment policy.

More importantly, perhaps, the communist threat to western Europe has completely disintegrated and evaporated since 1947. Western Europe has recovered its economic and political strength and has achieved far more spiritual and political unity than anyone would have dreamed possible in 1945. In addition, Western Europe has become again a central area in world politics. This astonishing advance has given hope to the peoples of Eastern Europe that they may one day achieve the political arrangements and the economic prosperity that their Western neighbors now enjoy.

Remarkable though the achievements of containment were by 1952, a great deal of dissatisfaction in the United States existed because of its various failures. When Americans looked at Eastern Europe, for example, they noted that the Soviet Union had achieved full authority or what Lenin used to call the commanding heights. Indeed, they realized that the Soviet Union was heavily engaged in reshaping the cultural values of the conquered peoples, developing a heavy industrial base in each country, tightening Soviet control over the police and armed forces, promoting agricultural collectivization, exploiting the area efficiently, and using all of Eastern Europe as an instrument of pressure against Western Europe and Yugoslavia. Moreover, the creation of the puppet "people's democracies," by the Soviet Union in Eastern Europe, and the seizure of control over the mainland of China by the Chinese communists led to the belief among communists and among many opposed to communism that communism did, in fact, represent the wave of the future. In other words, Soviet successes in Eastern Europe and communist success in China strengthened the conviction of the communist fanatics and tended to weaken the will of those who were in opposition.

Finally, of course, Soviet control of Eastern Europe, particularly of East Germany, divided the great continent of Europe and gave the Soviet Union a veto on any solution to the unification of Germany.

Soviet control was so great in the early 1950s and information within Eastern Europe about developments in the rest of the world was so fragmentary that the Western Allies were driven to the incredible tactic of trying to float balloons into Eastern Europe, particularly Czechoslovakia and

Poland, from various positions in Western Europe, using the winds to carry the balloons over occupied territory, where mechanical or chemical devices loosed leaflets upon the isolated peoples below.

The apparent failure of containment to help free the peoples of Eastern Europe from Soviet control led to such dissatisfaction by 1952 that General Eisenhower was elected to the presidency of the United States in part because of his statements and those of his future Secretary of State, John Foster Dulles, concerning a "new positive foreign policy" and a program for the liberation of the captive peoples. During the summer and fall of 1952, there was a great deal of talk by responsible American leaders about liberation, roll back, and an aggressive foreign policy. Liberation remained the slogan of the Republican Party and the Eisenhower administration until the summer of 1954, when it was quietly abandoned and replaced again by the older containment policy.

The popularity of the idea of liberation during these two years in the United States can be explained not only by the extended Soviet control over Eastern Europe, but by other important factors as well. The success of the Chinese communists by late 1949 was a massive blow to the entire policy of containment, one which could be easily explained because the American Government had wisely concentrated upon Europe, but one which nevertheless excited rage among many Americans. Moreover, by the summer of 1952 the United States had been involved for two years in a very costly war in Korea, one fought under the banner of the United Nations, but one which the Americans for the first time in their history did not bring to a successful conclusion. The Korean War, the rebuilding of American military strength, and American economic and military assistance to the states of Western Europe and to peoples of other parts of the world constituted an enormously expensive program, and the American taxpayer by the summer of 1952 resented its extraordinary cost. Moreover, these costs seemed particularly paradoxical at a time when the United States was the strongest military power in the world, and when she still possessed overwhelming superiority in the nuclear field. The inability of the American Government to use its military and economic might to attain its goals helped lead to a sense of bafflement and dismay, and therefore to the flirtation with liberation and with a positive foreign policy. Generally this was believed to mean increased application of external pressure upon the Soviet system in order to hasten its collapse and thereby hurry the emancipation of the peoples under Soviet domination.

President Eisenhower, Secretary Dulles, and the American people in general learned within two years that liberation was not a possible policy, if only because it might lead to a third world war. Therefore, the program was quietly abandoned. These two years, however, had a very unfortunate impact upon American policy and upon the image of the United States held by peoples in other parts of the world. Aggressive American talk, for example, enabled the Soviet leaders to portray the United States as an aggressive and militaristic country. Such talk consequently frightened American allies and millions of neutrals, while having no impact whatsoever within the system, except that these noisy doctrines did persuade even many communists that the American state was in fact a militant one. The prominence of Senator McCarthy in the United States at this same time gave some substance to anti-American charges that the United States was becoming a fascist system with the same kind of aggressive policies that Hitler had followed ten years earlier.

The death of Stalin in March 1953, set in motion a series of events in Soviet and world politics which helped lead to the quiet abandonment of liberation, brought a new series of achievements or triumphs to the policy of containment, and ultimately led to a very serious crisis in world affairs in October and November 1956. The men who succeeded Stalin began by describing their system as one of "collective leadership," but Khrushchev within two years had emerged as the dictator of Russia. Both the collective leaders of the first year or two and Khrushchev were quite eager to divest themselves of any connection with Stalin and Stalinism, and they therefore launched a number of programs within the Soviet Union, within the area dominated by Soviet power, and within Soviet foreign policy which ultimately created a great crisis for Khrushchev and his colleagues.

The "relaxation of tensions," the so-called new course for Eastern Europe, and the general thaw which followed Stalin's death led Khrushchev and his principal colleagues to visit Belgrade on May 26, 1955, to confess to Tito that he had wrongfully been discharged from the Cominform in 1948 and to urge him in a penitential way to return to the international communist movement. This extraordinary visit to Canossa and the other changes in Soviet policy were culminated by the Twentieth Congress of the Soviet Communist Party in 1956, a congress in which Khrushchev enunciated the doctrines that war is not inevitable, that communists can use peaceful means in democratic states to attain rule, and that there are various roads to socialism. He thereby destroyed the principle that there was only one road and that that road had to be defined by the Soviet Party. Khrushchev also attacked Stalin in a particularly vigorous way for many military and economic disasters, for the death of many leading communists, and for causing the 1948 break with Tito.

The new doctrinal innovations and the de-Stalinization program which Khrushchev launched let loose a chain reaction throughout the international communist system which brought it to a crisis that summer and fall. The crisis began with revolts or uprisings in Poznan and then spread to a skillfully conducted "palace revolt" in Poland late that summer and to a violent revolt in October and November by Hungary against Soviet rule.

The Polish revolt against the communists was remarkably successful; indeed, it was the only successful revolt that the Poles have been able to carry out in modern times. The first steps included the removal of many Soviet officers and advisers, notably Marshal Rokossovsky as Minister of Defense; the elimination of many Stalinists from important positions in the party and the government; and the release of Cardinal Wyszinski from prison and the almost immediate negotiation of a treaty between the Polish state and the Catholic Church, freeing the church from many controls and allowing again the introduction of religious education. Finally, in Moscow on November 18, 1956, an agreement was signed between the Polish and Russian Governments which recognized the full independence and integrity of Poland, promised that the Soviet Union would not interfere in Polish domestic affairs, and began the reorganization of all the political and economic arrangements between Poland and Russia.

The Hungarians were neither so skilful nor so lucky, and the Hungarian revolt was crushed in very bloody fashion in November 1956, while the world looked on in horror. Unfortunately for the Hungarian people and for the peoples of Europe, the Eisenhower administration and the NATO countries were unable to provide any effective assistance in November 1956, to the embattled Hungarians. They sought the withdrawal of all Russian troops from Hungary, equal relations between Hungary and the Soviet Union, Hungarian withdrawal from the Warsaw Pact, neutrality under UN protection, and the end of the communist political monopoly and of collectivization. Even though the American Government had earlier talked about liberation, the 1956 crisis revealed that the language had been only rhetoric and that no preparations whatsoever had been made to assist people such as the Hungarians who tried to fight their way free. In fact, in the spring of 1956 even Ambassador Kennan, the man who created the philosophy of the containment program, had lost hope and had written that there was a "finality, for better or worse, about what has happened in Eastern Europe." The platforms of both the major American political parties prepared and approved in the late summer of 1956 were quiet on Eastern Europe, urging only "that the spirit of freedom be kept alive." Ambassador Kennan in October wrote that there had been "extensive disintegration of Moscow's authority in the Soviet bloc." However, his spring view reflected those of the American Government, and even those who advocated liberation were caught by surprise by the "extensive disintegration" and by the "sudden upthrust of liberty" which the Poles and the Hungarians had so dramatically demonstrated.

Even though the Western powers were inactive and even though the revolt in Hungary had been brutally and effectively crushed, most Western observers considered that the events of 1956 were political disasters of the first magnitude for the Soviet Union. Some wrote that the disintegration of the communist empire was beginning. Others called it a mark of the military power and spiritual weakness of the Soviet system. Others were impressed that the darlings of the communists, the workers, the intellectuals, and the students, had turned against the system, thus proving that the power and influence of communism had been exaggerated. The value of the disloyal area to the Soviet Union was put in question by the 1956 revolts, and the communist movement outside of communist countries suffered a kind of spiritual crisis because of 1956.

However, the Eisenhower administration, the American people, and their allies after 1956 returned to the defensive and reactive policy which they had in fact adopted again in the summer of 1954. The main emphasis of Western policy after 1956 was upon containment, upon strengthening the areas of the world most susceptible to communist pressure, upon persuading the communist rulers that the Western states would resist expansion, by war if necessary, but would not attack the communist states, and upon some effort to direct all of the energies of the communists and of the rest of the world toward a peaceful solution to the problems which threatened the peace of the world.

In fact, some Western leaders, including Ambassador Kennan himself, several members of the British Labour party, various continental socialists, and a number of European intellectuals, in 1957 and 1958 were much impressed by a new doctrine called disengagement, which suggested creating a "thinned-out zone" or a "mutual withdrawal from the heart of Europe in order to reduce tension and armament." Thus, Western and Soviet troops should move away from the line which separated them in East Central Europe, with the Western forces possibly evacuating all of West Germany and the Soviet troops moving back from East Germany and Czechoslovakia. The disengagement thesis was based on the belief that the real dangers which faced the world resulted from the confrontation of the rival armies in Central Europe and on the assumption that moving these armies back or disengaging them from each other would reduce the tensions. It assumed also that the Soviet Union would and could safely withdraw her forces from East Germany, Poland, and Hungary, surely an assumption no Soviet leader would support. Indeed, many critics noted that disengagement would create a vacuum and a neutral Germany living in great uncertainty and tension.

Above all, the disengagement thesis reflected the belief that the division of Europe was "a dangerous and unsatisfactory situation from everyone's standpoint" and that the Western powers could do little to change it. Indeed, Kennan wrote:

> If things go on as they are today, there will simply have to be some sort of adjustment on the part of the peoples of Eastern Europe, even if it is one that takes the form of general despair, apathy, demoralization, and the deepest sort of disillusion with the West. The failure of the recent popular uprisings to shake the Soviet military domination has now produced a bitter and dangerous despondency throughout large parts of Eastern Europe. If the taste or even the hope of independence once dies out in the hearts of these peoples, then there will be no recovering it; then Moscow's victory will be complete ...[1]

While Kennan and some other Western statesmen lost faith and urged disengagement, Khrushchev and other Soviet leaders took advantage of the West's indecision and this flirtation with a new appeasement to direct a remarkable recovery from the disasters of 1956. The Soviet economy and the economies of East European states continued to grow at the rapid rate begun earlier. Moreover, and perhaps most strikingly so far as the rest of the world was concerned, Soviet science and technology provided the Soviet system with an extraordinary boost on October 4 and November 3, 1957, when the first sputniks were sent aloft. Indeed, this dramatic demonstration of Soviet scientific skill and technological progress helped to conceal or to bury the political disasters of only the year before.

These achievements were supported also by the new diplomacy in which Khrushchev excelled. He traveled to various parts of the world as no other Russian leader had, visiting even the United States in the summer of 1959. He borrowed from the policies of the United States and her Western

Allies with his new program of trade and aid for underdeveloped countries, programs which promised a great deal more than was ultimately provided, but which created the belief that the Soviet Government was generous and that the Soviet economy was beginning to rival that of the United States in strength and wealth.

Within the Soviet Union, Khrushchev carried out a number of dazzling policies which removed the eyes of her citizens from foreign disasters and persuaded them that life would be more peaceful and sweeter. For example, Khrushchev launched several waves of decentralization of Soviet industrial, agricultural, and political activity, and the machine-tractor stations were abolished, leading some to think that even the collective farm would one day be removed. The Soviet Government placed renewed emphasis upon education and indeed forced the United States to engage in a race for improving education. Khrushchev launched a sensational program for agricultural production in the so-called virgin lands, and he placed far more emphasis upon consumer goods than earlier Soviet Governments had.

In addition, Khrushchev began to emphasize a new phrase, "peaceful coexistence," one which was designed to demonstrate that the Soviet Government and all communist states stood for peace and one which was designed also to weaken the resolution and unity of the allied peoples. This policy was supported by Khrushchev's travels, as well as by the new policy which allowed tourists to visit the Soviet Union and to review Soviet achievements in carefully guided tours. In fact, in 1958, the Soviet Union signed a cultural exchange agreement with the United States, under which American scholars, artists, athletic teams, and groups of specialists were able to visit the Soviet Union for various periods of time, and under which their Soviet colleagues could visit the United States. This new attitude toward travel and cultural exchange helped to persuade the Soviet people that Khrushchev did in fact seek a relaxation of tensions, that the Soviet state was being transformed into a less dictatorial one, and that the Soviet Union was becoming a full member of the civilized world.

As Khrushchev had anticipated, these new policies had some impact beyond the frontiers of the Soviet Union. Indeed, some American statesmen and scholars began to believe that the Soviet system and the American system were beginning to converge. The convergence thesis was based on the belief that the industrialization of Russia was creating a new class, the demands of which would force the Soviet Government to devote more attention to consumer goods and less emphasis to defense and to capital production. The thesis also rested on the belief that the growth of a complex Soviet industrial state with a new middle class would inevitably mean a mellowing or softening of Soviet policy. In addition, the convergence thesis assumed that increasing contact between the Soviet Union and the rest of the world would inevitably lead the Russians to adopt ideas and techniques from other countries which would so influence Soviet patterns as to make the Soviet system more like that of the states with which they were dealing.

The very considerable achievement of Khrushchev in rallying his forces and in recovering from the disasters of the fall of 1956 did not completely conceal the massive changes which were taking place within the

Soviet system and among communist parties all over the world and which tended to weaken communism. It was clear even to communists that those who had risen in 1956 were the darlings of the Soviet system, the students, the workers, and the intellectuals of the East European countries. The "children of 1956," in other words, had turned against Marxism-Leninism, and Marxists around the world were unable to explain how the favorites of communism had led the revolt against the system.

Moreover, both the achievements and the failures of the Soviet system and communist China led more and more communists to wonder about the validity of Marxism-Leninism, because of the very apparent contradictions between what in fact was happening and what Marx and Lenin had predicted only a century earlier.

Within Eastern Europe itself, Soviet power was obviously shaken by the 1956 events. It was clear both to the Russian rulers and to the West European people that the Soviet Union could not count on the loyalty of the satellite armies and the satellite peoples in any future crisis. In fact, both in Poland, where the revolution had been successful, and in Hungary, where the revolt had been unsuccessful, the communist states became more liberal than before 1956 and considerably more relaxed than the Soviet system was. Poland after 1956 abolished collectivization, gave new authority and power to the Catholic Church, tolerated criticism and expressions of ideas which had previously been forbidden, and opened up contacts in trade and in cultural exchange with the West which made Poland the freest communist country in the world.

Even more paradoxically, the beaten Hungary of 1956 received extensive Soviet assistance, increased the production of consumer goods in order to acquire additional popularity, and gradually relaxed the controls which had brought on the revolt in 1956. Consequently, Hungary by 1965 was also a relatively relaxed and free country. The illustration or examples provided by Poland and Hungary led other communist states in East Central Europe to work quietly for greater independence. Rumania, for example, in 1962 successfully resisted a Soviet effort to create an "international division of labor within the Soviet Union and Eastern Europe by assigning to Rumania the function of remaining an agricultural country and one which would have to import its capital goods from other countries." Rumania refused to accept the program assigned to her by the Soviet Union and has succeeded in establishing her own program for industrial development and in extensively widening her economic contacts with the West. In fact, Rumania by 1964 and 1965 had reached such a degree of independence that she supported communist China in her quarrels with the Soviet Union and refused to accept Soviet leadership with regard to the international movement. By the summer of 1964, Rumanian autonomy had reached the point that the Rumanian prime minister, Maurer, visited France and discussed increased economic and cultural exchanges with General de Gaulle.

The withering away of Soviet control over Eastern Europe was assisted enormously by one of the principal developments of the late 1950s, the growing friction between the two greatest communist states, the Soviet Union and communist China. In June 1959, the Soviet Union refused to honor an earlier agreement to provide assistance to communist China in developing nuclear weapons. This important step, preceded by other frictions, led to a growing gap between the two countries and ultimately to an almost open break by 1965. The issues between the Soviet Union and communist China are beyond the capacity of the leaders of these two great states to resolve in a peaceful way. The Chinese, for example, resent enormously that they have had to pay for the economic assistance received from the Soviet Union, while the Soviet Union has provided some free assistance to India, one of China's main rivals, and to other parts of the world. The two great giants quarrel also about the direction of the international movement, the Chinese arguing that their experience has more relevance for communist parties in underdeveloped countries than that of the Soviet party, which now rules a relatively well-developed country. The Chinese communists also feel that they have a particular priority in Asia, especially in Southeast Asia and South Asia, which they tend to view as a territory which ought to be under their general direction.

Other issues have also been of importance in creating the split. For example, there have been quarrels and perhaps even open conflict over the boundaries between Russia and China, which extend over 4,000 miles and which are not clearly defined. The countries have disagreed on policy toward India, where there has been open friction between communist China and India. The Soviet Union has not only refused to support the Chinese position in this conflict, but has provided economic and military assistance to India.

Finally, and perhaps above all, the Soviet Union and communist China have disagreed vigorously over long-term policy toward the United States. The Chinese communists believe that the United States and her allies can be overthrown only through the use of force, while Khrushchev and later Soviet leaders have been led to believe by the crisis of the last few years that peaceful coexistence is a necessary policy, that the use of force might lead to a third world war and obliteration of all the great states, and that there is a great opportunity for progress toward communism by the use of peaceful means. Consequently, Russia and China have quarreled openly since the summer of 1963. This display of disunity between these two great communist states has helped to bring about polycentrism, or the "extensive disintegration" of the international communist movement and to threaten its very survival.

The disagreement between communist China and the Soviet Union has inevitably affected the entire international communist movement, leading to disagreements and even splits within some of the major parties and causing a great deal of confusion in a movement which had prided itself upon its high degree of discipline and unity. In fact, the so-called communist bloc no longer exists, and careful observers foresee the creation of at least two communist groups, one headed by communist China and the other by the Soviet Union, with some communist states, such as Yugoslavia, remaining aloof from both assemblies.

This disintegration of the international communist movement has been assisted by the continued vigor of the Western states, as demonstrated by their remarkable recovery and renewed vigor and by American action in the

October 1962 crisis in Cuba. In that critical 1962 situation, the Soviet Government backed down under vigorous American pressure, removed her guided missiles from Cuba, and surrendered an important strategic advantage she had sought. This disaster for the Soviet Union helped to weaken the faith of communists around the world in the wave of the future. It also educated people in many parts of the world concerning the aggressive policy of the communist states. Since the crisis had exposed millions to obliteration because of a drastic aggressive Soviet action, it inevitably increased criticism of the Soviet rulers and of the Soviet system.

While the Cuban crisis was a significant defeat for Khrushchev and the Soviet Union, the removal of Khrushchev himself on October 15, 1964, was a political disaster for the Soviet Union, particularly so far as it affects Soviet control over Eastern Europe. It is almost certain that the bitter relationship which had developed between the Soviet Union and China played a significant role in this removal, and it is also obvious that Khrushchev's erratic and highly personal role alienated those closest to him. It is quite likely that the unfolding of a new policy toward West Germany contributed to this act. Thus, Khrushchev's son-in-law, Adzhubey, visited West Germany in July 1964, and wrote a number of articles which indicated that he believed West Germany was not a belligerent nation, that West Germany had made extraordinary economic progress, and that Soviet policy toward West Berlin might be changed in the future. Indeed, on September 3, 1964, Khrushchev announced that he was going to visit Bonn in the winter of 1965, leading many observers throughout the world to conclude that the Soviet Government was considering a new policy toward West Germany and toward West Berlin in particular.

Whatever the causes for the removal of Khrushchev, the action did weaken the Soviet system. Khrushchev had attained considerable popularity within the Soviet Union, as well as in Eastern Europe, where much progress toward autonomy had been achieved under his rule. Moreover, the way in which the removal was carried out and announced annoyed communist leaders, all of whom were as surprised as were their opponents. In fact, a wave of "shock, anger, consternation and regret," swept through the international communist movement with the sudden announcement of Khrushchev's removal. Moreover, since the ousting of Khrushchev occurred on the day in which the British general elections were being held, only a day before the communist Chinese exploded their first nuclear bomb, and only three weeks before the American national election, this system of changing political leaders put the Soviet Union in a very poor light.

Unfortunately, the Western states have not been in a position in recent years to take advantage of the extraordinary opportunities which Soviet and Chinese communist fumbling has provided for them. The last decade has been one of extraordinary economic and political recovery within the West, and Western Europe has only now begun to regain the world role in economic growth, trade, science, and technology which it held before 1914. However, Western strength has not been matched by Western wisdom or unity. Basically, Western policy has been dull and drab and has been marked more by negative anti-communism than by any positive policy.

Western peoples seem both confused and complacent about the world in general and to some degree seem to have been swallowed up or absorbed by their very considerable economic achievements. At the same time, the successes of the Soviet Union in science and technology have shaken the faith of the West in its superiority.

In addition, the NATO organization has not achieved the military strength or the unity which was sought when it was established fifteen years ago. None of the contributing states has supplied the forces which it had promised, and NATO has properly been called "the uncertain trumpet." The "delicate balance of terror" which is now maintained between the Western states and the Soviet Union finds the NATO organization continually in crisis and unable to provide the necessary leadership in this age of opportunity.

NATO has been racked by a number of competing nationalisms, which have prevented it from leading Europe toward greater unity. On various occasions during the last decade, suspicion and resentment between the United Kingdom and Germany have been very high, with the English, particularly those in the Labour party, unwilling to assume that the Federal Republic has earned her way to respect and trust, and with the Germans, especially among the Christian Democrats, resentful of English suspicion and fearful that England will accept the permanent division of Germany and will reach a private agreement with the Soviet Union. France and Italy have clashed on occasion. Greece and Turkey in 1964 were on the verge of war and almost wrecked the NATO organization in the Eastern Mediterranean. All of the NATO states in the 1960s seem to be turning inward, both with regard to adjustments in their economies, their attitude toward foreigners or outsiders, and their growing spirit of independence.

However, the principal demonstration of the weakness of NATO and of Western European disunion and confusion has been provided by General de Gaulle, the authoritarian leader of France since he assumed power in June 1958. General de Gaulle resolved the Algerian crisis for France, an achievement which no other French leader could have attained, but he has not been able to restore political unity in France, and it is clear that his death might produce a serious civil crisis in that great country. Above all, de Gaulle has threatened to wreck the foundations and prospects of Western unity which were at the center of Western progress and which represent the core of Western policy toward Eastern Europe. He alone decided in January 1963, for example, that the United Kingdom should not be allowed to join the Common Market. He has led a massive anti-American campaign throughout Western Europe designed to force the United States out of Europe and to create some kind of European unity under the French. His proposal for a *Europe des patries* has emphasized a new nationalism destructive of the principal efforts toward unity which were earlier made, and his effort to obtain a "Europe to the Urals" is a clear indication that he thinks the United States should leave Europe and that the Western part of the Soviet Union should be detached and should become a part of a new European community. In other words, General de Gaulle has roused the nationalism of the European states against the United States and has put under threat the immense political achievements of the last twenty years.

In the winter of 1965, the world faces a number of extraordinarily serious problems. In spite of the disasters which have afflicted the Soviet Union in recent years, that country remains a powerful, highly unified state with virtual control over Eastern Europe and with considerable influence over a number of communist parties in other parts of the world. Communist China, now a nuclear power, remains a mysterious and restless threatening state, with a great potential for creating mischief and serious crises in territories on her own borders and in distant Africa, where radicalism and racialism can be combined to create dangerously explosive mixtures. Critical problems burgeon everywhere, from Cyprus to Cuba, from the Congo to Viet Nam, all exposing the dreadful weaknesses of the United Nations. Thus, the disarray brought about by the new nationalism is not restricted to Western Europe, because the host of newly created countries which have appeared since 1945 are all afflicted by this disease, which tends to grow more and more out of control and to weaken the hopes which the new states themselves had placed in the United Nations.

Moreover, all are prisoners to some degree of a number of myths which have grown up about the Soviet Union. For example, Western policy toward the Soviet Union has been hampered by assigning exaggerated magnitudes to Soviet power and skill. For years, Western peoples believed that there was a highly centralized bloc of communist states, long after Soviet control had been seriously weakened and had even fallen apart before their eyes. Western peoples have also exaggerated the malevolence and ambition of communist leaders, who have had to devote far more attention to domestic problems and to maintaining control where it was already established than to expanding the system. Finally, Western states in general have often advocated negative anti-communist policies which have led to more talk of liberation than to discussion of ways and means through which communist authority over Eastern Europe and other parts of the world could be gradually and peacefully removed.

In general, the United States Government in the last few years has acted on the policy that it should provoke no crises, but should work instead for gradual change within Eastern Europe and within the other communist states. It has sought to hold high the hopes of the peoples of Eastern Europe for self-determination, and it has promoted contacts of all kinds between Western and Eastern European peoples. It has encouraged diversity, and it has been generous in providing economic and cultural assistance, particularly to Yugoslavia and Poland.

However, the main problem for Western policy-makers with regard to Eastern Europe is simply that of constructing a Western European union which will absorb the renascent nationalisms into a new community which will attract Eastern Europe and which will provide a base on which a European system of states can be peacefully constructed "within its historic boundaries." President Kennedy recognized this central issue on July 4, 1962, when he advocated the establishment of what he called an Atlantic partnership of interdependent states, a system of states which could ultimately be expanded peacefully to bring in those states in Eastern Europe now under communist control without at the same time threatening the proper sensitivities of the Soviet Union.

President Johnson on May 23, 1964, in a speech at the Virginia Military Institute urged that the United States and the Soviet Union recognize their common interest in a joint approach to certain basic problems which all the world faced. He urged continuous contact between the two great countries, the joint exercise of self-restraint in the critical areas, increased trade, agreements on arms control, and open discussion of the main difficulties which separated the two areas. He has also supported the mixed-manned nuclear fleet, an American proposal designed to restrict the spread of nuclear weapons and at the same time to give the West European states, including West Germany, some influence over Allied nuclear policy, which is now determined basically by the United States. Above all, President Johnson supported the suggestion that Europe be reconstructed "within its historic boundaries." He suggested that the United States stood ready to assist the countries of Eastern Europe in improving the conditions under which their peoples lived, opening "new relations to countries seeking increased independence" and giving "free play to powerful forces of legitimate national pride."

This renewed approach toward Eastern Europe, promising support and encouraging the evolution toward independence, peaceful cooperation, and the creation of open societies, faces serious difficulties of a political and economic character within the United States and within some states in Western Europe, notably West Germany, where many fear that the reunification of Germany will be sacrificed to a general effort to loosen communist controls over the other countries of Eastern Europe.

Unfortunately, the initiatives of Presidents Kennedy and Johnson, the efforts of other West European leaders, and the proposals made by important private citizens in all of the countries of Western Europe have not led to any significant increase in Western unity or produced any fruitful proposals which would attract East European states and significantly affect the way in which they are gradually changing. In fact, 1964 and 1965 witnessed a kind of undignified scramble among the West European states, both for political leadership over a system that was creaking badly and for trade with the countries of Eastern Europe. In fact, the anarchic Western approach toward these countries may lead them to become freer of Soviet rule at a time when there is no European or world framework into which they can fit and when pacifism and nationalism have undermined the foundations of Western unity and strength.

In other words, Western policy toward Eastern Europe in the winter of 1965 reflects the perils of prosperity. The very successes of Western Europe in economic and political recovery, on the one hand, and the various failures of the Soviet Union in Eastern Europe, on the other hand, together present the world with a splendid opportunity to progress toward a system under which peoples of Eastern Europe can gradually obtain more freedom from Soviet rule and find a secure position within a European structure which satisfies the legitimate aspirations of all European peoples without at the same time threatening the legitimate interests of the Soviet Union. However, right at this splendid but critical juncture, the states of Western Europe are deeply divided and uncertain of their own political future. Unsure of their joint economic goals, the kind of unity they need and how to achieve it, and the safest and most effective system of nuclear defense, they stand unready to benefit from their achievements and to assist their fellows in Eastern Europe, who have also made great progress but who also stand at another critical point.

There is a great need for a new concept of a world order, a new dedication by the United States and Europeans alike to the drive toward European unity. All nations need to return to the ideas and idealism of 1947, when the United States and the peoples of Western Europe faced a crisis far more serious than in 1965 but when they had a clearer concept of a world order than they have today. There is a pressing need to renew efforts to establish a European political community which will dampen and extinguish the Franco-German and other national conflicts; direct the spiritual, economic, and military forces of Western Europe into new channels; and create a political unity which can resist Soviet influence, pull Britain, Canada, and the United States into European affairs, and draw Eastern Europe from communist control and again into the European community. The United States and her allies must decide upon an alliance based upon the principle of integration rather than on immutable national sovereignty if they are to acquire the unity, strength, and good will necessary to assist the states of East Central Europe to win their way to freedom.

NOTE

1. George Kennan, *Russia, The Atom, and the West,* (New York, 1958), 35.

2

Soviet and Chinese Communist Relations with Yugoslavia

Yugoslavia's expulsion from the Cominform on June 28, 1948, came as a complete surprise to the Western world and was a great shock even to the Yugoslav communist leaders. Indeed, it was not until late 1949 that the Yugoslavs realized that Stalin insisted on full surrender and that they would have to rely upon their own strength and Western assistance to survive. The expulsion was due largely to Yugoslav insistence upon maintaining independence, but it also reflected Stalin's dissatisfaction with Yugoslav ideas concerning a Balkan federation and with the Bled agreement concluded with Bulgaria on August 4, 1947, with regard to Thrace and Macedonia.

During the years from 1948 through 1953, the Yugoslavs suffered from a Soviet and satellite economic blockade that seriously damaged their economy and their economic plans, heavy propaganda against the Yugoslav Party and Government, interruptions and delays in rail and shipping traffic, sabotage, military maneuvers on Yugoslavia's frontiers, and border excursions and alarms.

Shortly after the death of Stalin, the new Soviet rulers apparently decided to reduce or eliminate the political liabilities they had inherited. In the summer of 1953, they ended the Korean War. In the spring of 1955, they finally accepted the Austrian State Treaty; Porkkala was returned to Finland in the summer. At the Geneva Conference in July 1955, they exuded good fellowship in a meeting that they hoped would extend the new "atmosphere" so that negotiations on basic issues might be undertaken in a "friendly spirit." In September 1955, after a Soviet initiative, diplomatic relations were opened between Moscow and Bonn, which the Russians had previously denounced as a Nazi stooge of the United States.

Within the Soviet Union, they spoke of collective leadership, relaxed somewhat the severely repressive system, gradually reduced considerably the prison-camp population, and promised more consumer goods. In East Central Europe, the period after Stalin's death witnessed the slow birth of a new policy, called the New Course, which produced a slight political relaxation, releases of political prisoners, and the revision of economic plans to allow for production of more consumer goods. Above all, Stalin's successors adopted a new policy toward Yugoslavia.

Originally published in *UNITY AND CONTRADICTION Major Aspects of Sino-Soviet Relations*, Kurt L. London, ed. (Praeger Publishers, New York, 1962), pp. 159–184. Copyright (c) 1962 by Frederick A. Praeger, Inc. Reprinted with permission.

Stalin's successors were convinced that ousting Yugoslavia from the Cominform in 1948 had been a serious mistake, one upon which the Western allies had skillfully capitalized. Tito was a successful heretic and his survival had created an obvious crack in the international communist movement. Belgrade between 1950 and 1954 rivaled Moscow as the Mecca for communists and left-wingers, and many communists were confused by criticisms of the Soviet Communist Party by communists. The Soviet leaders apparently believed that Tito would return to the position he had held, particularly because he had been supremely loyal to the Soviet Union before 1948 and had been so resolute a dictator since that time. They also must have believed that this mission had to be accomplished to end the dangers of the heresy labelled "national communism" and to advance the refurbished "peaceful coexistence" propaganda line throughout the world, especially among Western socialists and in Southeast Asia, the Middle East, and Africa. The new Soviet line toward Tito may have been considered especially useful in 1954 in weakening the drive toward West European unity, particularly in helping to defeat the European Defense Community, which failed only in that year.

In any case, in the spring of 1953, the new Soviet policy of wooing Tito was launched. Step by step, diplomatic relations were resumed; Soviet jamming of Yugoslav broadcasts and Soviet radio war against Tito were abandoned; border skirmishes and threats ceased; trade was resumed and increased; easy credits were granted; and the Cominform was dissolved. Finally, on May 26, 1955, the principal Soviet leaders, led by Khrushchev but not including Molotov, made a sensational pilgrimage to Canossa by visiting the triumphant but wary Tito in Belgrade. At this meeting, they confessed that Tito had been wronged in 1948, assigned responsibility to Beria, and sought to resume the old party and governmental relationships. The Belgrade declaration of June 2 stipulated that both governments would respect the "sovereignty, independence, territorial integrity, and equality of states in their relations with each other and with other states," and would be guided by "mutual respect and noninterference in internal affairs for any reason - whether economic, political, or ideological - inasmuch as questions of internal organization, differences of social systems and of concrete forms of development of socialism are all exclusively the affairs of the peoples of the individual countries."[2]

The greatest surprises were yet to come. At the Twentieth Party Congress, in February 1956, the campaign of de-Stalinization reached its peak, particularly in the long Secret Speech by Khrushchev that assigned to Stalin responsibility for the break with Tito. Knowledge of this assault on the charismatic leader of the Soviet Union, published in the Western press early in June 1956, caused shock and confusion among millions of communists educated to revere Stalin. Khrushchev at the Congress played down Soviet primacy and cited four different forms of socialist construction - Soviet, People's Democratic, Chinese Communist, and Yugoslav - and he conceded others might appear. In one of his speeches he said: "In the Federal People's Republic of Yugoslavia, where power belongs to the working people and society is founded on public ownership of the means of production, unique specific forms of economic management and organization of the state apparatus are arising in the process of socialist construction." One of the resolutions of the Congress acknowledged that "great successes in socialist construction have also been achieved in Yugoslavia."[3]

This Party Congress also introduced several crucial doctrinal shifts - there are several roads to socialism, war is not inevitable, and communists can use peaceful means in democratic states to attain rule. In June 1956, in the course of a triumphal visit by Tito to the Soviet Union, the Soviet leaders signed an agreement recognizing that Tito's stand was not heresy, that the Soviet Union had no monopoly on methods of attaining socialism, and that relations between communist parties should be "equal, frank, and free."[4] The new Soviet approach to Tito developed slowly and haltingly, and some Soviet leaders, particularly Molotov, were reluctant to move along the new path and were even critical of the program sponsored by Khrushchev and Mikoyan. Thus, even after the Soviet trip to the Yugoslav Canossa, in May 1955, Molotov in the July 1955, Plenum of the Soviet Central Committee pointed out the hazards involved in the new policy, said that Tito was no longer a communist, and asserted that the Soviet Union no longer had the capability of influencing him. Molotov also argued that Poland would have followed Yugoslavia's path in 1948 if Tito had not been expelled from the Cominform at that time.[5]

The new communist minuet required two partners, and Tito's policy and attitude shifted in the same manner as did those of the Soviet leaders. However, during the period between 1948 and 1954, particularly after 1950, the Yugoslavs developed a number of concepts and institutions that made a return to the "normalcy" of 1947 impossible. Most important, the Yugoslav experience after expulsion from the Cominform had been such a shock and had so educated the Yugoslav communists on the realities of Soviet policy that Tito and his colleagues had developed a clear definition of the limits in friendly relations and alliance beyond which the Yugoslav Government would not go, no matter how skillfully and vigorously pressed. While Tito noted with pleasure "a great relaxation" arising from "a changed Soviet foreign policy," he gloried in his position as the doughty David who had stood up to Goliath.[6] He was, therefore, even more firmly determined than in 1948 to defend the battlements of Yugoslav independence and to maintain the prominent role Yugoslavia had achieved as a neutral in world politics.

After the spring of 1950, the Yugoslav Party slowly developed a new set of economic and political institutions. Somewhat later, the Yugoslav communists produced an "ideological cloak" to cover the apparent retreat from communism that the new procedures involved. The first step toward what became known as Titoism was the 1950 Basic Law on Management of State Enterprises by Workers' Collectives, and perhaps the clearest and most effective outline of the Yugoslav system and theory was Edvard Kardelj's speech in Oslo in September 1954.[7] Decentralization and pragmatism were the keys to the Yugoslav approach, and the Yugoslavs denied that it was possible to invent political and economic patterns to which all must conform. They called the Yugoslav system "socialist democracy," and they deliberately avoided creating a highly organized theoretical foundation for their stand, which they asserted sought to return to the original, unadulterated concepts of Marxism-Leninism. In industry, they introduced the "workers' councils" and decentralization of the state economic administration. They separated the party and the bureaucracy, abolished eighty percent of the collective farms in existence in 1948, increased religious and cultural freedom, and modernized and codified civil law. Careful observers noticed, however, that the communists maintained full control through the armed forces, the police, and a monopoly over the political and judicial systems.

For those Soviet leaders who hoped to create a new relationship between the Soviet Union and Yugoslavia, the theories that Tito used to justify the changes he introduced constituted a significant barrier, particularly as the Yugoslavs - rejoicing in the skill with which they maneuvered between the two great power blocs - delighted in slinging darts into the hide of the tough and rigid Soviet rhinoceros from behind this barrier. The Yugoslavs labeled the Soviet system "state capitalism," called the Soviet bureaucracy "one of the most centralized and bureaucratic state apparatuses" in the world, ridiculed rigid Soviet planning and coercive penalties, and mocked Soviet Marxist thought for its sterile rigidity.

Consequently, by 1954, when the thaw began to soften the Soviet view of Yugoslavia, Tito and his colleagues had erected a number of obstacles that made full and gracious reconciliation difficult for both sides.[8] However, while reserved, the Yugoslavs moved toward the new Soviet leadership, persuaded that the harsh policy had died with Stalin. Tito apparently believed that the domestic problems the Soviet and satellite communists faced were similar to those the Yugoslavs had confronted and that, as every heretic dreams, the mother church would adopt the sensible and practicable concepts of the rebel. Tito also naturally saw an opportunity to increase his power and influence in world politics by strengthening his "positive neutrality" position between the great power blocs. Finally, he was apparently convinced that mass weapons had reduced the likelihood of war and had created a new balance of power, in which Yugoslavia and other neutral states could play a more active and effective role.[9]

The Twentieth Congress of the Soviet Communist Party, sometimes called the Titoist Congress, dissolved any reluctance the Yugoslavs may have had before early 1956. Enormously pleased at Khrushchev's attack on Stalin and convinced that he was now Khrushchev's main ally against the remaining Stalinists, Tito supported Khrushchev within the Soviet Union and applied full pressure on the various satellite governments to abandon their campaigns directed at him. Thus, *Borba,* on March 20, 1956, published many details of Khrushchev's famous Secret Speech (*The New York Times* published a more complete text on June 5, 1956) as part of its effort to destroy Stalinism, and Yugoslav journals, newspapers, and radios hammered at the satellite governments to follow the lead of Khrushchev, whose speech had said nothing about Soviet politics in the satellites.[10] In foreign policy, after several years of cautious silence, Tito even jeopardized his relations with West Germany by hinting that he was about to recognize the German Democratic Republic, which would have been a great advantage to the Soviet Union.[11]

The reconciliation was so exhilarating that Tito may have become excessively offensive. Moreover, his knowledge of the policy divisions within the Soviet hierarchy acquired from discussions with the Soviet leaders, his criticism of satellite leaders, his ready pronouncements on every aspect of communist life in every communist country, and his eagerness to share ideas with other communists led the Kremlin in September to issue an appeal for solidarity and a secret warning to the East Central European parties against "mechanical" imitation of the Yugoslavs. Even so, on September 19, 1956, Khrushchev flew to Belgrade to visit Tito. The two spent the period from September 27 through October 5 in the Crimea with other communist leaders; in these sessions, the Soviet leaders tried, unsuccessfully, to persuade Tito to abandon some of his resolute positions, coordinate his policies in East Central Europe with those of the Soviet Union, and return to the "socialist camp"; Tito in return sought to assure the Russian leaders that they must further dismantle the Stalinist system or face revolts.[12]

The calculated risk the Soviet leaders took toward Tito and toward relaxing control over East Central Europe led to a chain reaction. Thus, in the June 16 issue of the *Nuovo Argomenti,* Togliatti, the Italian communist leader, who had visited Tito in May, wrote: "The Soviet model cannot and must not any longer be obligatory. The whole system has become polycentric, and even in the Communist movement itself we cannot speak of a single guide but rather of a progress which is achieved by following paths which are often different." This relaxation culminated in a successful Polish revolution, which limited Soviet control, and in a bloody revolt in Hungary, which was crushed in November 1956, by thousands of Soviet troops and tanks.[13]

Generally, most Western observers considered the successful Polish revolt and the tragic Hungarian revolution political disasters of the first magnitude for the Soviet Union. Some wrote that we might be witnessing the disintegration or the breakup of the communist empire; Milovan Djilas considered Hungary the beginning of the end of communism. Some saw 1956 as a mark of the military power and the spiritual weakness of the Soviet system. Others noted that the darlings of the communists - the workers, the intellectuals, and the students - had led the revolts, and considered this proof that the influence of communist doctrine and control had been vastly overrated by those living outside the bloc.

While East Central Europe obviously retained its strategic significance for the Soviet Union, its value was believed to have declined. Larger Soviet forces would be needed in occupation, at a time of growing manpower shortage. The satellite armed forces could no longer be considered reliable. In addition, Soviet economic aid and credits would be necessary to prevent increased dissatisfaction.

Finally, 1956 had a fearful impact upon the international communist movement, with most parties outside the bloc divided over Soviet policy in

Hungary and with many prominent leaders leaving the party. Communism in Western Europe in particular suffered a spiritual crisis, which threatened to put a permanent blight upon its prospects. Throughout the world, the carefully nurtured campaign for "peaceful coexistence" was apparently dealt a massive blow. Developments in Hungary in particular destroyed many illusions and educated many peoples and their leaders concerning the realities of communist rule.

Since the bitter day in November 1956, when Soviet troops completed the destruction of the Hungarian rebellion, one of the most startling and remarkable developments in world affairs has been the Soviet recovery from its blunders and the skill with which the Soviet Union has leapfrogged into a position of increased power. However, the issues raised by the policies of Yugoslavia, the problems involved in the effort to "put Humpty Dumpty back on the wall" by re-creating bloc unity, and the emergence of communist China in European affairs have thrust Soviet and Chinese communist relations with Yugoslavia up to a new level.

The motive forces of the Soviet recovery have been the continuing rapid growth of the Soviet economy, the dramatic achievements of Soviet science and technology, particularly in outer space, and the skill and daring of Soviet diplomacy. The Soviet Union has been particularly astute in its recovery in East Central Europe. Hungary has been a millstone, but economic aid, staunch diplomatic support, and a diplomatic offensive which has scored triumphs in several other parts of the world have diverted attention from Hungary and have created for Khrushchev a position from which he could deal more effectively with Tito.

The Polish and Hungarian revolts in the fall of 1956 created policy problems for Tito almost as complex as for Khrushchev. Both revolts proved Tito's advice to Khrushchev correct, but Tito ultimately condemned Nagy and the Hungarian revolution and reluctantly approved Soviet military action. Both political and ideological considerations led him to this decision, which he explained in a speech at Pula on November 11. The success of a multiparty neutralist government in Budapest would have constituted as serious a threat to communism in Yugoslavia as it would have to Soviet control over East Central Europe. Moreover, if Tito had not approved Soviet intervention in Hungary, he would have lost his power to influence Soviet policy and he might have opened Poland to Soviet intervention.

Tito therefore sought to balance, asserting that the "Hungarian bureaucratic state machinery" had created the discontents which led to the revolution, but condemning Nagy for his actions and for his appeal to the UN. At Pula, he declared the second Soviet intervention an "error," but, "if it saves socialism in Hungary, then, comrades, we will be able to say, although we are against intervention, that Soviet intervention was necessary." Yugoslavia twice abstained on November 4 in the UN on the resolution calling on Soviet forces to withdraw. These actions saved Tito from Soviet denunciation and delayed a sharp break with the Soviet Union. However, they also cost Tito the opportunity to stand forth as a "national communist" who acted on high principles, who sought for others the status Yugoslavia had achieved, and who was willing to continue working for gradual change within the communist movement. In particular, Tito's policy reduced his ability to influence the leaders and peoples of East Central Europe and contributed to the success Khrushchev has had in isolating Tito there.[14]

The 1956 revolts forced the Soviet leaders to put their policies toward Yugoslavia and East Central Europe through an "agonizing reappraisal." The Soviet Government decided that the Hungarian revolt had to be crushed at all costs and the Polish revolution kept within bounds. At the same time, these policies had to be carried out without driving Yugoslavia into active hostility or so destroying the position of Yugoslavia that it could not support other Soviet policies.

In this situation, the Soviet leaders groped and hesitated. Relations with Yugoslavia were kept open, but Soviet policy remained both unclear and irresolute until the spring of 1958, when publication of the Yugoslav party program either caused, or was used as a pretext for, a new conflict. In the meantime, Yugoslav domestic policy and ideology were subjected to heavy criticism. Albania and Bulgaria were particularly unrestrained in their propaganda attacks, while the Poles were moderate and conciliatory. Indeed, the satellites' campaign was so diversified that it gave the impression of a carefully controlled orchestral piece, with each player assigned a different theme.

During the first four or five months of 1957, Soviet criticism of Yugoslav policy was sharp, but not virulent. Thus, Khrushchev noted in *Pravda* in January 1, 1957, that the "so-called national Communists" sought to connect the transition from capitalism to socialism with specific national features, but that this was a one-sided approach and that the national features of no one country could "cancel the basic laws governing socialist revolution." A Yugoslav trade mission in Moscow was kept waiting in an undignified way, and some satellites broke off trade negotiations. However, Khrushchev spoke hopefully of Yugoslavia on occasion, and criticism was kept within limits. On their side, the Yugoslavs were equally restrained in their replies to all but the Albanians.[15]

In August 1957, following a visit by Kardelj and Rankovic to Moscow in June and apparently at the request of the Yugoslavs, Khrushchev, Mikoyan, and Kuusinen met with Tito, Kardelj, and Rankovic for two days in Bucharest in an effort to bridge the gap that separated the two parties and countries. The two groups were able to reaffirm the 1955 agreements on "separate roads to socialism" and on relations on the basis of "equality, mutual assistance and cooperation, the respect of sovereignty, and non-interference in internal affairs." They also agreed to subordinate their differences and disagreements in favor of "comradely cooperation" in major foreign policy areas. In addition, Tito accepted an invitation to attend the celebration of the fortieth anniversary of the Revolution in Moscow. However, the two groups could not agree on the means by which unity should be ensured. Moreover, Tito's request that satellite attacks be moderated was met by Khrushchev's rejoinder that Yugoslav attacks "against the countries of the socialist camp and the fraternal parties" would not go unanswered.[16]

Yugoslavia supported the Soviet Union in the UN debate on Hungary in September 1957. It also recognized East Germany in October of that year, thereby destroying a significant planned West German program for opening limited contacts with Poland and other East Central European states. These efforts to reassure Khrushchev were not sufficiently impressive, however, and the November anniversary meeting in Moscow laid bare the fundamental disagreement.

At the 1957 Moscow meetings, the Yugoslavs signed the Peace Manifesto, but refused to sign the "Declaration of Representatives of Communist and Workers' Parties of the Socialist Countries." This document stressed the "basic laws" that applied to all countries developing a socialist society and the leading role of the Soviet Communist Party in the communist movement. Tito did not attend the Congress, claiming illness, but he and his representatives insisted that Yugoslavia be "an equal among equals." They viewed the Declaration as an attack upon "revisionism," or Yugoslav concepts, and as another attempt to impose a Soviet orthodoxy upon them. Khrushchev and the Russians were obviously disappointed, but he declared that the ideological differences had been reduced and that he remained active and hopeful. However, *Pravda* on January 17, 1958, noted a "growing tendency" among "unstable elements" to reject "the basic tenets" of Marxism. *Moskva* in a January 1958, issue said even more clearly: "Revisionism and national Communism must be beaten and destroyed ideologically. . . . Either we bury revisionism, or revisionism buries us. There is no third course."[17]

Even at the times when Soviet propaganda was thundering vigorously at Yugoslavia's "revisionists," the leaders of the two states exchanged cordial birthday and party-anniversary greetings, signed trade protocols, and arranged cultural, scientific, and technical exchanges. Indeed, at the height of the tension over the Ljubljana Program in April 1958, Mikoyan and Furtseva in interviews with Western newspapermen emphasized that relations between the Soviet and Yugoslav Governments were and would remain excellent, although there were "ideological differences."[18]

After a precarious peace that had existed from the fall of 1956 between Yugoslavia, on one hand, and the other communist states, on the other, a conflict broke out in the spring and summer of 1958 almost as dramatic and complete as that of 1948. This conflict was launched by Tito, who apparently believed that the ideological confusion within Yugoslavia caused by the developments of the previous few years must be ended and that a clear and firm description of the Yugoslav position must be made. The League of Communists of Yugoslavia therefore circulated to the other communist parties a draft of the Yugoslav program prepared for discussion at the Seventh Congress of the League at Ljubljana from April 22 to April 26, 1958. The Yugoslavs dropped from the original draft the charge, which had particularly irritated the Russians - that both blocs shared responsibility for world tension - but the draft described policies and made proposals that ran directly contrary to Soviet and other communist positions. Moreover, the Yugoslavs commented freely on developments throughout the world in a way most irritating to orthodox communists. The draft itself so annoyed the Soviet and most other parties that they sent only observers to the meeting.

Only the Norwegian and Danish parties sent official representatives, and the observers appointed by the other parties, except for the Poles, withdrew when Rankovic said Yugoslavia would not accept Soviet leadership.

The Ljubljana Program, published early in March 1958, criticized the bureaucratism and "bureaucratic-statist deformities" which prevailed in the Soviet Union under Stalin and the dogmatism and "cult of the individual" which had developed from it. It contrasted this with the pragmatic decentralization of state functions in Yugoslavia. The Yugoslavs found state capitalism emerging in Western Europe and North America, with the state assuming the role of regulator of social and economic life and with capitalism, therefore, moving peacefully toward the era of socialism.

The Program also summarized what the Yugoslav communists considered the improvements they had made on Marxism-Leninism. In essence, it described Yugoslavia as the most advanced socialist state. It lauded Yugoslav decentralization of industry, the system of "worker self-management," the "liquidation" of the bureaucracy, and the "socialist free market," which the Yugoslavs claimed combined the advantages of a nationalized "planned economy" with those of a capitalistic free market.

The Program confirmed the correctness of the concept of "different roads to socialism." Socialist goals are everywhere the same, but the different conditions existing in the different countries inevitably influence the means used. Cooperation among the socialist states must be based on the principle of full equality, and the Program cited "ideological monopoly and political hegemony" as among the greatest obstacles to socialist development. Indeed, the Yugoslavs asserted that declaring one particular "form of socialist development in any single country as the only correct path and form" is unwarranted and dangerous dogmatism.

Finally, the Yugoslav Program described the existence of two political and military blocs as the main source of world tension. Some responsibility for world tension was therefore ascribed to the Soviet Union, because its policies, including its effort to subjugate Yugoslavia, had led the Western powers to unite. The document urged coexistence between states of different social systems, and not between blocs, if peace were to be assured. Moreover, it emphasized the contributions toward reducing tensions made by states such as Yugoslavia, which stood outside all military and political blocs. As Tito put it, if Yugoslavia should join any bloc, it "would lose the role which [it] plays in the world and which enables us to take an independent attitude in expressing our thoughts on all issues ... This role of ours is what most irritates the Soviet comrades."[19]

The attack against the Ljubljana Program was launched by the Soviet journal *Kommunist* on April 15 in an article that defended Stalin and ridiculed Yugoslav criticism of Soviet bureaucratism and dogmatism. It asserted that the proletariat must conquer power, not receive it as the process of a peaceful transition. It declared that all communist parties must subordinate themselves to the over-all requirements of the struggle for socialism ("true proletarian internationalism"), emphasized the need for leadership and unity, and declared that Soviet experience should be a model for other socialist states. It ridiculed the idyllic descriptions of the Yugoslav political and economic system. Above all, it pointed out that those whom it labeled "revisionist" ignored the division of the world into two ideological blocs, with capitalist monopolies and imperialism constituting the main dangers to international peace. The Yugoslavs had thus erred in "putting the peaceful policy of the socialist countries on a level with the aggressive policy of the ruling circles of the imperialist states."[20]

The *Kommunist* article was followed by a general drumfire of attack from the Soviet and satellite press and radio and from the Chinese communists as well. Indeed, the Chinese communist opening assault, in *Jen Min Jih Pao* (*People's Daily*), was even more bitter and ruthless than the Soviet critique.

Tito, in his opening address at the congress, apparently sought to appease those whom he had so irritated by a confident review of recent demonstrations of friendship for Yugoslavia, by strong condemnation of Western foreign policy, by denunciation of his own democratic critic, Milovan Djilas, by stating that Yugoslavia adhered "to the socialist world and its ideas in the broader sense," and by firm but mild defense of Yugoslavia's independence and concepts against Soviet criticism. The Yugoslav press was quite moderate in its defense until after the Chinese communist assault on May 5. Even the principal summary speech Tito gave in this period, that at Labin on June 16, emphasized both Yugoslavia's determination to pursue an independent foreign policy and to remain friendly with all states. Indeed, in November 1958, after reciting the list of sins committed by communist states against Yugoslavia, Tito asserted that the Yugoslavs still hoped to "return to the closest possible and most constructive cooperation with the parties of the other socialist countries."[21]

In addition to making press and radio attacks, the Russians responded by postponing President Voroshilov's planned state visit to Yugoslavia and canceling other such engagements. Khrushchev, late in April, wired congratulations to Tito on his re-election to the Presidency, however, and it was not until May 28, directly after a Soviet Central Committee meeting, that the Soviet and East German Governments "postponed" until 1969 credits of $285 million granted Yugoslavia in 1956. This was a heavy blow to Yugoslav plans and a strike against Tito, who, in his opening address at the congress, had cited these credits as one of the marks of greater mutual understanding and confidence. On June 3, in Sofia, Khrushchev, who had previously remained aloof from the conflict, found correct the expulsion of Yugoslavia from the Cominform in 1948, called Tito a "Trojan horse" of the imperialists in the "socialist camp," and accused him of major responsibility for the Hungarian revolution in 1956. These charges were repeated in more detail in East Berlin at the Fifth Congress of the Socialist Unity Party in July.[22]

The most forceful blow was still to come. On June 17, *Pravda* announced the execution as traitors of Imre Nagy and several of his colleagues. This act ended any hopes Tito might have had for reconciliation, because Nagy had left the asylum of the Yugoslav embassy in Budapest in November 1956, under a pledge from the Hungarian Government of his personal security. In addition, Tito, in Rumania, in August 1957, had accepted assurances from Khrushchev that Nagy would not be harmed. The Yugoslavs denounced the execution "with profound indignation," pointed out its resemblance to similar staged trials and executions in the recent past in Hungary, and noted that most of those responsible for the earlier infamous trials had themselves suffered later.

Since the announcement of the execution of Nagy, Soviet policy toward Yugoslavia has been remarkably consistent, with the conflict more sharp during the Twenty-first Party Congress in January 1959, and during May 1960, when the Paris Summit Meeting was torpedoed by Khrushchev. There was a lull in the early summer of 1959, when CEMA (Council for Mutual Economic Aid) held its tenth-anniversary meeting in Albania. The latter part of 1959, when Khrushchev visited the United States, was also quiet, as was most of the fall of 1960, particularly those weeks during and after Khrushchev's visit to the UN General Assembly session in New York.

During the past two and a half years, satellite leaders, except for those of Albania, have continued to exchange ceremonial greetings with Yugoslavia, trade pacts have been negotiated and honored, and delegations have been exchanged. The Soviet and satellite press have emphasized "the very friendliest of feelings for the fraternal people of Yugoslavia," and the Hungarian Government in the fall of 1960 even invited the Yugoslav Ambassador to speak over the Hungarian radio.

Albania and Bulgaria, particularly the former, have deviated to a considerable degree from the line established by the Soviet Union and followed by the other states of East Central Europe so far as Yugoslavia is concerned. These two states have been most blatant in the propaganda war, charging persecution of the Albanian and Macedonian minorities. These states have also charged Tito with old fashioned imperialism, in an apparent effort to reduce his influence in Asia and Africa. Hoxha, the First Secretary of the Albanian party, has even called Tito a Trotskyite.

An Albanian deputy premier was the only important representative from East Central Europe at the Chinese Communist National Day celebration in the fall of 1960, and both communist China and Albania attacked the Yugoslav role at the UN General Assembly that fall. Indeed, the Albanian press charged that "the effort of the Yugoslav revisionists to create a 'third bloc' was an ignoble, dirty maneuver carried out only for the purpose of getting more dollars, and, no doubt, millions of dollars will be paid to the Yugoslav flunkies for their valuable services." The bitterness of the Albanian attack is measured also by the denunciation of Gomulka for his "excessive spirit of personal initiative" in seeking to improve relations with the West at the General Assembly meetings.[23]

On occasion, the Soviet Party and Government have sought to ignore Yugoslavia. Thus, the Khrushchev speech in Moscow on October 20, 1960, on his return from the UN General Assembly session, did not even mention Yugoslavia. Tito protested, particularly in 1959, about "the conspiracy of silence" directed against him. Some Soviet propaganda has been petty.

On a different level, Khrushchev and the Soviet press in 1959 tried to demonstrate that the Yugoslav economy was stagnant, if not regressive, particularly in agriculture, and that the alleged failure of the Yugoslavs to match the industrial growth of other communist states reflected the mistaken policies of Tito. American aid contributed, in the Soviet view, to the failure of the Yugoslav economy to advance effectively, and accepting American aid, of course, made Tito an agent of the imperialists.[24] The main charges, however, have been that Yugoslavia bears the infection of "revisionism" and that it seeks to dissolve the vital unity of the socialist camp.

The conflict bubbled again late in the spring of 1960. In May, Tito condemned the United States for launching the U-2 over the Soviet Union, but assigned the Russians some of the responsibility for the resultant tension and the failure of the Summit Conference. Yugoslavia, he said, must therefore cooperate "with all peace-loving forces in the world in the struggle to preserve the peace. You can see for yourselves that the great powers are not exactly those in whom one might have full confidence."

Moscow struck back hard at Tito in the May issue of *Kommunist*. This article, presumably written before the Paris meeting collapsed, called Tito an apostate. It denounced Tito for trying to obliterate the difference between socialism and capitalism, declared that Tito's "outside-of-blocs" position was aiding the imperialists, and said that no socialist country could remain neutral without harming itself and the international socialist movement.

This line was also strongly pressed by Khrushchev at a meeting of communist parties in Bucharest in June 1960, and at the conference of parties after the November 7, 1960, celebration in Moscow. Observers felt that the stiffer note in the Soviet line at both meetings may have helped bring the Soviet Union and communist China closer together in their view of world affairs. The main Khrushchev speech in Bucharest was especially interesting because the Soviet leader emphasized that Tito was a revisionist and a member of a bloc. He then went on to defend the Soviet revision of Lenin on the inevitability of war. Lenin's tenets on capitalism were true, he said, but "were put forward and developed by him decades ago, when many phenomena that have now become decisive for the development of the historical process and for the entire international situation did not exist ..... We must not now repeat mechanically what Vladimir Ilich Lenin said about imperialism many decades back ....."[25]

Khrushchev in return was at least obliquely criticized by Tu Ting-yi, a deputy premier in communist China, who told the Third National Congress of Artists and Writers in July 1960, that modern revisionists chart their domestic and foreign policies "to suit the needs of imperialism." Revisionists who declare "that Lenin's theory concerning imperialism and his principles on proletarian revolution and proletarian dictatorship [are] now out of date," according to him, are trying to end the struggle against imperialism.

The Yugoslav position in the last two years has been considerably stronger than in 1948, and the tactics used by Tito in the new crisis reveal his awareness of the changes that have occurred in his favour. He remained remarkably restrained until the late fall of 1958, shortly before he left for an extensive tour of Southeast Asia.[26] He adopted a judiciously firm stand in a sweetly reasonable tone. He maintained the formalities, determinedly negotiated trade treaties, approved those Soviet domestic policies that resembled those of Yugoslavia, and defended Yugoslav economic growth. In addition, he immunized Yugoslavia by denouncing American action in Lebanon, by applauding Soviet scientific and technical achievements, by voting for the admission of communist China into the UN, and by supporting the policy Khrushchev announced toward Berlin in November 1958.[27]

On the more aggressive side, Tito, in April 1959, described the impact Stalin's purges in the 1930s had had upon the Yugoslav party. He noted that the Soviet Union criticized Yugoslavia for accepting American economic aid, although Mikoyan on his visit to the United States in January 1959, himself sought credits. He also pointed out that Khrushchev was himself a "revisionist," and that the Soviet leaders had modified a number of vital Marxist-Leninist doctrines. Yugoslav writers praised Dudintsev and Pasternak. Yugoslav journalists provided the world with important information concerning life within communist China, especially on the impact of the communes.[28]

In addition, probably the most clever and effective device chosen by the Yugoslavs was the publication, first in a number of articles in *Borba* and later as a book, of a series of essays by Edvard Kardelj, Yugoslav First Vice-President. Kardelj's book, *Socialism and War,* was an attack upon the Chinese communists for their assertion that war between the capitalist and socialist camps is inevitable. He pointed out that this ideological position would divide the "socialist camp," strengthen "reaction" in the rest of the world, which considers itself the defender of both peace and national independence, and lead to serious political defeats for the socialist states.

This volume posed special dangers for the Soviet leaders because it stated the Soviet point of view in the muffled debate between the Soviet Union and communist China concerning the "inevitability of war." The Chinese communists naturally denounced the Kardelj volume. The Soviet communists almost certainly would have preferred to ignore the book. However, *Pravda* restated the Soviet thesis that war could now be prevented, assailed unidentified "dogmatists" who believed war was inevitable, and denounced Kardelj and the Yugoslavs as revisionists who charged the Chinese communists with dogmatism and aggression and who "white-washed American imperialists." Imagine, it thundered, the charge "that a socialist state could wage an aggressive war"![29]

Finally, Tito sallied forth from his Adriatic retreat to tour Asian and African nations, where he provided other neutral leaders with concrete information concerning Soviet policies and past political and economic relations between the Soviet Union and Yugoslavia. He was on an extended tour of Southeast Asia and the Middle East (Egypt, Ethiopia, Sudan, Indonesia, Ceylon, India, and Burma) when Khrushchev launched his most bitter attack in January 1959, and Nasser was returning a visit in June 1960, when the Bucharest meeting erupted against Tito. In other words, Tito was able to undermine the Soviet and communist Chinese "peaceful coexistence" drive and to point out that the Soviet attacks on the Yugoslav position concerning the two blocs applied equally well to "the

Asian and African countries which do not belong to blocs." Thus, on his return in 1959, he noted:

> It has become fairly clear that they are disturbed by our policy - the policy of coexistence, the policy of an energetic struggle to establish among nations, among states, equal and good relations, and to reduce international tension. We represent the idea that cooperation is possible between states and nations regardless of their internal systems, but they do not like this idea. And what else do they dislike? They know that Yugoslavia is not a great power which endangers the African and Asian peoples and which goes there to impose on them a colonial system. They know that very well. But what upsets them? They are disturbed by Yugoslavia's influence. They are afraid that we may "corrupt" those peoples and that they, to, would be in favor of coexistence, that they, too, would be in favor of equality. ... That is what upsets them. It was fairly clearly shown during this entire time in writings and attacks on our country and on us who were on this trip.[30]

Tito's tours of Southeast Asia and his skillful work among the Afro-Asian nations probably irritated the Chinese communists even more than they did Khrushchev, for they struck directly at the concepts concerning the uncommitted nations that the Chinese communists were propounding widely. In fact, I believe that Tito's ventures in Southeast Asia and the Middle East were the principal factors that brought communist China into the conflict.

Communist China strongly supported Stalin's policy toward Tito from 1948 through 1953. Yugoslavia was among the first states to recognize communist China in 1949. However, Mao refused to enter into diplomatic relations with Tito until late 1954, just before Tito began a trip through the Middle East and Southeast Asia. There Tito presumably sought to persuade those whom he visited that an important shift that should be encouraged was under way within the Soviet Union and within the Soviet bloc in general.[31] Beginning in January 1955, Yugoslavia and the People's Republic of China began to exchange delegations of journalists, pianists, philatelists, and acrobats; trade protocols were signed; soccer and basketball games were played. Communist Chinese journals and newspapers carried sympathetic accounts of Yugoslav achievements, including the workers' councils. More important, *Jen Min Jih Pao,* on April 5 1956, confessed that Stalin had "made a wrong decision on the question of Yugoslavia."[32]

Communist China's role in the crisis of 1956 is still obscure, but certainly the Yugoslavs, and even more the Polish communists, considered the Chinese communists their special advocates and defenders. There is some evidence that in the summer of 1956, Mao encouraged Ochab, then First Secretary of the party in Poland, and exercised a restraining influence upon Khrushchev and his colleagues in October. The Chinese, like the Yugoslavs, then reversed their position and endorsed Soviet intervention in Hungary. The Yugoslavs were particularly pleased that the Chinese communist press printed their views after the Hungarian crisis, praised the workers' councils, sent the Vice-Minister of Foreign Affairs to Belgrade for a visit in January 1957, and were mild and moderate in the principal statement on Hungary, published in *Jen Min Jih Pao* on December 29.[33]

This statement, apparently written by Mao himself, emphasized the importance of bloc unity and Soviet primacy, and asserted that all discussion must proceed from "the most fundamental fact, the antagonism between the imperialist bloc of aggressors and the popular forces in the world." It was gentle with Tito, whose "attitude ... cannot be regarded as well-balanced or objective," but it noted that the Yugoslavs "understandably" resented recent Soviet policies.

Chou En-lai's trip into Eastern Europe - "the first Asian initiative in Europe since the siege of Vienna" - may have helped inform the Chinese communists of the dangers that unorthodoxy posed and probably contributed to the "rectification" campaign that was launched in June 1957. This drive, the shock administered by the Yugoslav refusal to sign the Declaration in Moscow in November 1957, and the Chinese communist emphasis after 1956 on bloc unity were probably the main reasons for the vigor with which the Chinese communists denounced the Ljubljana Program in the spring of 1958. However, to the Chinese communists, Tito's main heresy was his refusal to join the "socialist camp," which would have ensured its unity and more rapid triumph. Even the Russians were surprised at the ferocity with which the Chinese communists lashed out at what they called "revisionism."

The Chinese communists, and the Russians, too, may have used the Ljubljana Program simply as a pretext for launching a new attack against Tito. It is important to note that communist China entered the campaign with great zest at the same time its massive collectivization and industrialization drive began. The Quemoy crisis in the summer of 1958 and the fear that Khrushchev might "relax" too much at a UN Summit Meeting not attended by his Asian allies also probably increased the fervor with which the Chinese communists struck at the Yugoslavs. The Chinese communists' interest in Yugoslavia strengthened their foothold in East Central Europe, perhaps as a balance against Soviet influence elsewhere, and assured them a more prominent position in the international communist movement.

Economic interests may also have exerted some influence. Communist China entered CEMA in May 1958, the year in which Yugoslavia ceased to attend as an observer. The forced-draft drive launched in May increased communist China's need for credits, and the communist Chinese must have wished that the Soviet Union were as active in its aid to communist China as it was with India. The Yugoslavs pointed out on a number of occasions their belief that communist China excited pressure against Yugoslavia and increased world tension in order to pry more economic aid from the Soviet Union.[34]

Moreover, by 1958, communist China had an important economic stake in East Central Europe. It is a heavy importer of machinery from East Germany, Czechoslovakia, Hungary, and Poland. In fact, more than half of satellite machinery exports in 1957 and 1958 went to communist China, and the trade of the countries of East Central Europe in 1958 with communist China was almost one-half as much as that of the Soviet Union with communist China.

Another motive for the Chinese communist attack against Yugoslavia has been concern to preserve the Afro-Asian territories from "revisionist" ideas. After 1957, Tito was active spreading ideas among the neutral states, especially the newly independent states of the Middle East and Southeast Asia. He made a special effort to emphasize that the entire world should not be divided into blocs and that the uncommitted nations could and should play an important independent role in world affairs. In fact, Tito argued that the two great powers and their blocs were showing ever more clearly their inability to lead the world to peace.

Tito was thus not only weakening the "socialist camp" by refusing "to serve the cause of peace" and by raising the hazards of confusion and infection, but he was also invading territory that the communist Chinese had come to consider theirs. Moreover, Tito's views concerning the role which the Asian and African nations could play was quite different from that of the communist Chinese. Tito believed that the neutrals should remain aloof from the great conflict that dominated world affairs and should, by their example and by their policies as independent states, serve to reduce tensions.

The Chinese communist view of the Asian and African nations was quite different. To them, neutrality and "peaceful coexistence" were temporary stages. They suggested that the Chinese communist "liberation struggle" had especially fitted them to be mentors of the colonial peoples, and they have sought consistently to establish "militant friendship" with the new states of Asia and Africa.

In the long run, the Chinese communists saw these new states and peoples first as adjuncts and later as parts of the communist bloc, under the special wing of communist China. Tito, therefore, represented a menace, because his doctrine had a genuine appeal to the nationalism of the uncommitted states.

Consequently, the Chinese communists label the 1948 expulsion of Yugoslavia from the Cominform "basically correct and necessary." They call Tito a "fascist hireling" and an "American tool." They have accused Yugoslavia of instigating and intervening in the Hungarian revolution. On the more petty level, they refuse to attend receptions which even Soviet representatives attend, they refuse to address Yugoslav party members as "comrade," and they have called Tito "a dwarf kneeling in the mud and trying ... to spit at a giant."[35]

Tito, in return, has emphasized the inhumanity of the communes and accused the Chinese communists of seeking war to conceal domestic difficulties. He has also called attention to the Chinese communist conviction that 300 million Chinese would survive a nuclear war and that such a war would therefore destroy capitalism, but not communism. He has therefore raised doubts concerning the Chinese communist definition of "peaceful coexistence."

It is interesting and even exciting to speculate on Soviet and Chinese communist policy toward Yugoslavia: what the policies in fact are, why they have been adopted, why they have been modified, what the connections are between the two sets of policies, what the relation is between policy and propaganda, and what insight this throws on the fascinating puzzle of Sino-Soviet relations. However, it is also difficult, even impossible, to make judgments with confidence because of the nature of the evidence and because so many other issues and forces, often concealed, affect particular policies. Even so, one can identify some of the main characteristics of the relationships and can perceive in outline the main issues and trends.

First of all, the differences between the Soviet-Yugoslav relationship from 1948 to 1953 and relations between the Soviet Union and communist China, on one hand, and the Soviet Union and Yugoslavia, on the other hand, from 1957 to 1960 are very considerable. The weapons in the second period are entirely verbal. Relations have been maintained between the governments, although not always between parties. Throughout the last four years, trade has continued and exchanges in the fields of culture, sport, science and technology, trade union affairs, and youth movements have flourished. There has been no sabotage, economic blockade, maneuvers, or military pressure. In fact, while the conflict is often labeled ideological, and there are ideological issues involved, the struggle has been primarily one of propaganda.

Second, in some ways Tito has campaigned in the second period as a more powerful and more assured competitor than in the first. His position has been far stronger; he has considerable popular support; his party has faith in its system and pride in its new concepts; and he is certain of Western support. Actually, one of the new characteristics of the relationship is the restrained confidence with which Tito has performed in the propaganda battle.

The current disagreements are especially significant because they constitute the first ideological conflict of any import within the international communist movement since the 1930s. In these ideological disputes, however, Yugoslavia is not always aligned against the Chinese communists. Some of the most significant though muted disagreements are between the Chinese and the Russians. Moreover, Yugoslavia plays the very special role of lightning conductor in the dialogue between the Soviet and Chinese communist leaders: Many of the comments directed by both against the Yugoslavs are in fact indirect criticisms of each other in a new kind of "Aesopian language." The Yugoslavs by their actions, therefore have helped bring important issues to the surface. They have contributed enormously to the discussion now raging over the communist goals, Marxist-Leninist economic policies, the role of the party and of the state bureaucracy, the development of capitalism in this new era, the inevitability of war, and the role morality and humanity ought to play in socialist society.

On the other hand, one could argue that the disputes of the last four years have not been ideological, but reflect power politics. Most of the Yugoslav domestic changes which the Soviet and Chinese communists now criticize as "national communism" or "revisionism" were introduced between 1950 and 1954 and were in effect when the Soviet leaders made their pilgrimage to Belgrade in May 1955. Tito's policy toward Soviet hegemony was not different in 1958 from what it had been in 1955. *Pravda* and the Chinese communist press both wrote approvingly of Yugoslav foreign and domestic policy in 1955 and 1956. Moreover, Yugoslavia was receiving economic and military assistance from the United States before and during the years of reconciliation, without Soviet complaint. Finally, of course, some of Khrushchev's most impressive and effective achievements in domestic policy in recent years bear a striking resemblance to actions taken earlier in Yugoslavia. In other words, while ideological issues are involved and provide powerful evidence of the disagreements, the most important issues are not ideological.

The first key factor in the current dispute between the two most powerful communist states and Yugoslavia is the question of organization of the communist bloc, an issue which all participants have quite successfully concealed behind the smoke screen of the discussion concerning the inevitability of war. 1956 and the years since have been marked by the steady erosion of the unity and discipline of the bloc, in spite of the energy and skill with which Khrushchev has sought to revitalize communist doctrine and has labored to cement the cracked monolith together again. The communist leaders have discovered that the "thaw" and the events in 1956 raised incredibly difficult problems. During two or three years, from 1955 through the spring of 1958, Khrushchev and Tito made a number of determined efforts to develop a new system of relationships among communist states. No satisfactory solution was reached, largely because, as *Pravda* put it on August 18, 1958, "Yugoslavia's leaders do not want to march in the common ranks of the champions of peace." In other words, Yugoslav refusal to accept Soviet hegemony is the main cause of the dispute with both the Soviet Union and communist China, which supports bloc unity even more fervently than does the Soviet Union.

The current dispute also illuminates another important development in world affairs in the 1950s, namely, the shift of interest from East Central Europe, indeed from Europe as a whole, to Asia and Africa. 1956 was a disaster for Tito as well as for the peoples of East Central Europe. However, even before, Tito had launched his drive among the Asian and African countries. Shrewd observers, such as Walter Lippmann, then foresaw that Tito's main effort in the next few years would be directed toward the "conversion" of Asia and Africa. Tito, of course, did not create the interest in the newly independent countries, but the communists' various campaigns to influence Asia and Africa have helped raise the present conflicts into a new world framework, to a new level above and beyond Western Europe and NATO, where American eyes have generally been riveted. Consequently, the relationships of the Soviet Union and communist China to Yugoslavia reflect the struggle for the uncommitted nations. At the moment, at least, the possible impact of Yugoslav policies in Africa and Asia is of more concern to the Soviet Union and communist China than is the influence of Yugoslavia in East Central Europe. Communist China has been especially aroused against Tito because of the conflicting aims communist China and Yugoslavia have among the uncommitted nations. The reverse side of the new emphasis on Asia and Africa is the Khrushchev achievement of re-establishing the bloc in East

Central Europe. Tito, in effect, has been isolated or quarantined from his neighbors, though no one, not even Khrushchev, can be certain that the influence of Yugoslavia will not someday be reasserted. More important, Khrushchev has succeeded with considerable skill in subordinating Poland again to Soviet authority; one of the most important developments of the period since October 1956 has been the gradual return of Gomulka to the fold, no longer inspired by Yugoslav example or protected by communist China.

1956 and its aftermath in East Central Europe reflect Soviet skill and resolution, Tito's fatal ambivalence, and the inability of the West to act promptly and effectively. While Tito's influence has apparently been snuffed out among his closest neighbors, Tito's Yugoslavia still survives as a challenge to the communist thirst for unity. Yugoslavia's independence and the example and ideas it distributes around the world raise problems for the Soviet Union and communist China even more baffling than those of 1956. Moreover, the challenge will almost certainly become far more serious when the next crisis arises within the communist system, whether due to a new succession problem, popular unrest, troubles between the Soviet Union and communist China, or simply another effort to reorganize the bloc in the old monolithic unity, this time with communist China deeply involved in the decision.

NOTES

1. This paper is based upon an analysis of published Soviet and Yugoslav materials, mainly journals and newspapers, of translations from Chinese communist newspapers and journals, and of Western studies of developments within the Soviet Union, Communist China, and Yugoslavia and of relations among these states. However, I did not have access to all the published information. Naturally, some of the most significant information is available to none of us. The nature of the subject and of the evidence makes this paper largely one of speculation.

2. *For a Lasting Peace, For a People's Democracy*, June 3, 1955, 1.

3. *Current Soviet Policies - II: The Documentary Record of the 20th Communist Party Congress and Its Aftermath*, Leo Gruliow, ed. (New York, 1957), 37-38, 190.

4. *Ibid.*, 227-30.

5. Zbigniew K. Brzezinski, *The Soviet Bloc: Unity and Conflict* (rev. ed.; New York, 1961), 176.

6. *Borba,* October 25, 1954.

7. This speech is reprinted in *Yugoslav Facts and Views* (March 1, 1956). Probably the best brief summaries of the Yugoslav position are Charles P. McVicker, *Titoism: Pattern for International Communism* (New York, 1957), 306-20; and Vaclav L. Benes, "The Dispute: Ideology and Practice," in Vaclav L. Benes, Robert F. Byrnes, and Nicolas Spulber, *The Second Soviet-Yugoslav Dispute* (Bloomington, 1959), xxi-xxii.

8. Ernst Halperin, "Is Russia Going Titoist?," *Problems of Communism, and the Soviet Union 1948-1956* (Hamden, Conn, 1956), 12-16.

9. Brzezinski, *op. cit.*, 175; *Manchester Guardian Weekly*, May 10, 1956, 2.

10. Brzezinski, *op. cit.,* 179, 183, 190-93; Philip E. Mosely, "Soviet Foreign Policy: New Goals or New Manners?, *Foreign Affairs,* XXXIV, No. 4 (July, 1956), 541.

11 *Manchester Guardian Weekly,* August 2, 1956, 10.

12. Brzezinski,*op. cit,* 195-205; *Manchester Guardian Weekly,* October 4, 1956, 9.

13. "Soviet-Yugoslav Relations and Eastern Europe," *World Today,* XII (1956), 490-91. The frayed discipline within the international communist movement and the Polish and Hungarian revolutions came as a great surprise to even the most astute Western observers. In the 1956 Presidential campaign in the United States, both major parties urged "that the spirit of freedom be kept alive," but neither urged the satellite governments to become more independent or "national." Indeed, George Kennan, the author of the containment theory, noted in the spring of 1956 that there was "a finality, for better or worse, about what has happened in Eastern Europe." In October, 1956, observing events in Poland and Hungary, he described these developments as "an extensive disintegration of Moscow's authority within the Soviet orbit."

14. Brzezinski, *op. cit.,* 230-34.

15. Nikita S. Khrushchev, *Speeches and Interviews on World Problems, 1957* (Moscow, 1958), 32-33.

16. Elliot R. Goodman, *The Soviet Design for a World State* (New York, 1960), 349-50; Richard P. Stebbins et al., *The United States in World Affairs, 1957* (New York, 1958), 126; Brzezinski, *op. cit.,* 310-12; *Pravda,* August 4, 1957; *Manchester Guardian Weekly,* October 17, 1957, 3.

17. Khrushchev, *op. cit.,* 361-62; Donald S. Zagoria, "The Spectre of Revisionism," *Problems of Communism,* VII, No. 4 (July-August, 1958), 15; Victor Zorza, "No Equality with Moscow," *Manchester Guardian Weekly,* December 12, 1957, 4.

18. *New York Times,* January 4, January 29, March 15, April 23, April 27, May 3, 1959; *East Europe,* VIII, No. 8 (August, 1959), 33; No. 9 (September, 1959), 43; No. 10 (October, 1959), 43; No. 11 (November, 1959), 42.

19. This is a summary analysis of some of the main points of the Ljubljana Program. The most important part of this document, the first three chapters, is reprinted in Benes, Byrnes, and Spulber, *op. cit.,* 29-91.

20. This article is reprinted in Benes, Byrnes, and Spulber, *op. cit.,* 95-130.

21. "Concerning the Speeches of Comrades Gomulka and Khrushchev," *Yugoslav Facts and Views,* No. 71 (November 19, 1958), 4.

22. There was much speculation throughout May, especially in Poland, that Khrushchev's inaction in the campaign at a time when the Chinese communists were most vociferous revealed a split within the Soviet leadership and between the Soviet Union and communist China. See *New York Times,* May 11, June 1, 1958; Victor Zorza, "Tito, 'A Trojan Horse,'" *Manchester Guardian Weekly,* June 5, 1958, 2.

23. *Borba,* September 6, 1960; "What Are the Real Facts?," *Yugoslav Facts and Views,* No. 87 (February 3, 1959), 1-2; *East Europe,* VIII, No. 3 (March, 1959), 37; No. 8 (August, 1959), 8, 34; Victor Zorza, "Tito Insists on Independence," *Manchester GuardianWeekly,* April 24, 1958, 3; Liliana Brisby, "Bulgaria: Leaping Forward Without Communes," *China Quarterly,* No. 3 (July-September, 1960), 80-84.

24. Nikita S. Khrushchev, *Control Figures for the Economic Development of the U.S.S.R. for 1959-1965* (Moscow, 1959), 107; *Pravda,* October 21, 1960.

25. "Speech by Comrade N.S. Khrushchev at Third Congress of Romanian Workers' Party," *Pravda,* June 22, 1960, 1-3, cited in *Current Digest of the Soviet Press,* XII, No. 25 (July 20, 1960), 3-9, 25; B. Ponomarev, F. Konstantinov, and I.U. Andropov,

"On Old Revisionist Positions," *Kommunist,* No. 8 (May, 1960), 24-48, cited in *Current Digest of the Soviet Press,* XII, No. 25 (July 20, 1960), 10-17; "Eastern Europe: Hot Water," *The Economist,* May 28, 1960, 850; "Bucharest Jamboree," *The Economist,* June 25, 1960, 1319-20.

26. Tito noted in October, 1958, that the Soviet Union and the satellites had published 670 attacks on Yugoslavia in six months, but they complained when the Yugoslavs replied. ("Excerpts from President Tito's Speech Made in Largest Yugoslav Steel Plant at Zenica, Bosnia, on October 12, 1958," *Yugoslav Facts and Views,* No. 67 [October 22, 1958], 3.)

27. Josip Tito, "Forty Years of Revolutionary Struggle of the Communist Party of Yugoslavia," *Yugoslavia Facts and Views,* No. 100 (April 24, 1959), 7-10, 15-18.

28. See, for example, the following translations: "China Through Yugoslav Eyes: Recent Reports from Peiping," *East Europe,* VII, No. 11 (November, 1958), 11-16, 27; Maks Snuderl, "From a Journey Through China," *East Europe,* VIII, No. 1 (January, 1959), 31-39; "China Through Yugoslav Eyes," *East Europe,* VIII, No. 7 (July, 1959), 16-22; No. 10 (October, 1959), 26-31.

29. *Borba,* August 12, August 15, September 12, 1960; *Pravda,* September 2, 1960.

30. *Yugoslav Facts and Views,* No. 81 (January 14, 1959), 2-3. It is interesting to note that the Chinese communist press devoted very little attention to Khrushchev's visit to India and Indonesia in February, 1960.

31. Relations between communist China and Yugoslavia were considered so unimportant in 1956 and early in 1957 that the excellent study by McVicker, cited in n. 7, refers to China only once, and that time obliquely in the introduction, which is dated May, 1957.

32. Chen Yung-wen, "Yugoslavia's System of Workers' Own Management," *Jen Min Jih Pao,* November 29-December 1, 1956, cited in *Survey of China Mainland Press,* No. 1435 (December 20, 1956), 38-45; Allen S. Whiting, "Contradictions in the Moscow-Peking Axis," *Journal of Politics,* XX (February, 1958), 146; S.F. Hudson, "Communist Ideology in China," *International Affairs,* XXXIII (April, 1957), 178; *Survey of China Mainland Press, No. 1549 (June 13, 1957), 30.*

33. Whiting, *op.cit.,* 152-57; *Manchester Guardian Weekly,* February 7, 1957, 9; *Survey of China Mainland Press,* No. 1464 (February 6, 1957), 46; Victor Zorza, "China's Declaration of Orthodoxy," *Manchester Guardian Weekly,* January 3, 1959, 7. There were rumors in April, 1957, that Chou En-lai would visit Yugoslavia that June (*New York Times,* April 9, 1957).

34. Brzezinski, *op. cit.,* 283-84, 286-366; Goodman, *op. cit.,* 363, 364; *New York Times,* June 17, 1958, 8.

35. *Jen Min Jih Pao,* June 5, 1958, cited in *Survey of China Mainland Press,* No. 1787 (June 9, 1958), 9-12; *Jen Min Jih Pao,* June 14, 1958, cited in *Survey of China Mainland Press,* No. 1795 (June 19, 1958), 14; Victor Zorza, "Kremlin on the Cold-Warpath Again," *Manchester Guardian Weekly,* June 26, 1958, 3.

3

Russia in Eastern Europe: Hegemony Without Security

Even in an age of nuclear weapons and intercontinental missiles, the states of Eastern Europe now dominated by the Soviet Union constitute an important element of Soviet national security, a kind of *cordon Stalinaire*. The one hundred million people, and the resources their governments command, contribute a significant increment to Soviet economic, technological and military power. Soviet control of these areas provides forward military bases and possession of the traditional invasion routes into Western Europe, especially across the northern plains. The Soviet position, in fact, constitutes a threat to the security of Western Europe, a pistol held at its head.

The division of Europe and the perpetuation of tension have assisted the Soviet Union by restricting the role which West European states play in world politics and by increasing the American burden. At the same time, the Soviet position provides a veto over the unification of Germany and also over the reconstruction of Europe as a whole. Soviet control over East Germany maintains the fear of another Russian-German alliance and provides opportunities for Soviet diplomacy. It almost guarantees crises over West Berlin, in circumstances the Soviets choose. In short, Eastern Europe remains at the heart of the struggle between the Soviet Union and the NATO states.

On the surface, the Soviet control over Bulgaria, Czechoslovakia, East Germany, Hungary and Poland appears tighter and more effective than ever, and the independence of Rumania in foreign policy is severely hedged by its geographical position. The close ties between the parties and the governments are supported by chains of command which run from Moscow into the various capitals through the armies, the police, the trade unions and the diplomatic service. Soviet armed forces are stationed in East Germany, Poland, Czechoslovakia and Hungary.

From two-thirds to three-quarters of the trade of each of these countries except Rumania is bound to the Soviet economy, and Soviet hegemony is exercised also through the coordination of economic plans. East European leaders, except those in Rumania, accept the Brezhnev Doctrine, which provides the Soviet Union formal authority to interfere in

Reprinted with permission from *Foreign Affairs,* II (July, 1971), 683-697.

the affairs of the other states. Finally, of course, the force and skill with which Soviet-led forces crushed Czechoslavakia in 1968 demonstrated that the Soviet Union is ruthless, and will not tolerate significant modification of the Soviet position in those countries.

Even so, however, Soviet authority in these states has declined notably since its peak late in 1947, when Stalin said, "I will shake my little finger and there will be no more Tito. He will fall." Tito survived, and Yugoslavia has emerged as an independent national communist state with significant influence within Eastern Europe and among communist parties throughout the rest of the world. The political and ideological shifts connected with de-Stalinization and the rise and overthrow of Khrushchev have weakened the Soviet grip on other communist states and parties. The emergence of deep hostility between the Soviet Union and communist China has promoted polycentrism.

Unfortunately for the Soviet rulers, the problems reflected in the Polish uprisings in 1970-71 and in the earlier Czechoslovak crisis represent only one of a large number in an area which lacks uniformity and whose peoples have always proved troublesome to rule. Rumania, for example, has a staunch authoritarian government, but it maintains a resolutely independent foreign policy. Yugoslav relations with the Soviet Union on occasion have been friendly, but Yugoslavia remains irrepressibly free, little subject to Soviet influence. Tiny Albania has even withdrawn from the Warsaw Pact and is a kind of mouthpiece of the People's Republic of China in its violent hostility to the Soviet Union.

On the other hand, Bulgaria represents no problem for the Soviet Union, except for the small subsidy it requires, and the economic and political recovery of Hungary under Kadar constitutes a bright spot. Hungary is experimenting successfully thus far with economic reform, careful to ensure that its changes do not spill over into the political system from the economy or make Hungary too conspicuously liberal or successful.

The most critical problems reside in the so-called "Iron Triangle": East Germany, Czechoslovakia and Poland. Poland's problems were illustrated by the riots and strikes. The Soviet Union crushed Czechoslovak socialist humanism in 1968 with remarkable speed and skill, and it has quietly supervised the removal of Dubcek, Smrkovsky and their chief supporters and introduced substantial change in the Czechoslovak leadership and political system. The Soviet Union, in short, has carried out an effective political counterrevolution, but the economic and social problems which created the "spring" in Czechoslovakia remain more serious than ever.

Finally, the German Democratic Republic represents special difficulties, symbolized by the Berlin Wall, now almost ten years old. Few governments could more resolutely maintain control over their society. On the other hand, Ulbricht was an extremely stubborn defender of the interests of the German Democratic Republic, and he succeeded in delaying Soviet initiatives in its relations with the Federal Republic. Above all, the political situation in East Germany is most unstable, and the Soviet rulers must wonder whether Honecker will follow Novotny and Gomulka, both of whom also seemed secure in their positions.

The situation within Eastern Europe cannot be isolated from that in the remainder of the communist world. The Twenty-fourth Party Congress was in many ways soothing and reassuring. However, a number of important communist states, including the People's Republic of China and Yugoslavia, were not represented, and Soviet policy was criticized by leaders of parties as important as those of Rumania and France. The French and Italian parties in particular exercise a significant influence throughout Eastern Europe.

Finally, communist China has now decided to return to the world and to great-power politics, increasing again the attractions of national communism as well as the ability of the East European regimes to manoeuvre against the Soviet Union. Its recent tactics have elevated ping-pong to an important position in international diplomacy, and the Soviet nightmare of a combination of China and the United States must now recur more insistently. In addition, the communist Chinese, who maintain five embassies in Eastern Europe, have set out to reduce Soviet authority there.

The basic Soviet problem in Eastern Europe is simple: its military and political role is threatened by powerful economic, social and intellectual forces not susceptible to the controls which have proved effective in the Soviet Union (and which will remain effective within that country). First of all, nationalism is a rising force throughout Eastern Europe, as it is in most other parts of the world. The peasants kept it alive during the dreadful years under Stalin and his puppets. The affection for the national history and culture, and for the national interest, has now been adopted by the workers, the professional groups, and the students, all favored by their regimes. In fact, communist success in creating new classes has helped to erode the earlier gratitude for liberation from the Nazis. Many direct more of their animosity against the Russians for recent restrictions than against the Germans, who were the hated enemies for the first two decades after the war, especially in Czechoslovakia and Poland.

At the same time, the economic achievements have enabled the peoples to devote their attention to issues other than simple survival. The approaching retirement of that generation which felt most grateful and loyal to the Soviet Union as well as the population explosion have created a homogeneous and predominantly youthful population with ideas and interests quite different from those who ruled or even survived in the 1940s and 1950s. (More than half the Polish population, for example, is under thirty.)

The economic problems which produced the "spring" in Czechoslovakia and the riots and strikes in Poland remain unresolved. Basically, the East Europeans at enormous effort, including the sacrifice of most civil liberties, have modernized their economies quite significantly and have made substantial progress in industrial production. However, they have found that the command economy methods have "taken them as far as they can go," and that the West Europeans in the same two decades have moved into a new economic era, one which leaves East Europeans further behind than before.

Moreover, the economic and social problems of Czechoslovakia and Poland are even more fundamental and challenging now than before the crisis. In fact, the invasion of 1968 deepened the Czechoslovak depression, and the sterile and bleak leadership worsens it. The troubles in Poland have simply indicated that massive economic reforms are mandatory. Internal resources to meet the economic needs do not exist. In addition, neither the Czechoslovak nor the Polish Government has the intellectual understanding, the political sense, the popular support, or Soviet approval now necessary to carry out economic change. At the same time, the Soviet Union lacks the material resources and the understanding to provide assistance. Indeed, it is hampered by the same scientific and technical lag. Consequently, the stagnant Czechoslovak economy must stagger on, with a working class ever less disposed to obey the commands of its rulers and with an industrial base ever less competent to meet the demands of the last third of the twentieth century, when the revolution of rising expectations will become ever more important throughout Eastern Europe.

In addition, an intellectual and philosophical vacuum has grown. Briefly, Marxism-Leninism is considered less and less relevant even by communist leaders in those countries. Many of them now consider Western management techniques and equipment more useful for their ailing economies than ideas imported and imposed from the East.

Above all, Eastern Europe, is unstable because of the remarkable recovery and the growing vitality of the neighboring states in Western Europe. At a time when the silence in Russian culture which Sir Isaiah Berlin noted fifteen years ago has become even more profound, Western ideas and ideals are overwhelming Eastern Europe and producing a significant impact upon the Soviet Union as well. Movies, music, fashions, novels, economic theory, social relations between generations, and the qualitative achievements of Western science and technology are known, respected and envied. The sunflower turns to the West now rather than to Moscow. Moscow must on occasion see Eastern Europe as a carrier of Western infections rather than as a barrier.

Unfortunately, from the Soviet point of view, Eastern Europe cannot be isolated from Western Europe and the rest of the world as it was during Stalin's time. The striking changes in transportation and communication and the massive expansion of education, even highly technical education, have created interests, appetites and needs which have shriveled the old controls and increased Western influence. Indeed, the very highest levels of the communist parties have been deeply affected by Western ideas and this influence has spilled into the Soviet Union as well, especially among the minorities, such as the Jews and Ukrainians. Louis XIV's comment that nations meet *only* at the top does not apply in the age of mass culture, increased education, international travel and study and a series of revolutions in communications. However, nations still meet *first* at the top and foreign influences are absorbed first by today's political leaders and scientists, as they were earlier among aristocrats. Soviet dissidents, such as Sakharov, Medvedev and Amalrik, were all influenced by developments in Eastern Europe and in the West.

In some ways, the Soviet dilemma in Eastern Europe is like that which the regimes of Alexander I and Nicholas I faced one hundred fifty years ago, except that the Soviet Union is more deeply involved in European state politics and more influenced by European ideas and economic vitality that was the other old regime. The Decembrists and the Polish Revolt in 1830-31 alarmed the early Tsars just as the Budapest, Prague and Polish revolts have frightened their successors. Today's dilemma is even more fundamental, because the communists are trying to catch up with Western Europe on the material plane and to shake off its influence on the political and psychological plane. As Christopher Dawson pointed out years ago, "Given the nature of Western political philosophy, which is a philosophy of freedom, this dilemma, and consequent conflicts are inevitable."

Those who make Soviet policy decisions with regard to Eastern Europe are, first of all, Soviet communists, with a view of themselves, of the world, and of history which derives from their interpretation of Marxism-Leninism. Seen through Soviet-tinted glasses, Eastern Europe has no doubt been undergoing slow, steady progress, hampered on occasion by "capitalist remnants," which caused difficulties such as those with Yugoslavia in 1948 and the various eruptions since that time. The forces of history and the guidance of Big Brother, however, will thrust into the dustbin of history those not sufficiently loyal or submissive. They will also assure that the danger threshold will never be crossed and that these states will continue their progress toward communism under vigilant Soviet leadership.

This view, which reflects imperfect knowledge of the peoples in this complex area as well as the inability to understand others which paralyzes all of us, is a serious limitation on Soviet policy. Moreover, the Soviet Government is profoundly conservative and unimaginative, handicapped by its philosophy and persuaded that force in the last analysis will overcome any shortcomings. In addition, the Soviet Government is to some degree restricted by the Soviet public, which was convinced by the Second World War that Eastern Europe, especially East Germany, remains essential to the security of the Soviet Union. The millions of veterans in particular would fail to understand a Soviet policy which surrendered or weakened the Soviet position. Moreover, the "hard-liners" in the party, particularly at the upper levels, have a significant impact on Soviet decisions in this central area and therefore limit the options available.

The Soviet Government also realizes that the national interests of each of the states of Eastern Europe differ frequently from those of the others and that they cannot be treated as a bloc. It also assumes that the leaders of these states are experienced in Soviet ways of dealing with others and that, even though loyal to the Soviet Union, they will on occasion defend their national interests against insistent Soviet pressures. Moreover, while Moscow retains the capability to use ancient dislikes and current ambitions to divide Budapest from Bucharest and Warsaw from Prague, and even to use anti-Semitism, it must know that the leaders of these states on occasion will band together to defend their interests, perhaps simply by stalling. The Soviet leaders also realize from experience that their relations with these leaders can no longer be shielded even from the rest of the communist world. Yugoslavia in particular obtains access to even the most confidential information, thus demolishing one of the great strengths the Soviet leaders used to enjoy.

The existence of other independent communist states, particularly communist China but Yugoslavia as well, also exerts a limiting influence upon Soviet policy. The Chinese charge that "peaceful penetration of Western capitalism" into Eastern Europe is occurring under the blind eye of the Soviet Union. Its other charges of ideological softness naturally affects Soviet views and policies, as do those of Western communist parties alert to Soviet "sectarian, dogmatic attitudes" and harsh, restrictive Soviet policies which will affect their own electoral prospects. The Soviet Government can and usually does ignore these criticisms or protests, but such actions exact a penalty and in the long run can circumscribe Soviet freedom of action.

Above all, the Soviet Government must fear Western influences and the effect any relaxation of controls in Eastern Europe would have throughout that area and within the Soviet Union as well. The "Great Fear" is that any unbinding of Soviet power in this critical borderland would erode communist power within the Soviet Union and begin a withering away of the myth that international communism led from Moscow is an invincible wave of the future. It would destroy the true faith of communists and at the same time encourage the "savage" Americans and Chinese. Thus, any weakening in Eastern Europe would be interpreted by the Soviet rulers themselves as an assault upon the inexorable forces of history, as well as upon the ultimate security of the Soviet Union.

To help meet the various challenges posed, the Soviet leaders have a number of choices. Thus, with regard to arrangements between those states and the Soviet Union, they might reconsider establishment of a socialist commonwealth of nations, including the states of Eastern Europe, except for Albania and Yugoslavia, and any other communist states which might wish to join. This dramatic and vague proposal, made originally just before Soviet armed intervention into Hungary, would bind the various states of Eastern Europe more closely to the Soviet Union in an ostensibly free federation. It would help establish clear lines of policy and political arrangement. It would divide those who supported the Soviet Union from those who refused to join it. It would also establish a framework into which a repentant or revised Rumania and a new Yugoslavia, Albania and communist China could join.

On the other hand, Rumania would almost certainly refuse to join such a "federation" and would resent its establishment. Some of the other states would certainly fear that such a commonwealth would constitute a step toward absorption as a Soviet Socialist Republic. Yugoslavia, Albania and communist China would not only refuse to join but would attack it as the re-establishment of the Cominform, while those foreign communist parties already critical of Soviet efforts to establish a coordinating system would be vociferously critical.

Another option - incorporation of one or two of the states of Eastern Europe into the Union of Soviet Socialist Republics - would enable the

Soviet Government to deal most effectively with the people so absorbed. The Soviet Government apparently considered the incorporation of Slovakia in 1968 as one way of resolving the Czechoslovak issue. However, such an action would create enormous opposition throughout Eastern Europe and among other communist states and parties. It would especially create fear and hostility among Germans, East and West, for they would conclude that it meant that the German Democratic Republic might one day also be swallowed, thereby ending "forever" any hope of German unity.

A third option is maintaining the status quo throughout Eastern Europe, supplemented by a gradual and almost imperceptible general tightening of control within each country and of Soviet hegemony over all the countries. This slow and almost invisible kind of re-Stalinization would be concealed by amenities and would consist of small steps, with the carrot always concealing the stick. It might be reflected in revised treaties such as that concluded with Czechoslovakia in May 1970, which increased Soviet authority and obligated Czechoslovakia to assist the Soviet Union in conflicts even in East Asia.

Such a general tightening would strengthen Soviet controls, at least temporarily. It would alienate the privileged classes which Russia seeks to persuade. It would also, of course, arouse communist parties such as those of France and Italy, and it would clearly raise tensions throughout Europe and the world, thereby endangering the detente and Soviet hope for increased trade and for Western technological assistance to the USSR.

Economic stagnation, especially in Czechoslovakia and Poland, the ever more visible lag of the science and technology of Eastern Europe behind that of Western Europe, and the pressure for diversion of increased resources to satisfy the needs of the urban classes constitute the most direct and serious challenge throughout Eastern Europe. The Soviet response, and that of the Novotnys and Gomulkas, has not been impressive. When the Soviet Government has provided substantial aid, as it did in Hungary in 1956, in Czechoslovakia in 1968, and in Poland in 1971 - after crises had erupted - it has done so on a crash basis. So far as we know, it has never considered anything like the Marshall Plan, or any long-term proposal which sought to advance the interests of each country in a co-ordinated long-term aid program designed to raise the general economic level.

Such a policy is beyond the capacity of the Soviet leaders. Their interest in the Soviet Union and in Soviet advance is single-minded. They have a pyramidal view of world communism, with the Soviet Union at the top, at the highest stage of development. Stalin's view concerning the construction of socialism in one country still fetters them, as the Chinese communists discovered a decade ago, when they urged that all states ruled by communists share resources and move toward communism at the same pace. Moreover, both the Soviet economies and those of the East European states are in such straitjackets from centralized controls that a multinational program would be immensely difficult to administer, even if the political will existed.

Another possibility is transforming COMECON, the Council for Mutual Economic Assistance, into a joint supranational economic organization of the communist states, one designed to establish a "Socialist integration." Such an approach, which would probably be modeled on the Common Market, is also beyond practical Soviet capabilities. Establishing a supranational organization of reformed and unreformed economic systems would be extraordinarily difficult. It would require each state to surrender part of its sovereignty, which Rumania already has refused to do. Each country would have to introduce substantial institutional changes, remove entrenched bureaucracies' grips from the national economy, and coordinate its own national economic plans with those of the other countries. Each currency would have to be revalued, and a uniform price system established which escaped from the arbitrary and inflexible national systems which now prevail. Above all, the communist states would have to establish a multilateral payments system with a convertible ruble. These steps are almost inconceivable, so that COMECON is condemned to stumbling along as it has since 1949, with slow and minor improvements.

Another possibility is Soviet promotion of economic reform along the lines which the Kadar government in Hungary is now following or those which the Czechoslovak Government sought to establish in 1968. This would decentralize the economies, give more authority to individual enterprises and to the market, provide increased national incentives, and elevate the role of qualified specialists as compared to bureaucratic party managers. It would pay significantly greater attention to consumer expectations, and it would lead almost inevitably to relaxed controls.

The Soviet Government is likely to tolerate some economic reform in Poland and Czechoslovakia, if the trusted governments of those countries can overcome fears of change within their own beleaguered administrations. However, the Twenty-fourth Congress of the Soviet Party in March 1971, especially the speeches of Kosygin, "the reformer" within the Politburo, revealed that the Soviet Government itself has turned against economic reform. It instead re-emphasized administrative centralization, spiced with devices modeled upon American business schools such as the Institute for Management of the National Economy, and Western technology acquired through increased trade and through arrangements with firms such as Fiat.

Thus, the Soviet rulers believe that "Liberman reforms" almost inevitably lead to Sik and that Sik almost inevitably leads to a crisis such as that of August 1968. Moreover, reformed communism represents a direct threat to traditional socialist planning. The bureaucrats who would lose power and positions would oppose it, as would those who fear the impact of reform upon communist party rule. Continued success in Hungary without any threatening political consequences alone offers hope. However, even the Hungarian reform involves increased trade with the West, and Western investment, and raises the specter of the influence of foreign ideas. Moreover, the Hungarians must walk a very narrow path, somehow containing their changes within the economy and not becoming so successful as to attract the fear and wrath of Soviet or East German conservatives.

Another possibility is significantly increased trade with the West, including Japan and the United States. In fact, rejection of internal economic reforms would increase the need for expanded trade, because the centralized command economy could be revived only through Western technology - but Western equipment and ideas could be acquired only through trade. However, from sixty to seventy-five percent of the foreign trade of the East European states is committed to the Soviet Union by long-term agreements, so they have little freedom of action. The arrangements which the Soviet Union has established constitute a form of imperialism which further cripples the Poles, the Hungarians and others in trade with the West: generally, the East European states are obliged to ship their finest industrial products to Moscow, receiving in return various raw materials, such as oil, gas and iron ore. In addition, the quality of the goods produced in Eastern Europe is generally below the level sought by Western consumers, and East Europeans lack the marketing skills international trade requires. In short, prospects for greatly increased trade are dim. Increased Western aid is also unlikely, for economic as well as political reasons.

The East European states not only lack the capacity to increase trade significantly with the West, but the Soviet leaders realize that trade is a most serious cause of infection. It would introduce fresh air, new contacts, and ideas. Moreover, any increase in trade would lead inevitably to pressure to reform the economy in order to produce the kind and quality of goods and services required in payment by the West. As Toynbee revealed in his "Study of History," no society can borrow an idea, a technique, a piece of equipment from another society without also importing that society's spirit and values.

In contemporary terms, the Soviet Union and Eastern Europe are a closed system facing a modernization crisis of special severity because it is compounded by imperial problems. The Russians are facing a hazard which de Tocqueville foresaw for any autocratic government which sought popularity or greater productivity. In an old Russian phrase, "They seek a fire which will not burn." Moreover, this new fire might not succeed in warming up the stagnant economies but might only stimulate appetites and intensify problems.

During the past few years, the Soviet Union has followed a policy called detente, one designed to weaken the resolution of Western Europe, to break up NATO, to weaken and destroy the Common Market, and to remove American forces and influences from Western Europe. The Moscow treaty between the Soviet Union and the Federal Republic of Germany in August 1970, the trade and aid agreement completed in October between Bonn and Warsaw, and the agreement signed in Warsaw in December 1970 between Germany and Poland are the outstanding illustrations thus far of this process.

However, neither the Federal Republic's *Ostpolitik* nor the Soviet Union's *Westpolitik* has yet passed the major test, because the Moscow agreement has not yet been ratified or even placed before the West German legislature. In fact, the absence of progress in West Berlin has increased opposition to the treaty. German ratification of the August 1970 Moscow agreement still depends on a satisfactory solution of the West Berlin situation, one in which the Soviet Union would recognize special ties between West Berlin and the Federal Republic and guarantee access of West Germans to West Berlin and of West Germans to East Berlin. If the

Soviet Union should reach agreement on West Berlin, the Moscow and Warsaw treaties would be ratified, thereby providing official West German recognition of the permanent boundaries of Poland and acceptance of the German Democratic Republic. It might also lead to a European Security Conference, which would strengthen the apparent legitimacy of East Germany and would, in short, provide apparent additional security on the Soviet western borderland at a time of prolonged tension with communist China. It would also lead to increased trade and substantial loans from Western Europe, perhaps even from the Common Market, to the economies of Eastern Europe, a goal even more important to the Soviet Union than legitimacy.

On the other hand, as the Soviet rulers no doubt realize, the policy of detente raises serious hazards. It would expose the Soviet western borderlands to developments they may be unable to control. Basically, West German acceptance of the present boundaries of Eastern Europe represents no real change: no Western states hope to change those boundaries, and no treaty can guarantee their permanence, any more than the Congress of Vienna ensured the permanence of the status quo of Europe then. Moreover, the West German agreements with the Soviet Union and Poland, the trade agreements completed in 1970 with five countries of Eastern Europe, and the discussions going on with Czechoslovakia reveal that Eastern Europe no longer fears that West Germany seeks to revive Nazi ambitions. Indeed, even if the Moscow and Warsaw agreements should not be ratified, no one in Eastern Europe could doubt that the goal of the Federal Republic's policy is peace. This new relationship might even lead to genuine understanding and reconciliation with Poland and especially with Czechoslovakia, completing the isolation of East Germany. It might even lead to the abolition of the Berlin Wall, a prospect which no Pankow government could face without fear. Thus, the "outbreak of peace" would destroy the ideological foundations of the German Democratic Republic. The desire for reunion, shown by the tumultuous greeting given Willy Brandt on his first visit to East Germany, would exert tremendous pressures for some form of German reunification, even if the German Democratic Republic had been recognized as an independent state and were a member of the United Nations. In short, Soviet controls lose their justification and some of their potency when fear is reduced, while those elements of Western strength become ever more effective as peaceful relations are more widely accepted.

Another possibility for Soviet diplomacy is linking disarmament and German unification. Reducing armaments would help lessen tension, significantly decrease the heavy military burden on the Soviet budget, enable the Soviet Union to devote more attention to China, and weaken the resolution and verve of the West. It might also lead to large credits for the Soviet Union and Eastern Europe as Western Europe and the United States relaxed their fears.

However, no contemporary Soviet government could accept a reunified Germany, even if disarmed, because such a Germany would raise such uncertainties in the center of Soviet defenses. In addition, a unified Germany, even a neutral and unarmed Germany, would open Eastern

Europe to increased Western influences. It would be interpreted by the Chinese communists as a defeat for the Soviet Union, and it would reflect the first step backward from the massive expansion of communism which began after the Second World War.

The Soviet Union must have made preparation for opportunities which may arise in Yugoslavia after the retirement of Tito. It must assume that the end of Tito's rule will expose the Yugoslav Federal Republic to very heavy internal pressures and that the Republic may break up, providing the Soviet Union with an opportunity to make arrangements with one or another of the republics or with groups of Yugoslav communists who seek Soviet support to advance their own interests. An action such as this would have enormous advantages for the Soviet Union. It would end the threat of the heresy and even the examples posed by Tito. It would encircle Rumania and bring it back into the Soviet fold. It would strengthen Soviet hegemony in Eastern Europe and provide a new threat toward Albania, Greece, Italy and the Mediterranean. It would increase enormously the threat to Western Europe, while at the same time it would diminish the attraction of national communism and would vault the Soviet Union into a stronger position throughout the communist world.

Such an action could be undertaken only under most favorable auspices: an invitation from a Yugoslav Republic or from a group of Yugoslav "leaders" for aid; extreme disarray in Western Europe because of national elections, the presence of weak governments in critical countries, or some crisis within the West or in a part of the world critical to the West; and a divided, irresolute, and unprepared United States. In fact, a situation might occur similar to that which led to Munich in September 1938 or to further Nazi action, without opposition, in March 1939. However, in spite of the immense advantages such a step would offer, the circumstances would have to be most favorable to persuade even a dynamic and vigorous government to intervene. Moreover, Soviet intervention in Yugoslavia would raise difficulties similar to those encountered by the Nazis and would create a world crisis even more tense than the Cuban missile threat in 1962. Such intervention does remain an option, though, as the Yugoslav and Rumanian alerts after August 20, 1968, demonstrate.

Pressure against West Berlin, such as that which led to the blockade of 1948-1949 or to the Khrushchev ultimata of 1958 and later years, constitute another Soviet option, the likelihood of which will increase as the advantages of detente decline. West Berlin remains such a critical point and symbol for the West that significant harassment is unlikely, unless another crisis within the West should occur. In fact, the critical factor with regard to West Berlin will remain visible, unified Western determination to secure its security and Western access. If the Soviet Government has no doubts concerning Western resolution, neither it nor the German Democratic Republic will create significant pressure.

The Soviet Government now holds the commanding heights in Eastern Europe. The advantages of maintaining the status quo are immense, ensuring the Soviet Government the benefits outlined earlier and increasing the time for transforming and integrating the area and eroding the peoples' hopes. Moreover, in time, the strength and power of the West, especially the United States, may wither. In this situation, an occasional crisis might even be salutary, enabling the Soviet Government to identify the flowers of opposition as they bloom and to demonstrate Soviet determination.

However, maintaining present arrangements is not possible, while actions taken to resolve pressing issues are almost certain to raise even greater hazards. Control of the commanding heights provides political hegemony without security in an era as profoundly revolutionary as that of the Renaissance and Reformation. The vast changes under way threaten Western societies too, but Western Europe and the United States are equipped for change, lead in it, respect it, assume it. This is one world for the Soviet Union as well as for the United States. In the contest between the old titans, geography and force, and lively new ideas, the great changes in education and communication spread these ideas and help undermine the bases of all established, conservative systems, including that defended by the Soviet Government.

These changes are occurring at the same time the world is entering a new diplomatic era, one as pregnant with change as the 1850s and 1860s, when the Concert of Europe and federalism collapsed. Soviet diplomacy will no doubt remain skillful, but progress toward some form of West European unity, the emergence of Japan as a great power, the return of the People's Republic of China into world politics, and the steady rise of countries such as Mexico, Brazil and India will create a new situation, one which will help unbind all bonds of empire. This will give the East European states more maneuverability at the same time it makes the Soviet role less defensible. Thrashing critical leaders, crushing rebellions, and providing lavish short-term economic aid will not meet these issues, any more than tightening the command economy will stimulate innovation and new energies.

These changes and challenges are likely to strengthen the instinct of the Soviet leaders to make the system more repressive, darkening prospects of the Soviet peoples for greater freedoms and more consumer goods. The Soviet leaders, as the Twenty-fourth Party Congress demonstrated, will thus seek to "safeguard and strengthen" their rule. The new "impersonality cult" will seek the gray middle of the road, buttressed by the conservative instincts of an elderly ruling group which feels itself threatened. Policies reflecting these postures will not provide economic dynamism, respond to growing claims for the right to self-determination, or provide other acceptable solutions, even safety-valves, to the problems posed by Eastern Europe.

Thus, the Soviet position in Eastern Europe is an unstable one. Fundamentally, this reflects the conflict between the ideas of Wilson and those of Lenin concerning the ways in which societies should be organized and should deal with each other. No area in the world is more important than Eastern Europe in resolving these great issues, and none under Soviet hegemony is more precarious.

4

United States Policy Toward Eastern Europe: Before and After Helsinki

The signing in Helsinki of the agreement on security and cooperation in Europe has led to bitter criticism of President Ford and of the policy under which the United States drifted into recognizing Soviet acquisition of 114,000 square miles of Finnish, Polish, German, Czechoslovak, and Rumanian territory, apparently sanctified as well Soviet domination of Eastern Europe, and recognized the "permanent" division of Europe. In return for endorsing these Soviet conquests, the Western states received some vague promises that the Soviet Union and the East European states would take a "positive and humanitarian attitude" towards applications from their citizens to rejoin their families in the West, would "facilitate the improvement of the dissemination" of publications from other countries, would provide three weeks notice of large military maneuvers within 156 miles of frontiers, and assured that every European state would be free from "external influence." All these phrases seem small recompense for such great concessions and from two years of negotiation by 492 diplomats, especially when hope in Western Europe in particular had been high for an end to jamming, censorship, and control over travel. Critics noted in particular that the formal summit agreement awarded the Soviet Union prizes it had sought since 1954, while the parallel discussion of reducing military forces in Eastern and Western Europe, in which the Soviet Union and its associates maintain immense superiorities, has long been stalled. Indeed, now that the West no longer has the lever of the Geneva talks, it has little pressure to persuade the Soviet Union to discuss mutual balanced force reduction. Many now fear that the Soviet Union will press instead for a collective security agreement, which would have no meaning, but which would totally demolish NATO, while leaving the Soviets on the commanding military heights in Eastern Europe.

Defenders of the Helsinki agreement profess surprise at the uproar, especially because the Geneva talks had attracted so little attention. They argue too that the agreement is not a treaty and is not legally binding. Moreover, it changes no policies. It recognizes no arrangements which West German treaties with the Soviet Union, Poland, and East Germany had not accepted in 1970-1971. They note too that no Western leader since John Foster Dulles has even talked of liberating Eastern Europe and that our

Reprinted with permission from *Review of Politics*, XXXVII (1975), 435-463.

strategy on this agreement is a continuation of our established efforts to liberalize communist rule in Eastern Europe. Moreover, the agreement does provide some kinds of assurance against Soviet pressure against Rumania and Yugoslavia, ensures that accredited journalists may obtain multiple entry visas, and establishes a "code of conduct" against which Soviet performance can be measured at the 1977 conference in Belgrade. Above all, no formal agreements, no matter how high-sounding, can preserve the East European regimes against the political, economic, and intellectual forces which are pulling them towards Western Europe. Indeed, they note the irony of the Soviet concern with "pieces of paper," with having their position recognized and ratified when increased contacts allowed by that very agreement will raise new problems for the Soviet Government.

The Helsinki agreement is an important link in the chain of American policy towards Eastern Europe, one into which we drifted without careful thought or successful bargaining. It is very important to the Soviet Union because it recognizes conquests and governments which had no legitimacy, but it does not resolve Soviet problems in Eastern Europe, any more than resolute and forceful Soviet military action did in 1956 and 1968. Moreover, it does not remove Eastern Europe from its central position as an issue between the Soviet Union and the West. The verve which the West Europeans demonstrated at Geneva alone demonstrates this. At the same time, it does provide the United States an opportunity to review its goals and policies and to refine new ways and means of assisting the East European peoples gradually to make their way toward more freedoms and greater independence in a struggle which will clearly be long and hard.

Since 1945, most of the states and peoples of Eastern Europe have lived under Soviet control, producing a situation which many observers consider the foundation of the tense relationships between the United States and the West, on one hand, and the Soviet Union, on the other. Even today, when Soviet and American interests often collide elsewhere in the world, many believe that Eastern Europe remains the heart of the struggle between the Soviet Union and the United States. Most also remain convinced that peace and security will not return to Europe and to the world until "the Red Army can be prevailed upon to evacuate Europe," in the words of Walter Lippmann in 1947. Western inability to help obtain independence and freedoms for the peoples of Eastern Europe has consequently played an important role in American domestic politics, and has constituted one of the principal shortcomings of American foreign policy in the last three decades.

The plight of the Eastern Europeans reflects in good part their geographical location between the Germans and the Russians. The present situation derives from the destructive impact of the war which the Nazis launched upon the political institutions of Eastern Europe. The flow of Soviet military power into the vacuum created by the defeat of the Nazi forces placed the Soviet Union in occupation of all the area now called Eastern Europe, with the exception of Yugoslavia and Albania. Yugoslavia under Tito was able to remain free of Soviet power after 1948 because the armed forces which Tito created had themselves freed Yugoslavia from the Nazis. These forces and Yugoslav nationalism under Tito enabled that country to survive Stalin's ousting Tito from the Cominform in 1948 and the subsequent military and economic pressures directed against Yugoslavia. Albania was able to maintain its freedom from the Soviet Union and later from Yugoslavia because of its special isolated position, the balancing of forces among its neighbors, and the formal protection which the People's Republic of China has provided since 1960.

Awakened from their long isolation by the Japanese attack at Pearl Harbor, American leaders and the American people had only a shallow understanding of the importance of Eastern Europe and of the ways in which the modern state must combine its military and political strategies. President Roosevelt concentrated entirely upon winning the Second World War, delayed facing the political problems which arose over Eastern Europe during the war, and relied upon the United Nations to resolve them after the conflict had ended. He therefore separated politics and political arrangements from military strategy. Soviet forces then flowed over Eastern Europe and consolidated Soviet rule, while we failed to use our economic and other resources to support a strong diplomatic position. The efforts of American and other Western statesmen late in the war and in the two or three years after the war to preserve the independence and liberties of the East European peoples were therefore almost doomed to failure, because of Soviet determination to retain the territories occupied. The Western powers and the East European peoples have therefore been condemned to a basically uphill and unsuccessful effort to deprive the Soviet Union of what Soviet leaders and peoples both consider a prize of victory and a guarantee of peace.

Until the beginning of the Second World War, American policy towards Eastern Europe was marked by neglect and ignorance. During the war, President Roosevelt in effect appeased Stalin, in the hope that benign behavior and consistent acceptance of Soviet requests and demands would persuade Stalin of the benefits of close and friendly relationships after the war, when the political issues could be decided in an amicable way. By 1947, President Truman and the great majority of the American people had recognized the massive failure of Roosevelt's efforts. We then devoted our resources and energies to the policy known as containment, an effort to erect an "unalterable counterforce" against the Soviet outward thrust, in the hope that marshalling Western military, economic and political resources would ultimately bring about a moderation and mellowing of Soviet policy and perhaps the break-up of the Soviet empire.

Containment has been more successful than most Americans realize. The outward thrust of the Soviet Union has thus far been contained in Europe, which remains the most critical area in the world. The expansion of communism since 1947 has been limited to the People's Republic of China, Cuba, South Viet Nam, Laos, and Cambodia. At the same time, Soviet policy, particularly since the death of Stalin, has generally been somewhat cautious and prudent and has mellowed to a degree. However, Soviet military power continues to grow and the Soviet Government continues to encourage other governments and political groups in the use of violence and to stimulate crises, in the Middle East in particular. Meanwhile, although Soviet authority has remained in command in Eastern

Europe, serious cracks have appeared on a number of occasions, beginning with the riots in East Berlin in 1953. The Polish revolt in 1956 and the Hungarian rebellion later that year led some to conclude that extensive disintegration of Moscow's authority within Eastern Europe was under way. However, the Soviet Union was able to effect a satisfactory compromise in Poland and to crush the Hungarian rebellion later that year, while the outside world watched helplessly. Similarly, the extraordinary effort of the Czechoslovak people, led by most of their communists, to create a "socialism with a human face" was crushed by the Soviet Union and its allied military forces on August 20, 1968, while again the United States and its allies stood by helplessly. In December 1970, dissatisfaction over long autocratic rule, rising prices, and new work quotas led to strikes, riots, and violence in ports and northern industrial cities in Poland. This forced the replacement of Gomulka by Gierek, reversal of the offending policies, and a new effort by the Polish Government to establish closer relations with the people and to remove the economic causes of these bitter discontents. This change in government policy forced from below revealed again the depths of the dissatisfactions which seethe in Eastern Europe, the readiness of even the privileged workers and students to rise against the government, and the brittle character of the regimes.

The Soviet interventions in 1953, 1956, and 1968 crushed revolts and led many to believe that a spirit of hopelessness and complete surrender would overcome the East Europeans. Curiously, the Soviet repressions and the Polish developments in 1970 and 1971 all led to improved economic and political conditions for the peoples who had risen against their rulers. Thus, the so-called Thaw and the New Course prevailed throughout Eastern Europe after the riots in East Berlin early in the summer of 1953, and the new government in Warsaw after the successful 1956 revolution was for several years more attentive and relaxed in its relations with the Polish people and with the Catholic Church than the Bierut government had been. Similarly, the challenge raised by the Hungarians in the fall of 1956 persuaded the Soviet Government to invest massive resources in Hungary to try to resolve some of the basic economic problems and, later, to tolerate another effort toward economic reform under Kadar called the New Economic Mechanism. Finally, the Soviet effort towards relaxation of tensions or a detente with the West picked up speed after the crushing of "the Prague spring."

Political and economic arrangements and conditions remain different in each of the East European countries, with the political and economic controls most intensive over the Bulgarians, Czechoslovaks, and Rumanians. However, conditions throughout Eastern Europe have generally relaxed and improved since the August 1968 invasion of Czechoslovakia. The reasons for this most recent shift in Soviet policy are numerous. They include increased Soviet understanding of the problems with which they deal in Eastern Europe, the flare-up of Soviet-Chinese hostility in 1969, the Nixon policy toward the People's Republic of China, the growing Soviet need for access to Western science and technology, and Soviet assessment of the most effective stance to adopt in order to advance Soviet interests throughout the world.

Whatever the causes for minor modifications of Soviet policy in Eastern Europe and whatever the nature of these changes, the Western states and peoples throughout the past three decades have continued to seek a set of policies which would assist the peoples of Eastern Europe and reduce the threat to security in Europe as a whole. Primary responsibility for this policy has rested with the United States, if only because the West European peoples have had to devote so much of their energies to economic, political, and spiritual reconstruction after the Second World War, to disengaging themselves from their imperial relationships, and to working towards some form of Western union. Basically, through all the changes in stance and in phraseology, our policy has remained one of containment. However, in Eisenhower's first term, Secretary of State John Foster Dulles urged a policy of liberation of the East European people. This more aggressive pose, which was shown in 1956 to represent only rhetoric, arose because the American people by 1952 were baffled by their failure to change the Soviet position in Eastern Europe, depressed by the high cost of the defense program, frustrated by the Korean War, and hopeful that a "positive new foreign policy" would somehow bring a quick end to Soviet occupation of Eastern Europe and to the high degree of tension.

Our inaction during the Hungarian crisis in 1956, when the United States and the United Nations both fumbled a splendid opportunity to recognize and assist the government of Imre Nagy, then persuaded some American and British leaders, including even the enunciator of the containment doctrine, George Kennan, to flirt with the idea of disengagement. This assumed that the cause of the tension was the presence of large armed forces facing each other in Central Europe and that disengaging these forces would reduce and perhaps even end the constant strain. It quickly became clear that the presence of the large armies was a reflection of the crisis and not the cause. The doctrine of disengagement never attracted large support, and faded away by 1958.

Our basic policy of containment has been supplemented since approximately 1960 by vigorous and imaginative efforts to improve relations with the peoples of Eastern Europe through "building bridges," peaceful engagement, and what the present Canadian Foreign Minister calls "dynamic coexistence." In short, for the past fifteen years, the United States and its allies have continued to concentrate on preventing further Soviet expansion in Europe and on increasing economic and cultural relations with the East European peoples, in the hope that these steps will reduce Soviet control and enable these peoples gradually and slowly to inch their way towards more independence and greater freedoms.

However, while Europe and Eastern Europe have remained properly at the center of our concern, we have naturally devoted even greater attention to the wider concentric circles which surround Europe. During the past decade in particular, the central nature of Europe's place has often been obscured by the prominence of many other areas and issues as the world has shrunk, as scientific-technical-economic revolutions have struck every part of the globe, and as crises reflecting changing power situations, ambitions, and local conflicts have risen elsewhere. The swirl and confusion produced by these rapid and numerous developments have made it difficult to analyze the nature of the Soviet role and the state of relations between the major powers. Clearly, the place of Europe is not so central as it has been for generations, and it will almost certainly continue to decline gradually in the years ahead. Even so, Europe will remain a central focus of world politics, and the world will not enjoy security until Europe itself has regained peace and freedom.

Reasons abound for gloom and pessimism. Western Europe, including the Common Market, seems forever in disarray. The NATO states have continually fallen short of their strength goals and show little resolution. NATO's flanks in the Eastern Mediterranean and Portugal are less secure than ever. Indeed, the entire Mediterranean underbelly of NATO is dangerously unstable. The United Kingdom may be lurching towards economic and social disaster and even division. Italy continues to totter on the brink of economic and political collapse, with the Communist Party moving from strength to strength in the confusion.

The United States has just emerged from a deep constitutional crisis, but the confusion and uncertainty which have marked recent years and which have reduced American interest and power in other parts of the world are likely to remain for some time. This central state in the Western alliance is deep in a recession, and the social disintegration and violence which have scarred our recent history continue to gnaw at our vitals. Many of our allies have doubts concerning our ability to sustain our power and policy. At the same time, while we have in some ways helped transform the character and climate of international politics and introduced new hope into a fearful world by establishing new kinds of relationships with the Soviet Union and the People's Republic of China, our relations with our major allies have deteriorated.

Soviet economic and military power continues to grow, and Soviet resolution and confidence both remain high, enabling the Soviet Government to continue to probe other areas of the world for ways and means of expanding its influence and power. Eastern Europe seems a secure element in the Soviet empire, with the state structure in each instance ever more solid and party rule ever more complete. The invasion of Czechoslovakia in 1968, the reshaping of Czechoslovak politics, and the series of treaties West Germany has made with the Soviet Union, Poland, and East Germany have apparently given legitimacy to the East German Government and to the Soviet position throughout Eastern Europe. *Ostpolitik* and the relationships between the West and the Soviet Union generally called detente have apparently served to strengthen the Soviet Union more than they have the West. While communist China remains a hostile heretic and the old unity of the international communist movement has been destroyed by many fissures, the Soviet Government retains great prestige among and considerable authority over many communist parties, some of which appear on the verge of power. It benefits also from the confusion and even anarchism which afflicts many other states and persuades some elite groups to look toward the Soviet Union.

Finally, a series of international problems torments the world in ways which tend to advance Soviet interests. The confusion and uncertainty over the world's major currencies have helped to produce a state of crisis in international trade, which threatens the stability of many major countries. Inflation, spurred by the oil embargo in 1973-1974 and posing ever more serious issues, threatens to wreck the economies and social structures of many states and the equanimity of relationships among them. Some old and new states beyond both alliance systems have developed new powers and ambitions which may undermine international stability, while others, wracked by economic disasters and dissension, are tempted into similarly dangerous ambitions. Moreover, the rise of authoritarian governments in most of these states shakes the structure of world politics, as does the anarchy which threatens the entire system. Anti-Americanism may become the most important unifying force in world politics in the last quarter of the twentieth century, as anticommunism was during the third quarter. Finally, pessimism may constitute our most crippling weakness, by blinding us to our opportunities and paralyzing our powers.

On the other hand, while the world, as always, faces serious problems, we may in fact be approaching the end of a long night. Indeed, a candid review of developments within the Soviet empire and beyond it as well could produce just as gloomy an estimate of Soviet and communist prospects. On the positive side, containment has in fact been remarkably successful in spite of all the disappointments of the past twenty-five years. Since 1959, communists have gained power only in South Viet Nam, Laos, and Cambodia. There the resolution of the North Viet Namese and their supporters, plus the aid provided by the Soviet Union and the People's Republic of China, overcame the resistance of the South Viet Namese, who were deeply opposed to communism but who lacked a strong sense of nationhood and political and social cohesion. The support the American people provided was remarkably generous, but the United States, which received little aid from its allies, ultimately proved to have neither the strategy nor the will to contain sustained communist pressure.

However, the fear that additional states in the Middle East or Latin America would fall into communist hands has not proved a reality, and some of the states most threatened are now among those most resolute in defense of their independence. The breakup of the international communist movement, particularly the hostility between the People's Republic of China and the Soviet Union, has significantly reduced the pressure which the old monolith used to exert against the rest of the world. It has also destroyed the myth that communism would bring peace to the world.

Largely because of these developments and reasonably shrewd and skillful Western diplomacy, we have made considerable progress towards arms control and crisis management. At the same time, the economies of the Western states have continued to grow, as has their military strength. In fact, who could have believed in 1962, when Khrushchev was threatening to surpass the United States in significant economic fields, that the Soviet Union in the 1970s would be desperately seeking Western aid in science and technology and burying its hopes of catching up with the Western economies?

In addition, the West European states have made remarkable progress towards European unity, particularly when one considers the situation in Europe only thirty years ago and the problems involved in even a slow march towards common institutions. With all of its failings, the West in general has shown remarkable resolution and determination in the face of the multiple crises which have afflicted the world.

Above all, the Western world has demonstrated extraordinary intellectual and cultural vitality. Western Europe and the United States together constitute the intellectual motor of the world. Their achievements in the arts and architecture, in music and literature, in philosophy (including Marxism!) and in all the sciences have demonstrated the verve and vigor of the West at the same time that Russian culture is marked by almost utter silence and has almost no impact upon life beyond the Soviet frontiers. At every level of culture, from jazz and pop art through hybrid corn and Holsteins to business management and computer technology, the Western world has shown vitality and has exerted significant influence upon Soviet and East European life. Imagine our position if we were wearing Russian-style clothes, eating and drinking Russian foods, listening to Russian music and adopting their dances, using their radio and television sets, and driving their automobiles.

Only twenty-five years ago, the East European states were violating recently concluded treaties with impunity, nationalizing Western property without compensation, closing news services, and imprisoning Western reporters and businessmen. Indeed, the only way in which the West could communicate with Eastern Europe was via radio, which was jammed consistently, and by floating free balloons, which were carried by prevailing winds from West Germany across Eastern Europe. During the entire period from 1936 through 1956, no American scholar studied in the Soviet Union, and very few were able to continue their work in Eastern Europe.

The transformation in the last two decades has been phenomenal. The differentiation among East European states is almost as great as in the 1930s. Nationalism is stronger everywhere, perhaps especially in the ruling parties. Some states, such as Rumania and Czechoslovakia, are as tightly controlled as twenty years ago, but still seek Western trade and allow some access to Western culture. Others, like Hungary and Poland, are experimenting with economic decentralization, tolerate reception of foreign broadcasts, allow some travel in Western countries, and encourage Western investment. In even the most restrictive countries, a certain amount of unbinding has occurred, and each of these states is on a higher level in the range from dictatorship to democracy than it was two decades ago.

The level of knowledge within Eastern Europe concerning developments within that area itself, the Soviet Union, and the rest of the world is much higher than in earlier years, demonstrating that the Soviet effort to control access to information has been a failure. Yugoslavia and Albania have acquired and retained freedom from Soviet control, and Rumania has been remarkably independent in its foreign policy and in developing economic relations with the West. Communist parties loyal to the Soviet Union control each of the other states, but economic and social policy varies from state to state. Thus in Poland, little land has been collectivized, and the Catholic Church retains its independence and even the right to maintain schools and provide religious education at all levels. In Hungary, the New Economic Mechanism has introduced substantial decentralization and some reliance upon the free market, and Hungarians are enabled to travel abroad far more freely than previously. In all of these countries, with the possible exception of Bulgaria, the desire for increased independence and greater freedoms exist at all levels of society and even within the highest levels of the communist parties. Above all, the hope and belief in independence and in freedom are stronger than thirty years ago. The survival of these hopes, amid the visible evidence of economic progress under the communists and the ineffectiveness of Western power, and at a time when other areas and issues have attracted the bulk of American and Western attention, reflects vividly the nature of the forces with which the Soviet Government and its associates have to deal.

The efforts of the United States and its allies to assist the East European peoples to free themselves have not succeeded, largely because the Soviet rulers consider the area so essential to the security of the Soviet Union and the survival and progress of communism. In fact, the Soviet Government would no doubt risk nuclear war rather than relinquish its control over any one of these states. Both the Soviet Government and the Soviet people see Eastern Europe as a symbol of the Soviet triumph over the Nazis and as a barrier against the West. No Soviet Government would find it possible to relinquish this territory and to surrender one of the principal conquests of the war, raising doubts concerning the survival and expansion of communism: the loss of any one of these countries would indicate that the wave of the future was going against the Soviet Union and communism, rather than ineluctably spreading communism throughout the world. These states provide an important increment to Soviet economic and military power. They also serve effectively as supply agents for the Soviet Union in the Middle East, Cuba, and other regions. Furthermore, so long as Soviet troops remain in East Germany, the Soviet Union will retain a veto over German unification and the reunification of Europe. In addition, the presence of ever more powerful Soviet forces in Eastern Europe constitutes a constant threat to the West European states, throws a shield over and strengthens the communist parties in Western Europe, and neutralizes the effectiveness of Western Europe in international politics. The Soviet leaders clearly perceive that the massive benefits acquired from the Soviet position in Eastern Europe significantly exceed the costs, including the large direct costs involved in maintaining extensive Soviet forces in that area, the disadvantage of supplying oil and other raw materials to Eastern Europe which could earn precious hard currencies in the West, the tensions with the United States and Western Europe, and the effects upon the communist parties of other countries, particularly France and Italy.

Soviet control over Eastern Europe seems impregnable. The communist parties, particularly their leaders, have been loyal and even subservient to the interests of the Soviet Union, even when their national interests have been in conflict with those of the USSR. The Soviet Government has thus been able to rely on the East European leaders, both those who were brought to rule against Soviet wishes, such as Gomulka in 1956, and those who were put in power by the Soviet Government, such as Kadar in Hungary and Husak in Czechoslovakia.

The bulk of foreign trade of each of these countries is tied to that of the Soviet Union. These states obtain the bulk of their raw materials from the Soviet Union and are committed to delivering their finest manufactured products to their Eastern neighbor. Soviet armies are located in each of these countries except Rumania, Yugoslavia, and Albania, and the Soviet Union controls the political police and the intelligence agencies. Finally, the resolute effectiveness with which Soviet forces invaded Czechoslovakia defined the limits beyond which no people shall be allowed to go and demonstrated the ruthlessness of the Soviet Government in defending its interests.

At the same time, Soviet hegemony is threatened by a series of forces, some of which are beyond Soviet control. Ironically, the very achievements of these communist regimes have created some of the problems, by bringing into existence new classes of people, technicians, skilled workers, thousands of students and intellectuals, who did not participate in the seizure of power and who do not share the revolutionary ambitions and enthusiasms of their communist elders. This is particularly true of "the heroes' children," because the generation gap in Eastern Europe resembles that of the capitalist countries, except that the flattered and spoiled youth in Eastern Europe are denied all access to power. The programs of these governments to modernize their economies have emphasized practical approaches and incentives which have weakened the role of ideology and created a powerful interest in material and national success. The decline of ideology and a new spiritual malaise have been increased by the doctrinal revisions made in 1956, which acknowledged several varieties of communism and tolerated several roads to socialism. The survival of Tito and Titoism and the appearance of polycentrism within the international communist movement with a break between the Soviet Union and the People's Republic of China have also accelerated division and revision. All of these developments have brought the political systems and their leaders closer to the people in a revived nationalism.

The mistakes of some of the governments, such as that of Rakosi in Hungary before 1956 and Gomulka in Poland in 1970, seriously damaged the system. The Soviet policies adopted to meet the various crises have paradoxically created a kind of slippage which tended further to undermine Soviet authority. Thus, the Thaw, the New Course, the New Economic Mechanism, and detente, all adopted in order to help resolve pressing problems, have tended to relax the controls of these governments and of the Soviet Union over the area and to create an ever more serious long-term threat to the system. On the other hand, the resolution with which the Soviet Government has crushed the various rebellions has disillusioned even communists, introduced fissures in communist parties outside the Soviet empire, and revealed again and again the true nature of the Soviet system.

Above all, the Soviet Union has discovered that the East European peoples cannot be digested as easily as the Central Asians were in the nineteenth century. The revival of nationalism throughout these societies, beginning with the older generations, particularly in the countryside, and rising gradually among the students, the workers, the intellectuals, and even the party bureaucracy itself, has been stimulated by Soviet exploitation, particularly between 1945 and 1960, natural resentment of governments imposed by a foreign power, and the immense authority wielded even now by massive Soviet embassies. The effort begun by Khrushchev to organize an "international division of labor" in Eastern Europe, assigning to Rumania the role of providing raw materials for the other states, also increased nationalism. The People's Republic of China has naturally fanned this movement, which has grown as polycentrism multiplied in the 1960s and 1970s and as national liberation movements in other parts of the world have been successful. *Ostpolitik,* which has made the Federal Republic a respected state, has reduced the traditional German menace. Thus, the series of treaties which the Federal Republic completed with the Soviet Union and the countries of Eastern Europe has reduced or even eliminated the main causes of fear of West Germany. The Federal Republic on December 7, 1970, recognized the Oder-Neisse boundary, signed a nonaggression pact with Poland, and agreed to the establishment of normal relations between Poland and West Germany. This treaty was supplemented before and after by trade agreements, which provide German economic and technical assistance, substantial German loans, and easy access to the German market for Polish industry and agriculture. These actions and *Ostpolitik* in general have weakened the reliance of these states upon the Soviet Union, and increased their appreciation of the price they have paid for Soviet control.

In addition, the East European states' economies have significant needs for modernizing which neither they nor the Soviet Union is able to meet. Their requirements for large amounts of capital, new technology in industry and agriculture, and managerial skills can be satisfied only in the West. The Soviet Union, which has a lower standard of living than most of these states, is not only unable to provide the assistance the East European states require, but is itself seeking Western capital, science, and technology. In addition, the Soviet Union seeks to harness East European industry to its own effort to expand production. Indeed, one of the great ironies of recent years has been Soviet insistence that the capital-poor East European governments invest in building heavy metal equipment factories, oil and gas lines, and other industrial installations in the Soviet Union, even providing extensive credits to their powerful neighbor.

Moreover, Soviet ability and interest to meet the needs of the East European states for critical raw materials, particularly crude oil and iron ore, have been declining since 1966, especially in the last two years, as Soviet needs for these raw materials have increased and as Soviet interest in expanding exports of these products to the West for hard currency has grown. In 1972, forty-seven percent of the Soviet Union's oil exports went to Eastern Europe. In that year, the Soviet Union provided ninety percent of Hungary's crude oil and iron ore, ninety percent of Poland's crude oil, and eighty percent of Poland's iron ore at a fraction of the world market price, because the prices for these materials were set before the 1971-1975 plan. The inflation of oil, gas, chemical, and metal prices in particular has increased the interest of the Soviet Union in selling its products in those countries from which it hopes to import scientific and technical systems.

Eastern Europe will therefore be desperately short of raw materials at the very time that its major exports to the Soviet Union will have to compete under unfavorable conditions with equipment of high quality produced in the United States and other Western countries. The East European states are therefore desperate for assistance in modernizing and supplying their economy and for new relationships with the West.

The long years of Soviet domination and the tragedies and failures of the efforts of these peoples to achieve greater freedom and abundance, the rise of nationalism, and the desperate need for access to Western capital, science and technology have all increased the interest of Eastern Europe in closer relations with Western Europe and the United States. These developments have therefore served to increase the power of the Western European cultural magnet at a time when the pervasive silence of Russian culture exerts almost no influence on East Europeans. West European culture at every level has simply overwhelmed Eastern Europe, while Soviet culture has almost no visible effect. Eastern Europe therefore turns to the West as a sunflower turns towards the sun, thus creating a great competition between Western culture and Soviet power.

The attractive strength of Western culture is especially compelling because of the changing nature of our universe, which in many ways is becoming one world for communists as well as capitalists. East European intellectuals and scientists have recognized this just as clearly as the Medvedevs, Sakharov and Solzhenitsyn, and they are just as eager to participate in the new technetronic age of interdependence as are their Soviet counterparts. This raises an inevitable conflict with the political system planted upon these people, and therefore threatens Soviet hegemony.

Whatever it is called, American policy has been and will remain based on American economic, military, and political power, and resolution. Indeed, while considering ways in which we can advance our interests and those of the peoples of Eastern Europe, we should remain aware that we must remain powerful and determined against continuing Soviet pressure outward. Thus, our resolution may be tested deliberately by East Germany, perhaps acting as a surrogate of the Soviet Union, over West Berlin, at a time when we have other preoccupations and our European allies are especially divided and weak. Our willingness to stand firm against direct or indirect aggression in a situation as hazardous as 1947 or 1948 may also be tested at the death of Tito. Such crises would illuminate, and test, the basic foundations on which our policy towards Eastern Europe and the world does and must stand.

Our second principal element remains our alliances with the NATO states of Western·Europe and Japan. One of the foundations of our approach towards Eastern Europe is the movement towards the economic and political community of Western Europe. Reviewed in the perspective of ancient animosities of the Second World War, and of the incredible complexities involved in bringing together a number of varied and proud peoples with long traditions of independence, remarkable progress towards European union has been achieved. Our capacity to assist Western Europe in pressing towards greater unity is very low, although this constitutes one of our most important objectives.

In recent years, in our policy towards the Soviet Union, we have concentrated upon developing and maintaining a world economy operating in such a way that our allies can remain prosperous, confident, and effective free associates. The immediate goal remains containment, but we seek to create and maintain an international order in which democracy can thrive and in which problems can be peacefully resolved. The creation of such an order and such a system will produce conditions under which peaceful change can occur everywhere, including within Eastern Europe.

The American Government has also concentrated extensively upon nuclear disarmament, an effort to reach a new balance of power by establishing new relationships with the People's Republic of China, and luring the Soviet Union into a new world order by increasing Soviet economic ties with the United States and the rest of the world. We have sought to persuade the Soviet Union and all advanced states to cooperate in a mass effort upon the new international problems caused by inflation, the resultant threat to economic order and stability, and such issues as the revolution of rising expectations among the underdeveloped countries.

At the same time, in order to introduce possibilities for peaceful movement towards greater independence and more humane and free government within Eastern Europe, the United States and Western Europe have sought to utilize the amazing vitality of their culture as an important instrument of their foreign policy and as a supplement to other Western strengths. We have thus sought to use our culture, including its reflection in creativity in the arts and in economic progress, to build bridges into Eastern Europe, creating new intellectual and economic relations with its peoples.

The present international situation and the increasing attention given to cultural and economic relationships provide us a splendid opportunity to advance our interests and to assist the peoples of the Soviet Union and Eastern Europe. We surely prefer to compete with ideas rather than with weapons. Cultural and scientific-economic exchanges enable us to compete with our strongest instruments in fields and areas in which we are especially interested and competent. In this contest, freedom is our best instrument and main strength. In an age of unprecedented change, we are particularly able to compete with a system of government which is extraordinarily rigid and brittle and suffers from conservative leadership. If we can use our other resources to maintain peace and establish some kind of stability, our enormous strengths in the cultural fields should enable us to encourage gradual and slow change in the Soviet Union and Eastern Europe in ways which should promote peace and security throughout the world.

Cultural relations can never be decisive in relationships between the Western states and the Soviet Union, but the role they play now is more important than ever, not only because of the present character of world politics but also because of the way in which the world has shrunk. The revolutions in transportation and communication, the significance of those economic forces which tend to make the world one, and the political transformation of most parts of the world all suggest that the increase in relationships of all kinds may be an inescapable and irreversible process. The new terrain of international politics may also be one which provides us an extraordinary opportunity because of what Christopher Dawson has called the "world hegemony of Western culture." Thus, we face mass possibilities for peaceful change within the communist states and in the relationships between them and other states. In fact, an era of peaceful coexistence will test whether the Soviet Union can endure peace.

Western radio stations have been and remain among our most important instruments in assisting the peoples of Eastern Europe. The Voice of America, the British Broadcasting Corporation, the Deutsche Welle, and other national broadcasting systems provide objective and accurate information to the peoples of Eastern Europe, increasing their knowledge of developments within the Soviet empire and in the world in general. Assisted by Radio Free Europe and Radio Liberty, the "unofficial official" stations of the American Government, they have forced the official communist mass media to compete and thus to improve the quality of news within Eastern Europe. These remarkably inexpensive instruments (Radio Free Europe and Radio Liberty together cost only $50,000,000 to operate in 1974-1975, approximately twenty-five cents per American citizen) have thus served as levers or instruments for free communication and for social change. They have been so effective in breaking through or evading the various expensive communist jamming devices and in increasing the level of knowledge that the East European states in 1973 finally ended jamming all but Radio Free Europe.

The influence these instruments have had within Eastern Europe and the Soviet Union demonstrates why the United States and its allies continue to press for a freer flow of information and ideas. In short, free access to Western publications would have even more revolutionary effect within Eastern Europe than do these important radio stations.

The Soviet and the East European governments benefit from these exchanges, through which they obtain important scientific and technological knowledge and instruments. These governments also obtain respectability and prestige from official exchange agreements with Western democratic states. Finally, both the Soviet Government and the East European governments clearly assume that they acquire some political influence through these programs, which may persuade some Americans that the Soviet Union is no longer a menace, that the political situation in Eastern Europe is forever frozen, and that peace is at hand.

At the same time, cultural exchanges of all types, from basketball teams through graduate students in history to senior scholars engaged in joint research on cancer, have an enormous political impact within Eastern Europe, and, to a lesser degree, in the Soviet Union. First, they remind East Europeans that they have not been forgotten or abandoned. They demonstrate the clear cultural superiority of the United States in particular and of the West in general. Above all, cultural exchanges persuade the East Europeans that life remains better and freer in the West. In any case, the East European states have been overwhelmed or flooded by Western culture, from consumer interest and life-styles to ideas of all kinds from movies, music, miniskirts and Levi's, Cokes, computers, input-output analysis, marketing and management, and even new versions of Marxism. Culturally, Eastern Europe is now again a part of the West, and it now sees the struggle as one between Western culture or civilization and Soviet military power.

Cultural relations therefore establish dilemmas for the East European and Soviet Governments, although not for their citizens, because they bring specific advantages but also carry deadly and even fatal infections. In short, in the nineteenth-century phrase, the Soviet and East European governments in their relationship with the West seek a fire which will not burn. They seek information, but not ideas. They want to borrow technology, but to keep out the culture which produced that technology. As a rigid, conservative, and backward political system in an era of great change, the Soviet Government therefore monitors cultural exchange programs very carefully. Indeed, expanding relationships require intensified controls over intellectuals, and the pattern of the past fifteen years almost reflects a political law: closer relationships with the West produce tighter controls. These concerns are particularly great because the Soviet Union is a society based on faith or dogma and has so little intellectual vitality.

The Soviet rulers therefore emphasize that detente does not mean "ideological coexistence," which they relentlessly reject. They insisted in the discussions at the Geneva Conference on Security and Cooperation in Europe that any agreements between the Soviet Union and the West "respect the principles of sovereignty and noninterference" and provide for "the strict observance of laws, customs, and traditions, of the participating countries." In short, the Soviet Union wishes to participate in cultural exchanges but on condition that it maintain its censorship and other forms of control. It seeks a fire that will not burn.

For the East European governments, cultural exchanges are both more attractive and more acutely contagious than they are for the Soviet Union, as the Soviet Government recognizes. The East European peoples, particularly the Poles, Czechs, Slovaks, and Hungarians, think of themselves as Europeans. Western Europe, particularly the thriving Western Europe of the past twenty-five years, therefore exerts a kind of magnetic attraction on the governments and peoples of Eastern Europe. This compelling attraction is greater even than in the nineteenth century because of the impressive vitality of the West, the isolation inflicted so long upon the East Europeans, and the tantalizing opportunities now available to taste the adjacent forbidden fruits. One shrewd British observer has pointed out that one can reach the Soviet Union only over a wall and across a moat. The Iron Curtain and its appropriate symbol, the Berlin Wall, remain as powerful and forbidding as ever, but entrance to (and exit from) Eastern Europe is now simpler, through a crisscross of turnstiles.

Increasing cultural relations also raise a dilemma for the United States and its allies, because the official cultural exchange agreements upon which the Soviet Union and East European governments insist constitute primitive barter arrangements, rather than the free trade in ideas which is at the foundation of Western culture. Signing restrictive agreements with authoritarian states is clearly a violation of our principles. Moreover, granting respectability and prestige to governments which imprison some of their historians and other intellectuals, systematically deny their citizens civil rights guaranteed by their own constitutions, and flaunt their violations of the United Nations Charter is a compromise which most Westerners regret, and about which we should always remain critical.

The vitality and dynamism of the American economy constitute another important instrument to assist the East Europeans, particularly because the Soviet Union and the East European states face such a desperate need to modernize their economies. In effect, the communist governments of Eastern Europe have established command economies and have sacrificed their citizens' living standards and civil rights in a sustained effort to transform these states from relatively backward into advanced and modernized ones. They have achieved significant rates of growth, particularly in heavy industry. However, in the last decade they have fallen considerably behind the West as a new wave of the industrial revolution, based on computers, automatic machinery, the application of new fertilizers and economic systems to agriculture, and the introduction of new methods of management has transformed the West.

Faced with this growing gap, their own stagnation in new industries, the pressures to raise living standards and the stagnation in productivity, the Soviet and East European leaders have a number of options from which to choose. They could continue the command economy, confident in its performance, although they realize that this system has not succeeded in producing new discoveries or sustaining continued growth. They could also reduce military investment and the provision of military aid to Third World countries, using the resources released in industry and agriculture. However, this would reduce Soviet influence on Third World countries, create disaffection among the military leadership, significantly reduce the capability to maintain control over the population, and weaken the force behind Soviet diplomacy. The communist governments could also choose economic reform, decentralizing industry and allowing the market price to prevail. However, they learned from the Czechoslovak experience before August 1968 that economic modernization leads to pressures for political pluralism, and they are therefore extremely reluctant to undertake such changes.

The final option, that which they have chosen, is to expand economic relations with the West and to borrow or buy Western scientific and technical knowledge, equipment, and skills, while at the same time somehow barring the introduction of the culture which produced these advances. This decision, like the policy of detente in general, is a necessary one for the Soviet Union and Eastern Europe, but it may also be fatal for the Soviet position in Eastern Europe.

The power and vitality of the Western economies and the shortcomings of those of the Soviet Union and Eastern Europe have therefore provided the United States and its allies an extraordinary opportunity to affect the policy of the East European states. Briefly, we should use our informational, cultural, and economic resources together in a coordinated way with our allies to our advantage and that of the East European peoples. We should seek the reconstruction of the European community within its historical boundaries in such a way as to increase the independence and freedom of the East European peoples and to reduce the Soviet threat to Western Europe, without alarming or threatening the Soviet

Union in any way. In short, we should use these instruments to end the Soviet empire over Eastern Europe slowly and gradually, creating no threat on the Soviet Union's Western frontiers but ending the empire which the Soviet Union has exercised for thirty years.

We can use these instruments of our culture in a number of ways. Thus, aware of the danger that the Soviet Union will use the energy crisis and its own capital shortages to tighten its economic grip over Eastern Europe, the United States should seek to expand East European trade with the rest of the world and its participation in the world economy. For example, the United States could grant most favored nation status to reward and encourage those East European states which are making most progress towards greater independence and increased freedom, as we did to Yugoslavia in 1957, to Poland fully in 1963, and to Rumania in 1975. We could assist Hungary, Poland, and Bulgaria to join Rumania and Yugoslavia in the World Bank and the International Monetary Fund. The first step would not be an important aid to these states to increase their exports to the United States, because our tariffs have not constituted an important barrier, but it would constitute an important psychological stimulus. Assisting East European countries to join and participate in the work of a number of international economic and financial organizations would help persuade them to abandon outmoded practices, provide access to increased international investment sources, weaken their dependence upon the Soviet Union, and bring them into fruitful, stimulating participation in the open world economy.

The American Government could also continue to encourage American businessmen to participate in joint ventures with organizations in Eastern Europe, allowed by law in Yugoslavia since 1969, Hungary since December 1970, and Rumania since November 1972. These cooperative ventures would enable American corporations to establish joint companies with East European firms, thus enabling the East Europeans to acquire access to American skills and knowledge and the Americans to obtain profits and the satisfaction of assisting others under conditions satisfactory to both. These steps would also weaken Soviet influence over these economies and bring these states more directly into the wider world.

In addition, we can complete trade agreements, such as those we established with the Soviet Union in the early 1970s and with Poland in October 1974. These provide for joint funding of cooperative scientific and technical research, cooperation on medical and health care, and cooperation on protecting the environment and on exchange crop forecasting.

Finally, the American Government through its export-import bank can assist American banks to provide short-term credit to East European state corporations, enabling them to purchase American equipment and expertise at low rates of interest in conditions favorable to all. We should not provide long-term credits, because these would reduce any influence we might have and would in fact increase the leverage of the debtor states upon us.

American trade with the Soviet Union has increased substantially in the past five years (but still remains less than one percent of our total foreign trade), particularly because of massive Soviet purchases of American grain and industrial equipment. Our trade with most of the East European countries has also increased significantly, under the same circumstances. We should continue to use our economic resources as instruments of American national interest, but we should be certain that this instrument is fully and effectively coordinated with other aspects of our foreign policy towards Moscow, where basic changes must occur if the East European states are to move even slowly towards self-determination. We should coordinate granting economic and scientific benefits to the Soviet Union and the East European states with the progress of the negotiations in Vienna on the reduction of forces in Europe and in Moscow, Washington, and elsewhere on nuclear disarmament.

Thus we should deny, or sharply reduce, access to American science and technology to those states which do not honor the Helsinki agreement to facilitate "free movements and contacts" and "the freer and wider dissemination of all kinds of knowledge." Similarly, if we should not succeed in the SALT II negotiations on nuclear weapons or in the discussions in Vienna to create an equilibrium of forces in Europe, the Soviet Union and those states which support its position should also be denied substantial access to those resources of the West necessary for revitalizing their economies. In addition, we should naturally not grant benefits to the Soviet Union or the East European states if they adopt an aggressive policy with regard to West Berlin or the Middle East, if the Soviet Union should exert substantial pressure on Norway to change the status of Spitsbergen, or if the Soviet Union should encourage the use of violence elsewhere in the world.

Finally, we should naturally use our economic and other resources to assist the East European and Soviet peoples to progress towards the civil rights guaranteed them by the constitutions and pledged by their governments under the United Nations Charter, because the creation of open societies will help enormously to reduce the distrust which is at the heart of our difficulties. After all, the right of self-determination has always been th core of our principle and of our foreign policy.

In short, the United States should not reiterate the error Roosevelt made during the Second World War, when he relied on his charm and our good intentions to persuade Stalin to accept governments in Eastern Europe which represented the freely expressed will of the people. We should also avoid his separating political considerations from our military strategy. Our policy, and that of our allies, should bring together our strengths, so that our diplomacy, and the fate of the peoples of Eastern Europe, will benefit from our greatest resources, our freedoms and our extraordinary cultural, scientific, and economic vitality. Such a policy will require more government control over international trade, the activities of American firms engaged in trade with Eastern Europe, and American intellectuals than we have been willing to accept in the past. Thus, after the celebrated grain deal in 1972, in which the Soviet Union took advantage of our open society and the competition among grain trading corporations to obtain millions of tons of wheat at low prices subsidized by the American taxpayer, the Department of Agriculture required these corporations to provide advance notice of large sales. The United States could easily drift into a situation in which the

American Government exercised full control over the grain trade, perhaps as part of some international grain reservoir agreement.

Of course, providing economic, scientific, and technical assistance to the governments of Eastern Europe strengthens them and makes their rule ever more legitimate in the eyes of their people and of the rest of the world.

In addition, balancing economic assistance of one kind or another against the various benefits upon which we should insist is a very complicated process in diplomacy. Our own government is so large and unwieldy, so many American interests are involved, and political considerations are so confusing in the United States that obtaining firm support for prolonged and complicated negotiations with an intractable authoritarian state will be a very considerable achievement. Moreover, such policies must receive the continued understanding and support of our allies, some of whom have views different from ours and are exposed to different temptations. All Western governments involved in a coordinated program such as this will be subject to pressure not only from Soviet and East European governments, but also from local communist parties and other political groups.

Recent history has demonstrated that obtaining satisfactory equivalents from the Soviet Union and Eastern Europe from Western benefits extended to them is a very difficult process. For example, the Federal Republic of Germany in 1970 recognized the Oder-Neisse boundary and ultimately the German Democratic Republic in the hope that granting legitimacy and recognition to that boundary and that government, and in effect to the Soviet position throughout Eastern Europe, would relax and mellow the East German Government, allow free movement between the two Germanies, and end all uncertainty concerning West Berlin and its relationship to the Federal Government. The treaties did not produce the effects desired: the East German Government raised new barriers, and the status of West Berlin remains under challenge. Similarly, the *Ostpolitik* treaties with Poland proved disappointing to the Federal Republic and the West. After agreements which recognized Poland's boundaries, arranged for substantial scientific and technical cooperation, and provided massive German loans at low interest rates, in return for an agreement permitting 50,000 Poles of German extraction to leave Poland for West Germany, the Poles raised new demands for compensation and larger loans and again restricted the flow of emigrants. The Vatican, in its negotiations with Hungary which led to the departure of Cardinal Mindszenty from the American Embassy in Budapest, and much later to the appointment of additional bishops, with Czechoslovakia, and with the Soviet Government, has failed to produce as many advantages for the Vatican or for the Catholic and other religious groups in the Soviet Union and Eastern Europe as the Vatican had expected. Indeed, even after long negotiations, only two of the twelve bishoprics in Czechoslovakia in the summer of 1975 had apostolic administrators, i.e., administrators formally approved by the Vatican, and only one seminary was open. Moreover, Lithuanian and East European Catholics are immensely critical of the Vatican for concluding agreements with governments which deny them their civil rights. Similarly, many Americans believe that the United States should not have recognized the

German Democratic Republic, granting it respectability, when the Berlin Wall serves as a visible symbol of that government's denial to its citizens of their basic rights and of its violation of the United Nations Charter.

Eastern Europe, which is more vulnerable than the Soviet Union to Western cultural influences, continues to play a central role because of its position in the Soviet empire and because it stands at the crossroads of European civilization. If the Soviet Union should succeed in absorbing the peoples of Eastern Europe as it apparently has those of Central Asia, the fate of Western Europe and of the United States would remain under growing threat. On the other hand, if the peoples of Eastern Europe should succeed in inching their way to greater independence from Soviet rule and to increased liberties, the peoples and the government of the Soviet Union would be directly affected and the future of Western Europe, and of the world, would become significantly brighter and freer.

The ultimate authority for developments within the Soviet empire resides in Moscow, and both East and West Europeans can only hope to influence that power in ways beneficial to all. The Soviet Union is locked in the same shrinking world as the rest of us. Its government may have absolute power over its subjects, but it also faces a number of problems, some of which are almost intractable. Above all, no government, however awesome and ruthless, can isolate its people from the world. In particular, it cannot borrow technology from other countries and cultures without simultaneously importing the larger culture which has produced those ideas and equipment.

We should naturally seek to press the Soviet leaders towards a policy of rejoining the world and both benefiting from and competing in a competition of ideas and systems on a peaceful field, with intellectual and economic weapons. In such a situation, Western strengths, unity, and resolution will remain fundamental. However, our policies on economic and cultural exchanges and basic human freedoms will also play a central role.

The success with which the West has protected Soviet dissidents illustrates the significant way in which we can marshal our resources to assist Eastern Europe. The presence of 240 Western correspondents in Moscow, the skill with which these men and women and the Soviet dissidents have kept in touch with each other, the diffusion of information about the dissidents throughout the world, and broadcasting back into the Soviet Union information about the dissidents and their views have provided an umbrella for them, restricted Soviet action against them, and protected them. Thus, the Soviet decision to expel Solzhenitsyn in February 1974, rather than to exile or imprison him, reflects in part his courage and in part the pressure exerted upon the Soviet Government by the information made available to the world and then to the Soviet public, at a time when the Soviet Government was (and is) desperate for Western scientific and technical aid.

Similarly, the National Academy of Science's message to the Soviet Academy of Sciences in September 1973 that the continuation of scientific cooperation between American scientists and the Soviet scientific establishment would be jeopardized by any Soviet action against Sakharov clearly has helped to defend that man's life and activity.

In short, we should use all the elements of our culture and strength to obtain our goals. We should consider every aspect of our life a part of our culture and should allow the communist states to benefit from one aspect only if they accept the other elements relevant to our relationships and to hopes of creating a peaceful and secure Europe.

The continued vitality of Western Europe and the firmness of the West European governments' positions at the Geneva conference suggest that the West European states should play an ever more important role in exchanges with the communist states. The various ties which bind individual Western states to particular East European states have regained their old strength and should be further developed. *Ostpolitik*, for which most of the Western price has already been paid and the dividends not yet collected, the various treaties West Germany has completed, and the "new face" of West Germany should encourage that state in particular to become more active throughout the Soviet empire.

Cultural and economic exchanges between the Soviet Union and the other communist states and the Western states therefore constitute a very important part of international politics. We face a long, hard, and dangerous road in maintaining and increasing these exchanges, but the Soviet and East European need for important elements of our culture provides us important negotiating strengths. We will all need the toughness, practical sense, imagination, and compassion we can muster in order to help us achieve our goals. Crises such as those of 1956, 1961, 1968, and 1970 are almost certain to recur, because the relaxation of tension within the Soviet Union and Eastern Europe almost inevitably creates pressures such as led to these crises.

While such lurches are dangerous, they do represent the painful progress of the Soviet and East European peoples towards greater freedom. In a sense, the earlier efforts to press dramatically towards greater freedom or towards "socialism with a human face" were all successes in the long run, although apparent immediate failures. Progress has been substantial since Stalin's death. The level of information throughout Eastern Europe is substantially higher. In spite of all the restrictions in Czechoslovakia and Rumania in particular and of general disappoint-ment over the Helsinki agreement the overall picture is brighter, and East and West Europeans are mastering the turnstiles which have been separating them.

In a way, the recent history of Eastern Europe resembles a canal, with a number of locks through which these peoples move slowly, gradually, from one level to another. Canals carry traffic two ways, of course. We are particularly well-equipped in the cultural field to help direct the barges upward through a series of locks to a new level from which all people, although not the Soviet system, will benefit.

5

East Central Europe: Present Situation and Principal Trends

The phrase East Central Europe describes the territories between the Soviet Union on the east and West Germany and Austria on the west, an area with no geographic or cultural unity, even when Greece is omitted. The concept dates from the end of the Second World War, when statesmen and observers needed a term that included all communist-ruled countries and peoples in Europe. The Yugoslav-Soviet split in 1948, Yugoslavia's subsequent success in maintaining its position as an independent communist state, and later the appearance of an Albanian state ruled by independent communists hostile to both the Soviet Union and Yugoslavia introduced still other confusions.

Generally, East Central Europe now refers to those states between the Soviet Union and Germany and Austria ruled by communists subservient to or dominated by the Soviet Union: the German Democratic Republic, Poland, Czechoslovakia, Hungary, Bulgaria, and Rumania. Mention of Rumania introduces still another ambiguity: geographically it is in the area; politically it is ruled by a communist regime at least as repressive as those of the other countries; militarily and economically it participates in many but not all activities of the Warsaw Pact and of the Council for Mutual Economic Aid (CMEA); yet it vigorously defends its independence from the Soviet Union. Moreover, the diversities among the six countries have grown throughout the 1970s. Poland and East Germany, Hungary and Czechoslovakia, Rumania and Bulgaria, are as different in many ways from each other as any two sets of West European states, and these diversities are likely to increase.

Whatever the definition of East Central Europe, determining what is happening and identifying the main trends are less difficult now than when Stalin died. The amount of available information concerning life in these countries, including Albania, is unprecedented. Moreover, Western journalism and above all Western scholarship have utilized the gradual expansion of access to these countries and to information about them to increase our knowledge and understanding greatly. Indeed, one of the great changes involving East Central Europe is the increasing quality as well as the quantity of Western scholarship on it.

Reprinted with permission from *East-Central Europe: Yesterday - Today - Tomorrow*, Milorad Drachkovich, ed. ((Stanford: Hoover Institution, 1982), 20-42.

However, our ability to understand the peoples and governments of these countries remains inadequate. Pre-Second World War myths about some peoples survive. Americans in particular still view the area from the standpoint of Moscow or Washington and see it as a dependent football, destined forever to be part of a Soviet empire, as various parts of it were in the past subject to the Germans, Russians, or Turks. The opinions of even our most experienced analysts often reflect shallow historical knowledge, flighty analysis, and the assumption that peoples of this area are far less interested in independence and self-government than are West Europeans and Americans. For example, in 1947 George Kennan, author of the "containment" doctrine, published the stirring words that helped provide the intellectual foundation of Western policy when he urged his country to form an alliance that would resist "with unalterable counterforce at every point where they [the Soviets] show signs of encroaching upon the interests of a peaceful and stable world." He estimated that such policies would "promote tendencies which must eventually find their outlet in either the weakening or the gradual mellowing of Soviet power. In the spring of 1956, just before the great events in Poland and in Hungary, the same observer wrote that there was "a finality, for better or worse, about what has happened in Eastern Europe." Six months later, he described the "extensive disintegration" of this part of the Soviet empire as a "sudden upthrust of liberty." In 1957, he was gloomy again and thought that the failure of the popular uprisings had "produced a bitter and dangerous despondency." He concluded that "there will simply have to be some sort of adjustment on the part of the peoples of Eastern Europe, even if it is one that takes the form of general despair, apathy, demoralization, and the deepest sort of disillusion with the West." He defined the major problem of international politics as the confrontation of Soviet and Western forces in Central Europe and advocated disengagement, establishment of a "thinning out zone," and "mutual withdrawal from the heart of Europe in order to reduce tension and armament." Later, in a paroxysm of self-criticism, he viewed Western civilization as a cancer of decadence and immorality, declared that the United States in particular had nothing to offer the world, asserted that Soviet occupation of all Europe would not necessarily constitute a disaster, and noted that "defensive rather than offensive impulses" explained the Soviet invasion of Afghanistan.[1] In short, the glasses through which we have examined East Central Europe have not always been in focus.

Even those scholars who possess sound historical knowledge and calm judgement have been surprised by many developments since the Second World War. Many skilled observers were stunned by Stalin's ejection of Tito and Yugoslavia from the Cominform in 1948. Some refused to believe it and for two or three years considered Tito a Soviet agent. In 1956, the Poznan troubles and the skillful and successful palace revolt in Poland and the revolution in Hungary surprised outsiders as well as the rulers of those countries and of the Soviet Union. No one in the spring of 1956 foresaw that Imre Nagy would advocate withdrawing Soviet troops from Hungary, establishing equal relations with the Soviet Union, leaving the Warsaw Pact, ending collectivization, re-establishing a genuine multiparty system, admitting noncommunists into a coalition government, holding free elections, and dismantling the secret police. The emergence of Janos Kadar as a communist "liberal" or reformer was an even greater shock. The Czechoslovak Spring stunned observers, although the Soviet invasion on August 20, 1968, did not. The ease with which Polish workers overthrew Wladyslaw Gomulka in December 1970 came as a shock.

Similarly, the effect on East Central Europe of the Helsinki agreement in the summer of 1975 astounded the majority of Western scholars and analysts. Most considered it a Western political disaster that recognized Soviet incorporation of 114,000 square miles of former parts of other countries (about three times the size of Indiana), noted the "permanent division" of Europe, and sanctified Soviet control of six other communist countries. In return, the Western signatories, it was thought, received a bundle of communist platitudes on a "positive and humanitarian attitude" towards the reunification of families, dissemination of publications from other countries, freedom from "external aggression," and three weeks' notice of maneuvers involving more than 2,500 troops within 250 kilometers of international borders. To the surprise of the West, the Soviet Union, and the East Central European governments, this "piece of paper," for which the Soviets had fought so long, raised hopes and encouraged political activities throughout the area, especially in the critical northern-tier countries: Poland, the German Democratic Republic, and Czechoslovakia. Charter 77 above all should humble outside observers. The show trials in the fall of 1979 demonstrated that "flowers continue to push through the cracks" among the most apathetic and downtrodden of the peoples of this area and that hope dies more easily in the West than among the peoples of East Central Europe.

The election of Pope John Paul II and the remarkable impact he exerted during his 1979 visit to Poland demonstrate how one totally unexpected election and one charismatic man can illuminate an entire landscape and bring into focus realities that observers had suspected but had by no means fully understood. He clearly deepened the ardor of Polish Catholics, increased appreciation of the church's role even among Marxists, and strengthened Polish nationalism among all groups, especially the young, the workers, and the intellectuals - the darlings of the regime. He humiliated the party by the magnetic popular attraction he demonstrated, inspired an already pugnacious church hierarchy, and strengthened Poland's traditional ties with the West. This visit contributed both clearly and significantly to the strikes and late in the summer of 1980 brought about the downfall of Gierek and recognition by the party and the government of free trade unions, and to a series of other steps, such as relaxing censorship and increasing access of the church to the media.

The 1970s were and the 1980s almost certainly will be ages of chaos and confusion in much of the world, with significant but unpredictable developments in East Central Europe and the Soviet ability to retain firm control unless its leaders are willing to use force. Moreover, the effects within East Central Europe of the rapid rise in oil prices since 1973 and of the recession in the West show that the area can no longer be sheltered from external events. Throughout the world, the rate of social and economic change has increased. Great uncertainties loom over NATO, South Africa,

Southeast Asia, the direction of the United States and of American policy, developments within Iran, the relationships between that volatile country and its immediate neighbors, the Muslim world, the United States, and other states dependent on Iran and the Organization of Petroleum Exporting Countries for much of their oil. The resistance hardy Muslim rebels waged against the Soviet invasion of Afghanistan in late 1979, the firmness of the Carter administration in leading major United States allies to boycott the Olympic games in the summer of 1980 and to reduce the flow of scientific data and technical equipment to the Soviet Union, the diplomatic vigor shown by the People's Republic of China in responding to the Soviet thrust into Afghanistan, and the overwhelming vote denouncing the invasion in the UN General Assembly must have struck an echo in Eastern Europe. Resistance anywhere to Soviet authority emboldens Eastern Europeans. The rapid changes in policy, foreign and domestic, of countries such as the People's Republic of China and Albania in 1978 and 1979 illustrate the character of the world in which we live. The latter country, after denouncing the People's Republic of China for its new relationships with the West, has followed the same pattern, sending a soccer team to Scotland and students to Austria, France, Italy, and Sweden, and establishing trade arrangements with Italy and other Western countries.

Not all is uncertainty and confusion. Some evident and important "sea changes" will remain significant as far ahead as anyone can see. First, the diversities among these states have continued to grow since the first relaxations of authority after Stalin's death. Economic and social policy and even political and intellectual freedoms vary from state to state. Yugoslavia and Albania have acquired and retain freedom from Soviet control, and Rumania remains remarkably independent in its economic and political relations with Western states and the People's Republic of China. In Poland, little land has been collectivized; the Catholic Church remains independent, maintains schools and provides religious education at all levels, and since the election of Pope John Paul II and his visit, has pressed with increasing vigor for more educational and social authority. In Hungary, the New Economic Mechanism introduced substantial decentralization and some reliance on the free market. Hundreds of thousands of Poles and Hungarians now travel west on their holidays; Vienna is once again a center for these peoples.

In all these countries, the desire for more freedom and increased independence exists at all levels of society, even within the highest reaches of the ruling parties, and is much stronger than in the late 1940s. The survival of these hopes, amid visible evidence of economic progress under communist rule and of the ineffectiveness of Western power, and at a time when other areas and interests attract the bulk of Western attention, reflects vividly the nature of the forces confronting the Soviet Government and its associates.

In addition, the level of knowledge and understanding of developments within each country, the whole area, and the world has increased enormously because of education and social change, the cumulative effect of various "thaws" (the last known as detente), the revival of national consciousness and nationalism, the very existence of the West, and the role Western radio broadcasts have played in providing information and in forcing the media of each country to improve qualitatively to compete with these outside sources. The effort of the Soviet Union and of the governments of these states to control access to information has failed fundamentally. The ingenuity of two families who floated in a balloon from East Germany to freedom in the German Federal Republic in the fall of 1979 recalls the early postwar era when the West could communicate with East Central Europe only by using favorable air currents to float balloons that, by mechanical or chemical devices, dropped leaflets over designated areas. Those days are gone forever. Few intellectual barriers remain, and many in Eastern Europe have begun to acquire the same level of knowledge and understanding of world events that many residents of Western Europe have long possessed.

Opinions on communism within this area and indeed throughout much of the world have also changed dramatically over three decades. Except for established fiefdoms in conservative communist parties in Western Europe, young radicals in the so-called Third World, and terrorists, Marxism has lost much of the attraction it once exercised. Moreover, the radicals and terrorists are as much a long-term menace to the Soviet Union as they are to the Western democracies.

Further, the Sino-Soviet split, which many Western observers refused to recognize for several years, is now twenty years old. Monolithic unity is long gone, and polycentrism is mature. Rumania, which in 1962 refused to accept either the "international division of labor within the Soviet Union and Eastern Europe [that assigns] to Rumania the function of remaining an agricultural country" or "Soviet control over its economy and its economic relations with the West,"[2] in 1978 refused a Soviet request to increase its military expenditures, a position other rulers no doubt also wanted to take. The visits of Hua Guofeng to Yugoslavia and Rumania in 1978 and to Western Europe in 1979 are symbolic of the change since 1956 and 1957, when the first Chinese visits to East Central Europe helped to reassert Soviet authority.

Finally, the Soviet Union and each country in East Central Europe face a succession problem in the foreseeable future; in Albania Enver Hoxha has been head of the Communist Party since 1943, and in the USSR an ailing Leonid Brezhnev heads a group of elderly leaders, all of whom must inevitably pass from the scene soon. Even in well-established political democracies, selecting and changing leaders often are painful and disturbing processes that produce some uncertainty before an election and some confusion or reorganization and redefinition afterwards. As far as we know, Yugoslavia has worked out a clear procedure for handling a succession. In the other states, all announced procedures have been abandoned, probably because the rulers feared that the designated successor would become restless. Even the Yugoslav system, tested after Tito's death in the spring of 1980, seems cumbersome and has yet to be put to a serious trial. The Soviet Union's peaceful transfers of authority in 1953 and 1964 do not ensure future Soviet success either within the USSR or in the most closely associated states. Moreover, the two or three years of policy uncertainties following these transfers of power helped precipitate the crises in 1956 and 1968. A disquieting air of uncertainty prevails in each country. Confusion and turmoil in one country could easily lead to widening ripples of indecision and crisis.

East Central Europe continues to occupy a significant position in world politics. Its geographical location, 133 million people, natural resources, and economic production make it critical. It remains a principal cause of Soviet-Western confrontation, even though Soviet probes into other areas have stimulated most recent crises. Walter Lippmann's 1947 dictum remains true: The world will not enjoy peace and security "until the Red Army can be prevailed upon to evacuate Europe."[3]

Moreover, East Central Europe is probably more important to the Soviet Government now than it was in 1945. It is both a prize of victory and a protective shield that enables the Soviet Union to utilize the peoples and other resources of the area to establish a barrier against the West, to veto German and European unification, and to neutralize Western Europe's role in world politics. It convinces communists and waverers that communism represents the wave of the future. Imagine the effect on communists and those waiting to see who will triumph if, say, the German Democratic Republic became a fully independent and free country.

The Soviet position seems even more impregnable now than it was ten or twenty years ago. The USSR maintains four air armies and approximately 785,000 ground troops, organized in thirty-one divisions, in East Central Europe (largely in the German Democratic Republic and Czechoslovakia), and provides direction to the six national armies in the Warsaw Pact, as well as fully standardized weaponry and training. Except for Rumania and Poland, it has infiltrated and in some way controls the armies and the police of these countries, and Rumania must be concerned about subversion of its forces. Its relations with party, labor, academic, and other social leaders are close and effective. In varying ways the Soviet Union has sought throughout these years to dominate the foreign trade of each country and to tighten trade bonds with them. Indeed, in the 1970s, it worked assiduously to create a "socialist economic commonwealth."

Above all, Soviet leaders, by their actions in 1968 and by their frequent demonstrations of power and resolution, have affirmed that the area is critical to the Soviet Union and that their determination to defend the Soviet position is as firm as Stalin's. The area is, however, extremely unstable. Some economic problems are so deep-seated, the social and intellectual changes so massive, and the gradual disintegration of political controls over the past three decades so great that the various regimes, except for Bulgaria, are brittle. They may appear firmly in power, but the pressures and uncertainties are so great that only continued Soviet presence, power, and resolution are indisputable. Even such hegemony does not provide the security or certainty it ensured as recently as the early 1960s.

In Lenin's phrase, the Soviets have retained the commanding heights in Europe. They have remained committed to their goals, simply introducing a little moderation, mellowing, or cosmetic change when appropriate to increase local popular support or to soothe concerned Westerners. After Tito's unpunished heresy in 1948 and his establishment of an independent communist state, Stalin tightened his control over the other countries and completed devastating purges of their hierarchies. Following his death, the new Soviet Government launched a gentle thaw, and the governments of East Central Europe adopted the so-called New Course. These developments led directly to the disasters of 1956, when the Poles not only removed their rulers, including the most important symbol of Soviet influence, Konstantin Rokossovsky, but also received assurance of frank and equal treatment, in effect ended collectivization, and relaxed controls over the Catholic Church. On the other hand, the Hungarian rebellion was effectively snuffed out, with Kadar the new Soviet man.

In spite of this apparently skillful recovery, 1956 was a catastrophe for the Soviet Union, demonstrating that the privileged groups the regimes had courted so ardently for a decade, the intellectuals, workers, and students, had not been converted. The black eye communism received led to doctrinal adjustments, particularly the recognition of several roads to socialism, and to Khrushchev's toleration and even encouragement of experiments in reform. The events of that year and the Soviet response also contributed to the Sino-Soviet split and the successful Rumanian bid for independence in the 1960s. The contemporary analyses of Milovan Djilas and others may have been correct: the revolts of 1956 perhaps marked the beginning of the end of the Soviet empire in East Central Europe.

The Czechoslovak effort to create Socialism with a Human Face, especially the abolition of censorship and the suggestion that the government might allow multiple political groupings or parties, led to the 1968 invasion. For the Soviet Union, this event was in some ways more detrimental than that of 1956 because it destroyed the appeal of communism and affection for Russia in the only country except Bulgaria where the Soviet Union had had a substantial number of supporters and because it produced a wave of criticism from even the most supine Western communist parties. But here again, the Soviet Government staged another remarkable rally.

Indeed, after Stalin, each of the crises in East Central Europe, however the Soviet Government handled the critical period itself, led to some relaxation of controls in an effort to alleviate the tensions that caused the explosions. The Czechoslovak Spring, the 1969 Ussuri River conflict between the Soviet Union and the People's Republic of China, and Soviet appreciation of the growing need throughout the area for massive Western economic, scientific, and technical infusions led directly to detente. This new period of relaxation was designed to provide the Soviet rulers time to remedy gross policy errors, particularly in Czechoslovakia, and to persuade the West that a substantial change had occurred so that Western governments and banks would allow and even encourage the expansion of trade and credits. All three relaxations proved the correctness of de Tocqueville's observation that the most dangerous period for a poor government occurs when it tries to reform. The Soviet response to the surprising reaction to the invasion of Afghanistan led to another period of reduced stress, and this again bred further disturbances in Eastern Europe, particularly in countries already deeply troubled, such as Poland.

The treaties the Soviet Union and some of the states of East Central Europe, especially Poland and the German Democratic Republic, signed with West Germany in 1970 and 1971 were important in launching detente in this area. They led to loans, trade agreements, and joint ventures, and by 1980 West Germany was the main Western trading partner of the Soviet Union and the states of East Central Europe. Indeed, in 1980 West Germany's economic relations with this area resembled German ambitions in the 1930s, with the great difference that the new Germany was no longer an aggressive totalitarian menace but an accepted associate. This alarmed the German Democratic Republic, which had long benefited from its trade with West Germany and from its sale of political prisoners to the Federal Republic. It understandably feared the role in East Central Europe of a vigorous, respected, and even admired democratic West German state.

Underneath the canvas of detente in the 1970s, the Soviet Union sought to resolve the recurrent problems of East Central Europe by pressing to bind the economies of the six states to that of the Soviet Union. By sacrificing some direct Soviet control in return for greater accommodation, cohesion, and stability, this effort to create a socialist commonwealth, or international relations of a new type, seeks to move toward a less rigidly controlled system than that which prevailed before 1968. Some see it as a complicated series of "entangling alliances" of "involuntary allies," with the German Democratic Republic and Bulgaria at one extreme as willing and even eager allies and Rumania as a most reluctant and unwilling partner at the other.

The Soviets have used every possible means to establish this commonwealth, especially a proliferation of economic ties. Through the Warsaw Pact the military arm seeks to unite the various national armies under Soviet direction and to increase cooperation, even in supplying military aid to Viet Nam. Politically, the Soviet Union has multiplied earlier methods for controlling top leaders and senior cadres by establishing personal and institutional contacts between Soviet and East Central European establishments for youth, workers, intellectuals, writers, scholars, and artists and by a joint ideological offensive.

Economic integration appears central to the program of the 1970s and 1980s. The Soviets have established contacts not just at the top through the ministries and main industries, but at every level. In 1970, the CMEA established an investment bank. In 1971, the Soviets advanced a proposal for interlocking the seven economic systems from the bottom. A 1976 addition to the CMEA charter stated that "socialist integration" was the council's aim. That same year, the seven countries implemented a coordinated economic plan for extractive industries, and in 1977 they established a voluntary "comprehensive program" to harmonize national economic policies, plans, and schedules on a supranational basis.

After 1973 the oil crisis encouraged the Soviets to accelerate their effort to tighten this infrastructure, particularly because the East Central European states are so dependent on Soviet oil and gas. In 1976, forty-seven percent of Soviet oil exports went to East Central Europe; Czechoslovakia and Bulgaria received 100 percent of their oil supplies from the Soviet Union, the German Democratic Republic ninety-five percent, Poland ninety percent, Hungary seventy-five percent, and Yugoslavia twenty-five percent. (Rumania is self-sufficient.) The growing need for oil and the 1975 Soviet decision to raise the price for its oil gradually to the world market price helped the Soviets obtain agreement for a series of joint ventures, all in the Soviet Union and all directed by Soviets. In these ventures, the East Central European states receive oil, gas, and other essential raw materials in return for credits to the Soviet Union, for construction of oil and gas lines linking the USSR and these countries, and for building heavy metal equipment plants in the Soviet Union that incorporate Western equipment purchased by the East Central Europeans with hard currency. This assures these states a supply of essential fuels and other raw materials and a market for their highest-quality manufactures. To some East Central Europeans, however, the new multinational production complexes curiously resemble the joint companies of Stalin's time.

It is difficult to estimate the past or future success of the Soviet Union in creating this web of arrangements, but the members of the Common Market have made far more progress in their slow and unruly march toward common institutions and policies than has the Soviet Union in East Central Europe. There each government has been stubbornly Gaullist in defending its remaining sovereignty. Moreover, larger concerns may force the Soviet Government to relax some of its economic constraints over East Central Europe and even lead these states to develop stronger economic ties with other nations. The oil supplied to East Central Europe reduces the quantity the Soviet Union can sell to Western Europe for the hard currency it desperately needs. In addition, most Western experts believe that although Soviet oil requirements will continue to grow rapidly, oil production will begin to decline in the early 1980s. In fact, the Soviet Government has already informed the other communist governments that they will no longer be able to rely so heavily on the Soviet Union for oil and that none will be able to obtain more than seventy-five percent of its needs from the Soviet Union after 1980. The rapid inflation in oil prices at a time when these states have little available currency is one of their most critical economic problems. This situation may increase their dependence on the Soviet Union. On the other hand, Soviet inability to satisfy their needs may increase pressures to revise their economies and turn them more toward the world market, particularly since the Soviet Government already requires payment in dollars for oil in excess of quotas.

Other problems within East Central Europe and between these states and the Soviet Union also handicap the Soviet dream of a new commonwealth. The varied economies of these states make it difficult to couple them to the Soviet economy. The national interests of each state differ to some degree from those of the Soviet Government, and each state and its bureaucracy insist on maintaining their own centrally planned economy. Collective decision making in any new community is problematic, but integrating controlled economies will be far more difficult than coordinating the economies of the states of Western Europe was. The system lacks a convertible currency, and none is in sight. In addition, the Soviet leaders themselves have no doubt begun to wonder if this system of integration is a liability or an advantage to the Soviet Union. If it is an increasingly costly economic liability, is it worthwhile, especially in view of the other strains on the Soviet economy? The Soviet economy's need for

Western capital and credits at a time when East Central Europe may require increased access to significant Soviet raw materials makes this an almost poignant problem.

The economic situation and trends constitute the most visible problem confronting East Central Europe and underlie political and other instabilities. Economic issues are increasingly serious for each government, though less so for Albania and Bulgaria than for the others. Ironically, these problems have arisen and are particularly troublesome because of the considerable progress of these states in the last three decades, especially in the first half of the 1970s. The growth of modern industry, the steady rise in living standards, the elimination of unemployment (but not underemployment), and tardy but substantial increases in production of consumer goods in the 1970s have led to "goulash communism" and at least temporarily increased popular satisfaction concerning economic trends. Although this progress has not been as sound or spectacular as that of West Germany, South Korea, Mexico, or the People's Republic of China, it has been substantial. But it has demonstrated the perils of prosperity or the new problems that progress creates by increasing appetites and dissatisfactions. Above all, the steady progress that began in 1950 and the spectacular advances that occurred for several years after 1970 both rested on nonrenewable foundations; this is the crisis each government now faces.

The original improvement was achieved under the centralized planning of a command economy that benefited from control and from the presence in these countries of a substantial surplus rural population that the governments could attract or drive into new industries. Basically, each state has reached the limits of a command economy in modern industrial society and has exhausted its inherited capital resources and those it was able to create in the frenetic drive toward modernization. Each now faces a labor shortage and basic structural problems in its economy. In every case, these have led to inflexible and unimaginative bureaucratic policies and attitudes, poor managerial skills, stagnation, low production, and inferior quality.

Some governments have demonstrated more skill and better sense than others in organizing economic development, but all face the same kinds of economic problems in the 1980s. For example, Hungary, under Kadar established the New Economic Mechanism, which led to substantially greater and easier progress and to a more satisfied populace than did the policies of Gierek in Poland or those of the Husak government in Czechoslovakia. Hungary granted partial autonomy to enterprises, increased the use of profit and other incentives, and turned more to pricing and a reliance on supply and demand as control mechanisms for its economy than have the other states. It therefore turned to the West earlier and used Western assistance more effectively than did the others; this has only sharpened its citizens' appetites and increased its interdependence on the world economy.

The surge of the early 1970s benefited from a concatenation of four elements that has since dissolved and is unlikely to form again:

1. The Soviet decision to adopt a relaxed policy toward Western Europe and the United States (detente), partly to obtain increased access to

Western science, technology, and credits and partly to avoid facing the need for internal economic reforms and for reducing expenditures on the armed forces and on aid to the Third World and so-called national liberation movements.
2. The simultaneous or earlier appearance in East Central Europe of similar essential needs.
3. The availability of surplus capital and credit in the West, in part because of the gradual slowing of Western economies and in part because of the increasing amount of capital for investment, especially with the flood first of Eurodollars and then of petrodollars.
4. The decision of Western governments and banks to take advantage of these communist needs in order to build additional bridges or to create what Henry Kissinger called "silken links of economic interdependence."

In the 1970s, the East Central European states took advantage of this financial and technocratic *deus ex machina* and the increased access to the West to expand their economies, especially the production of consumer goods. This reduced popular disaffection with the governments but increased economic and political appetites, which the governments are now less and less able to satisfy. Moreover, most of these states, particularly Poland and Bulgaria, have borrowed so heavily that they have reached the safe credit limits of Western governments and banks. Above all, the debt service and the approaching need to repay these loans not only reduce substantially the ability of these states to continue borrowing but also place their export industries under great pressure. For example, by mid-1981 the Polish debt to the West was approximately $27 billion. The interest on this debt consumed over half of the hard currencies earned that year by Polish westward exports, which themselves squeezed the Polish economy, especially the consumer sector. More than forty percent of Rumania's exports to the West are devoted to interest payments. One-third of Hungary's exports and one-quarter of Czechoslovakia's are assigned the same function - and these governments face repayments of the loans in the early 1980s. In the late 1970s each of these countries incurred a substantial trade deficit with the West; in 1978 that of Czechoslovakia was approximately $850 million, while Hungary's deficit was $2.2 billion, double that of 1977.

Beginning in 1977 or 1978, these governments recognized and sought to resolve the problems that heavy reliance on the West created by adopting austerity programs of increasing severity, phasing out subsidies for food, housing, and other consumer essentials, raising energy taxes, and tightening credits, but these measures had limited effectiveness and intensified political pressures. They have thus far refused to decentralize their economies, fearful perhaps of the example of the Czechoslovak Spring, which began after that government recognized its economic difficulties in the mid-1960s.

Unfortunately for the Soviet Union and these communist nations, the Soviet Union lacks not only the resources to assist (less than two decades ago Khrushchev was promising to overtake the United States in significant economic fields), but also what one might call the Marshall Plan mentality. Soviet inability to provide aid only underlines recognition of Western superiority, a factor that in the long run must trouble the leaders of all communist governments. Indeed, one of the most important phenomena of the 1970s was the number of communist states, beginning with the Soviet Union and followed by the states of East Central Europe, the People's Republic of China, and even tiny Albania, that have turned to the West for economic sustenance.

The evidence concerning the critical character of the economic situation and the need for massive economic reforms, which become more mandatory the longer they are delayed, is abundant. This is especially obvious in the countries of the northern tier, the German Democratic Republic, Czechoslovakia, and Poland. Moreover, the problems intensify, becoming political issues of growing gravity. They begin with shortages of labor, food, especially meat, consumer goods in general, and raw materials, particularly oil and gas. Each country long ago exhausted its labor surplus or reserves, and the declining rate of population growth at a time when labor productivity remains low outlines the nature of future problems. East Germany suffers in particular: from 1949 to 1977 its population declined by over 2 million (to 16.7 million) and its work force by thirteen percent. Meat has become a symbol for consumers in all these states, and the supply relative to demand continues to decline. Poland, for example, has to purchase, with hard currencies, millions of tons of imported feed grains and use special commercial price stores to try to meet this demand, but such policies are expensive and even counterproductive. As I indicated earlier, the oil and gas problem is especially ominous.

Growing consumer pressures aggravate political stresses. In many ways the problems resemble those of New York City in the late 1970s, but these governments have no Uncle Sam to provide temporary or long-term financial credit to tide them over a crisis created by years of economic boom. In each country, especially in Poland, the shortages of consumer goods in a population spoiled by recent progress have led not only to a second economy (a quasi-official black market), to special stores for large numbers of privileged citizens, to increased official tolerance and even encouragement of private enterprise - from pots and pans to housing, which is desperately short in the northern countries especially - but above all to increasingly open and vigorous expressions of political discontent. In short, these policies are producing some of the same social, psychological, and political consequences that the New Economic Policy produced in the Soviet Union fifty years ago.

Detente has introduced some Western economic problems into East Central Europe. In particular, the Soviet Union and the states of East Central Europe have not been able to isolate themselves from the recession in the West or from the rapid inflation stimulated by the oil crises since 1973. The recession has restricted access to Western markets, not only because of the general slowdown but also because the quality of many products of these states is not competitive, given the more stringent conditions in the world market. Soviet insistence that the East Central European states pay for Soviet oil, gas, and other raw materials in high-quality machinery, which often include Western parts, increases the difficulties. Moreover, the understandable Soviet decision to raise its oil and gas prices gradually to world levels has increased the strains on the other economies.

The seepage of inflation into these economies from the outside world has forced governments to admit the end of their self-imposed isolation and the beginning of their interdependence with the world economy and to adopt and then to abandon or reduce policies designed to protect their populations from its consequences. In 1979 Poland, especially sensitive to consumer dissatisfaction because of the revolt in 1970 and the riots in 1976, spent $7.6 billion on food subsidies. The government's ability to maintain this extensive program declined so much that early in July 1980, it sharply raised food prices. This action led to the nationwide workers' strike that produced the August 31 agreement recognizing workers' rights to form free trade unions and to strike and, a week later, toppled Gierek.

The other states face the same problems. In late spring 1979 Rumania raised food prices by about one-third. The increases in Czechoslovakia during summer 1979 averaged twenty percent: the price of oil rose 100 percent, of other fuels fifty percent, and of children's clothing 200 percent. In Hungary, which admitted a nine percent rate of inflation in 1979 and a food subsidy program of $2 billion in 1978, prices rose substantially in 1979; including five percent for bread, twenty-one percent for meat, twenty percent for milk, nineteen percent for sugar, and fifty-one percent for electricity.

In some cases, price changes, especially abandonment of food subsidies, may lead to an absolute decline in living standards. Growing interdependence with the economies of the West and of the rest of the world, especially the massive debts and the debt service problem, will increase pressures either for returns to tighter controls, which will increase dissatisfaction, or for even greater interdependence, which may be necessary but politically fatal in the long run. Even the revolution and the turmoil in Iran have deeply affected East Central Europe and will continue to do so, largely because these states had begun to turn toward Iran as an alternative source of essential oil. Bulgaria, Czechoslovakia, Hungary, and Poland had barter deals with Iran (in 1978 the University of Budapest even granted the Shah an honorary degree, with a fulsome and now embarrassing citation).

Relations with the West, particularly the Common Market, have therefore become increasingly important. Unfortunately for the states of East Central Europe, the recession in the West has led to a general decline in Common Market imports at the same time that the expansion of the Common Market and increased protectionism have emphasized restrictions. Moreover, in negotiations with these states the Common Market has a strong bargaining position and can force the Soviet Union to choose either greater opportunities for increased trade at the cost of recognizing the Western grouping and accepting relationships between the Common Market and individual East Central European countries or the denial of access to markets and capital. Thus, economic problems have been immensely critical throughout this area, raising issues of foreign as well as domestic policy and affecting internal intellectual, social, and political life. Economic stagnation, the ever more visible scientific and technical gap with the West, and pressure for division of increasing but still scarce resources to satisfy the needs of the urban classes constitute a direct challenge just when interdependence with the West has become a delicate economic and political problem.

The intellectual and social strains evident in East Central Europe are less significant than the economic pressures, but they are important. They reflect economic achievements as well as problems and have created social fissures apparent to the peoples of those countries and to the Western world as well. The successes of the past three decades have produced social classes, attitudes, and issues similar to those in the West, diminished any luster communism had, and revealed how East Central Europe has slipped into the general European pattern. The expectations and the development of attitudes among the youth, technicians, skilled workers, and women like those in Western societies and even the formation of interest groups are a tribute to the system's achievements as well as a threat to their continuing stability. These developments are particularly obvious among the "heroes' children," the sons and daughters of parents who devoted their lives to the party and to transform their societies; the generation gap in this region resembles that in Western countries. In Poland in particular, the disaffected groups have coordinated their oppositional programs, with the Catholic Church a silent, occasionally open, ally and protector.

Intellectual changes over the years have helped make such alliances possible and even more likely in the future. No kind of Marxism has any relevance or vitality in East Central Europe; interest in Marxist thought and revisions of it are far more common in France, the United States, and the underdeveloped countries than in the Soviet Union or Poland. Hungarians as well as others have spurned doctrine and doctrinal approaches for practical reasons: Kadar, his government, and most Hungarians are interested in what works best, not in how many workers can stand on the head of a pin. In Czechoslovakia, the events of 1968 destroyed any remaining interest in Marxism, forever associated now with invasion, not liberation, with Husak, not the human face of socialism. The utter collapse of the international movement, demonstrated not only in the hostility between the Soviet and Chinese Governments and their rival interpretations of communism but also by the conflicts between communist regimes in Ethiopia and Eritrea as well as in Cambodia, has completed the communist Reformation in just three short decades. Finally, Marxist materialism has come to a dead end; the religious revival among all groups illustrates the growing search for new answers to dilemmas that appear more eternal now that peoples have achieved substantial economic progress. Indeed, in most of these countries, the intellectuals see themselves as a surrogate opposition, one that repeated efforts have failed to crush or control.

The silence of Russian culture that Sir Isaiah Berlin noticed two decades ago has become even more deafening. In the competition of ideas, the West is simply overwhelming East Central Europe in art and architecture, jeans and pop music, hybrid corn and Holsteins, management techniques and input-output economic theories, genetics and ecology. Even the lowest forms of Western influence, reflected in movies and sex magazines, attract the peoples of this area and dissolve conservative controls. West German radio and television throughout most of the German Democratic Republic, cultural exchanges in all these countries, and Pepsi-Cola and Pizza Huts in Bulgaria are representatives of the saturation of these societies by Western culture.

The magnetic fascination of the West, due partly to the years of denial under Nazi and Soviet controls, and the increased interest in knowledge of the past and the present as well have led to vast audiences for Western broadcasts and to developments such as Poland's flying universities (classes, especially in modern history, offered in apartments). The expansion of travel opportunities from privileged supporters and hacks to hundreds of thousands reveals the character of the changes that have occurred and suggests the continued long-term effects these multiple contacts will have. Perhaps other communists can put their Humpty Dumpties back together again, but the dissolvent effects in East Central Europe of the years since Stalin can hardly be reversed or even reduced. The Soviet Union and the communist governments of this area have simply failed to reshape the established cultures and to create new social values. Instead, the national cultures have revived and Western influences have multiplied.

Western observers in general exaggerate the number and significance of the various dissident groups in the Soviet Union, noble though these men and women are and important as the evidence that they provide of the power and endurance of the human spirit is. In fact, these exemplars of the will to live and to be free are perhaps more significant in alerting and inspiring the West than they are as indications of powerful disaffection or threats to stability in the Soviet Union.

The peoples of East Central Europe are vastly different from those who have been inured by Soviet rule for several generations. Their histories and traditions, the conditions under which they have lived in recent decades, and their attitude toward Western Europe and its cultures differ so greatly from those in the heartland of Russia that the power and significance of the numbers actively and openly critical of their own governments also differ greatly. Considerable evidence sustains the general thesis that open opposition is thriving, even in the German Democratic Republic, whose repressive system is the most systematic and efficient, as the Berlin Wall continues to symbolize. The treaties of 1970 and 1971, the Helsinki agreement, the power of West German radio and television, and the flood of travelers (ten million West Germans visited the German Democratic Republic in 1976 and sixteen million made telephone calls) both opened up the state and necessitated a tightening of its savage control methods again in the late 1970s. The house arrest of regime critic Robert Havermann, the expulsion from the German Democratic Republic first of popular singer Wolf Biermann and then of party leader Rudolf Bahro, and the increasing mistreatment of West German journalists in violation of the Helsinki agreement are not so much the acts of a powerful and secure state as of a government that feels itself threatened despite its controls, its armed forces, the presence of large Soviet forces, and its particularly close ties to

Moscow. Similarly, the open violations of the Four Power agreement in 1971 by absorbing East Berlin into the German Democratic Republic in the summer of 1979 and arranging direct elections of deputies from East Berlin to the Volkskammer are acts of a state eager to establish its security by force, the only way possible. These actions reveal the illegitimate and brittle nature of the regime and make gradual change and peaceful resolution of the problems of this area ever more difficult.

The appearance of open criticism in placid Prague is even more remarkable than in East Germany. Charter 77, signed by over one thousand men and women, and the 1979 declaration of "respect for the rights of man" from the Czechoslovak Committee to Defend the Unjustly Persecuted are reminders that there is no "finality, for better or worse, about what has happened in Eastern Europe." Equally remarkable as these tiny but vivid Czech demonstrations has been the public support Andrei Sakharov and other Soviet citizens, Hungarians, and Poles have given the victims of "openly terrorist" repression. For the first time critics of these various regimes are beginning to cooperate, which reveals the weakening of controls and the flow of information among these societies.

Poland is of course the supreme illustration of national recovery and vitality among the East Central European peoples. Gomulka wasted fourteen years of opportunity to build a bridge between a communist government and its people. His replacement in 1970 following an incredibly stupid decision to cap years of increasingly autocratic rule by sudden price increases and changes in work rules demonstrated the depth of popular dissatisfaction, the powers workers can unleash, and the support such actions against repression and bungling can stimulate. Gierek's proposals late in 1975 to incorporate into the constitution a ringing definition of the United Workers' Party special role and Poland's links with the Soviet Union united intellectuals and the Catholic Church in effective protests. The violent June 1976 riots against new efforts to raise prices and to violate the pledge of 1971 forced another reversal of policy.

The government's part in stimulating these disorders revealed that Gierek had learned nothing from 1971, that the Polish Government was incompetent, ossified, and demoralized, and that it had lost both respect and authority. The explosion of *samizdat* publications; the formation of two free trade union organizations in 1976 (the Committee of Polish Defense and the Workers' Defense Committee), the Movement for the Development of Human and Civil Rights in 1977, and the Conference of Independent Poland in 1979; and above all the spirit and quality of Polish intellectual life in poetry, fiction, the theater, and films attest to the vigor and consummate skill with which the Poles have defended themselves and pressed for more freedoms. The emergence of the Catholic Church as a defender of human rights, even before the election of John Paul II and his dramatic visit to Poland, gained it the support of non-Catholic intellectuals and united much of the opposition to the government in a new kind of national front.

Faced with this informal alliance, the Gierek government early in July 1980 demonstrated once more that the new aristocracy had learned nothing from the 1971 and 1976 riots when it again suddenly raised food prices, especially of meat. This foolish action led to a series of strikes that spread from Gdansk and the Baltic littoral throughout the country, bringing the entire industrial economy to a halt by mid-August. This first nationally organized workers' strike in a communist-ruled country led to an agreement between the workers and the government on August 31. The agreement recognized the workers' right to strike and to organize independent trade unions, provided substantial pay increases and social benefits, relaxed censorship regulations, and gave the church increased access to the media, including television. This triumph of workers over communists revealed that the party and its governmental instrument had lost whatever legitimacy they had possessed and that communist rule would collapse except for national recognition that this would bring Soviet armed forces into action in Poland.

The new party and government leadership in the weeks after the agreement was deeply divided over the concessions and over economic problems, now more serious than before because of the work stoppages and the increased wages. Publicly committed to fulfilling the agreement, which the entire nation endorsed, but fearful that the agreement and its likely consequences meant such a serious threat to the "socialist system" that the Soviets would intervene militarily with consequences similar to those of 1831 and 1863, the leaders sought to delay recognizing and registering the free trade unions (ten million members strong by late October) and meeting the wage promises. However, the delay only increased the confidence and unity of the opposition that the August 31 agreement had strengthened. The church hierarchy remained especially close to the new unions, not only because it shared the workers' goals but also because it wanted to ensure continued responsible leadership. Moreover, the church, the workers, the intellectuals, and the students profited from cooperation. The government, already drifting and isolated and seeking church support, granted the embattled institution rights it had previously denied, to build new churches, to make Sunday radio and television broadcasts, and to enjoy greater freedom from censorship, more access to newsprint, and greater freedom in general.

The crisis of the summer of 1980 was by no means over by that fall. Indeed, in some ways it was more serious than ever because of Soviet fears that the Polish Party and Government would lose their tenuous control and that the Polish successes would spill across frontiers, not only into the German Democratic Republic and Czechoslovakia but into the Soviet Union itself. In short, freedom tends to expand. The ability of the Poles, their government, and their neighbors to live with the bubbling forces let loose in Poland constitutes one of the major problems of the 1980s.

As far as the Soviet Union is concerned, the steady revival of national consciousness and of nationalism in each of the countries of East Central Europe, with the possible exception of Bulgaria, renders these problems even more serious. The power of history and tradition is simply reasserting itself, even in the ruling parties. In short, the Soviet Government has discovered that the peoples of East Central Europe cannot be digested as easily as Russia absorbed the Central Asians in the nineteenth century - even Central Asia's Muslims may become restive.

In the 1970s, the Brezhnev administration's policies have destroyed the theme of the German menace and made the German Federal Republic respectable and popular throughout the entire area, even in Albania. The treaties, economic agreements, flow of trade and credit, and removal of old and potential problems by population transfers (125,000 ethnic Germans emigrate from Poland to West Germany annually) have helped demolish the barriers of distrust and fear and replaced them by fruitful economic and other ties. In the new nationalism ancient and honorable resentments are therefore directed against the Soviet Union, rather than against Germany. The renewed concentration on local and national economic interests, the return of the crown of Saint Stephen to Budapest, and John Paul II symbolize and strengthen national consciousness and nationalism in a way that inevitably weakens Soviet power.

Modern nationalism has not always been benign, and this force, like the others mentioned, has a fearsome as well as a hopeful side. The governments of these various states tend to emphasize national interests and will do so increasingly as each government concentrates on improving the condition of its people. National diversities are likely to continue to grow, on occasion enabling the Soviet rulers to play on the widening fissures in order to ensure the Soviet position. Thus, territorial disputes between some of these governments (for example, over Transylvania and Macedonia) may lead to diversionary crises, and the potential for the rise of men more like General de Gaulle than Jean Monnet is high, offering both advantages and disadvantages to the Soviet Union, but with the disadvantages outweighing the advantages in the eyes of Soviet leaders.

In any case, in the face of these problems and uncertainties, Soviet military power in and over this area will almost certainly continue to grow. The economic, political, and other ties the Soviets are weaving with ruling establishments, whose survival depends upon the Soviets, will no doubt continue to proliferate, integrating these states into the Soviet empire in ways that will receive less publicity than the discontents and dissatisfactions. However, in the last few years the Soviet gerontocracy has apparently lost whatever dynamism the Brezhnev system once had, and the visible decline of Soviet authority throughout this area may destroy whatever advances the socialist commonwealth may make. In a sense, the principal issue in the last part of the Brezhnev era and in the early years of the succeeding period is whether the unbinding of East Central Europe will continue slowly and gradually until some acceptable form of finlandization is achieved, or whether the area and the world as a whole will be pitched into a dreadful crisis, touched off by an accidental upthrust, a breakdown, or confusion and uncertainties connected with an unskillful transfer of authority. If progress toward more freedom proceeds quietly and even inconspicuously, and if Soviet rulers exhibit more understanding and sense than they have in the past, change in East Central Europe may remain peaceful. The area is still critical to the Soviet Union. Soviet rulers clearly possess the power to crush any uprising, regardless of the political cost, and the Soviet instinct will almost certainly lean toward the use of force, as it did in the case of Afghanistan. The very Soviet presence that is the main cause of instability in this part of the world may continue to prevent the growth of any force that could provide stability and peace.

As these important changes in East Central Europe were occurring, the United States, in its own assessment and in that of much of the world, stumbled from one disaster to another; the countries of Western Europe, especially the United Kingdom, France, Italy, Spain, and Portugal, tottered from crisis to crisis; the Common Market lost its vigor and enthusiastic support; and NATO was in disarray - an uncertain trumpet and a blind and leaderless giant. In the United States, the marvel of the moon landings, the progress in civil rights, and the incredible productivity of American agriculture were ignored or forgotten as pessimism blinded, weakened, and even paralyzed the most powerful state in the world. Instead, Viet Nam, Watergate, Iran, ineffective defense of national interests in diplomacy, the diplomatic and military bungling of the April 1980 effort to rescue the American hostages in Tehran, and the ravages of a seemingly invincible inflation dominated both domestic and foreign views of the United States. After 1965, moreover, anti-Americanism emerged as perhaps the strongest emotional political force in the world.

Yet during this same period, East Central Europe has skillfully inched away from Soviet control. This suggests, first of all, that the states of East Central Europe are acquiring a momentum of their own. It indicates, too, that Western values have been remarkably durable in this area and that the West has been overly self-critical. East Central Europe's existence as a group of lively states grappling with a series of new and complicated problems in an ever-shrinking world may constitute its greatest source of strength. But the West and its values have done more than survive: all the communist states, from Albania to the People's Republic of China, turn to it for aid. The economic and political recovery of Western Europe has influenced East Central Europe more than most Americans appreciate. That influence is likely to increase, even if the Reagan administration succeeds in unleashing the American economy, increasing American military strength, and producing a much firmer and more vigorous foreign policy, particularly toward the Soviet Union. Perhaps the most important sea change has been the growing respectability and increased role of the German Federal Republic, especially in Poland. This will probably continue to grow, almost independently of the political direction of West Germany.

Any discussion of the present situation and trends in East Central Europe inevitably turns to Western policy, even though its importance may decline in the 1980s. The United States and its allies, including Japan, can have little authority when a crisis erupts in this area and Soviet power exerts itself. However, the states of East Central Europe must remain tough, skillful, and above all confident if they are to move slowly toward greater freedom, if Soviet leaders are to abandon their dreams of empire, and if the world is to avoid another explosion. The West needs sensible and coordinated leadership in order to link its numerous strengths, especially economic aid, with moves toward the end of censorship, jamming, and restrictions on movement and access to information. Tying short-term credits, joint ventures, and participation in international economic organizations to lowering political and intellectual barriers in East Central

Europe should broaden the progress already made and pull these states into the world economy.

Such policies would force the Soviet rulers and their dependents in East Central Europe to face the dilemma that they have resolutely avoided but which pursues them relentlessly: either they must accept closer ties with the rest of the world, which would corrode a basically unstable Soviet position in East Central Europe, or they must try to re-establish the controls that once isolated and manacled the area.

NOTES

1. George Kennan, "The Sources of Soviet Conduct," *Foreign Affairs,* XXV (1947), 581-82; idem, *Democracy and the Student Left* (Boston, 1968); idem, "The Problems of Eastern and Central Europe," *The Listener,* LVIII (1957), 867-70; idem, *Russia, the Atom and the West* (New York, 1958), 35; idem, "Disengagement Revisited," *Foreign Affairs,* XXXVII (1959), 187-210, especially 190 and 194; and *New York Times,* February 1, 1980, 27.

2. *Economist,* April 20, 1963, 215-26.

3. Walter Lippmann, *The Cold War* (New York, 1947), 34.

PART TWO

The Soviet Union and the West

6

Russian and Soviet Attitudes Toward the West

Analyzing Tsarist and Soviet policy toward any country or area or issue is not easy; analyzing and describing the grounds or motives for policy is even more challenging. A discussion of "attitudes" is still more complex, for "attitudes" present a serious problem of definition in any society at any time. Even scholars from that part of the world which considers itself "the West" would find it difficult to reach agreement concerning what has been meant by "the West." Indeed, many would argue that use of the terms, "the West" and "the East," is a serious inaccuracy in definition and a costly political error.

Moreover, for few people does "the West" mean today what it did in 1947 or in any year before 1939. Definitions of the West change from year to year, from group to group, from country to country. The West itself is also not a constant; the West of Hitler or Picasso is not that of Gladstone or of Bismarck. Thus, an essay dealing with Russian attitudes toward the West inevitably deals with an almost infinite number of ever-changing variables.

In addition, of course, there are many different Russian attitudes toward the West. The different regimes, for example, have different approaches, and the attitude of the government is often substantially different from that of particular groups or classes. Finally, of course, the attitudes of the different classes or groups vary from each other and change from time to time.

Even if one were able to surmount these basic difficulties, the student of Tsarist and Soviet affairs must face other special problems. Russian history for the century before the 1917 revolutions offers an immensely rich fare of information, public and private. However, because of the most remarkable way in which the Soviet rulers govern and the devious ways in which the Soviet Government manages its foreign relations, it is sometimes difficult to identify particular Soviet policies or to determine their foundations. Mountains of information are available, but much of this is propaganda and constitutes more a handicap than an aid. It is often difficult to separate substance from shadow and to distinguish the ritual and rhetoric in Soviet language from the essential message.

Reprinted with permission from *Russian Foreign Policy: Essays in Historical Perspective*, Ivo J. Lederer, ed. (New Haven: Yale University Press, 1962), 109-141.

Analysis of Soviet propaganda has in recent years developed into one of the fine arts. We can now not only quite easily distinguish the "line" offered by the Soviet Government, but can even identify the basic foundation on which the propaganda rests. However, we are often quite helpless in determining even official Soviet motives or attitudes. Foreign policy has not been discussed in the Supreme Soviet in a significant way since 1929. The Soviet press does not fulfill the functions of the press in democratic countries in unearthing news but only describes the regime's basic approach to international affairs, its "line" on particular issues, and sometimes, usually discreetly, the circumstances in which a policy was determined. Memoirs and autobiographies in effect do not exist in the Soviet Union to shed light on the motives behind Soviet policies, the assumptions on which they are based, and the pulling and tugging involved in their ultimate determination.

Given these handicaps, one could adopt one of several approaches in analyzing Russian attitudes toward the West, in creating valid generalizations concerning the permanent and transient elements in these attitudes, and in suggesting some of the effects these attitudes have had on Tsarist and Soviet foreign policy. One could, for example, simply describe the way in which "the West" has been used at particular periods in Russian history. Thus, it is clear that Khrushchev means something quite different from Lenin when he refers to the West. One could also compare the attitudes before and after the Crimean War with those of the present time. One could describe the attitudes at particular critical points, tracing the shifts as they occurred. One could review the controversy between Westerners and Slavophiles in the 1840s, and compare it with developments in the late 1940s, when Zhdanov led the campaign against the "rootless cosmopolitans." One could analyze the attitudes of different classes or groups at different periods. One could analyze the treatment of the West in Russian histories, beginning perhaps with Solov'ev and ending with Pankratova and Zubok. Finally, if one had intimate knowledge of the subject and infinite grace and good judgment, one could write a learned and lively essay of the kind British scholars have sometimes written with such mastery. But only men such as the late B.H. Sumner could carry off such a feat with the necessary skill.

I have rejected these approaches and instead chosen one designed to define various ways of examining the problem, to identify some of the most interesting issues or questions, to provide some framework in which this complex problem can be studied, and to offer some generalizations or judgments for further research.

Thus, I have chosen four major subjects for review, in each case comparing Tsarist Russia from 1856 to 1917 with Soviet Russia: definition or conception of Russia; definition of the West; knowledge of the West; and attitude toward the West. For each of these subjects or factors, I propose to compare the position of Konstantin P. Pobedonostsev with that of Soviet leaders, with particular emphasis upon the period since 1953.

Pobedonostsev has been chosen for three reasons. First, I have studied the enormous amount of material available concerning him. Second, Pobedonostsev was both a significant and a representative figure in the last half-century of the old regime. A member of the bureaucracy for sixty years and an important state and court official from the middle 1860s through 1905, he was at the same time an unoriginal reflection of the "official" conservative point of view. Finally, Pobedonostsev is an excellent example of the Russian afflicted with an ambivalent attitude toward the West, an attitude that constitutes one of the most basic issues the Soviet Government faces today.[1]

I

Pobedonostsev's knowledge of urban and official Russia was extraordinarily deep. Born in Moscow, he was brought up in a warm, loving Slavophile home. He loved the theater from his youth, and he read widely in ancient and contemporary Russian literature. His father was a professor of Russian literature at Moscow University and one of the founders of the Society of Lovers of Russian Literature. The Aksakovs, Pogodin, and Lazhechnikov were among the family friends and neighbors. Pobedonostsev himself was a close friend and adviser of Dostoevskii in the 1870s, and he read everything of Leo Tolstoi's, whom he considered a menace. He devoted most of his time and energy from 1846 to 1865 to research in Russian history and law. His study of the history of serfdom led him into research on various kinds of landholding, property law, and Russian civil law, on which he published a three-volume study between 1868 and 1880.[2]

Pobedonostsev, however, knew little of rural Russia or of life outside court and academic circles. Except for visits to the estate of his father-in-law near Smolensk, there is no evidence of any knowledge of or concern with peasant life. Even when he traveled by train, he read constantly and did not view the countryside. The workers' world was also unknown to him until the last few years of his life. In other words, Pobedonostsev, like Marx, was a city man. Indeed, he was in this way a typical member of the Russian intelligentsia.

Pobedonostsev's lack of knowledge about and concern for the countryside and the peasant help mark him off from the Slavophiles, who had a special veneration for the peasant and for the *narod* and who had a dual image of Russia in which the state, an unavoidable evil, played an artificial and often arbitrary role. They saw Russia as a harmonious organic country, without classes or class divisions, distinguished by vigor, simplicity, love, Orthodoxy, and peaceful change, and they considered the Orthodox church free from and superior to the Romanov state. The Slavophiles spoke often of Holy Russia; Pobedonostsev never used the phrase. Indeed, the Slavophiles would have considered him and most other bureaucrats and members of the intelligentsia, conservative or radical, in the last third of the nineteenth century as non-Russians, city-dwellers who had been corrupted by Western ideas without realizing it.[3]

For Pobedonostsev, as for Karamzin and indeed for the communists, Russia meant the state. He thought first of the state, as naturally as an American thinks first of the individual. The state, and the government directing the state, represented the national will, with a mystical bond connecting the *narod* and the state. The state for him was also an expression of truth. Its purpose was to provide stability, harmony, and "rational direction" by means of a "calm, humane, indulgent, and arbitrary administration" and to prevent the rise of nationalism in the multinational Russian Empire, through providing both force and equality.[4]

The church was a servant and even a weapon of the state, designed to maintain the essential unity in faith and belief. Religion was to act as a homogenizing binder for society. A society could, therefore, have only one religion, regardless of the number of races it contained, for other beliefs and churches could only be "agents of disintegration." Basically, Pobedonostsev equated society and religion, and he would have accepted Toynbee's thesis that the great religions have created the different characteristics that make one civilization distinct from another.

The unity which the church provided he called the "community of believers." He asserted that "the church and the church alone has allowed us to remain Russians and to unite our scattered strength." Thus, when many of his contemporaries in Western Europe were developing systems labeled "integral nationalism," Pobedonostsev's might be described as "integral national Christendom." The Orthodox church more than any other was "a house where all are equal," and the church in thus satisfying one of man's elemental desires helped at the same time to strengthen the stability of society.[5]

Pobedonostsev was convinced that by nature men were evil and unequal. He repeated frequently that "every man is a lie" and that "every word said by man is an idle word of self-delusion." He shared the view expressed by Dostoevskii's Grand Inquisitor that man is "weak, vicious, worthless, and rebellious." He naturally condemned those who assumed that reason could be an effective tool for any but a tiny minority, whom he called "the aristocracy of Intellect."[6]

Pobedonostsev was as conservative in his approach to foreign policy as he was to political or social change. He saw Russia as a member of a European state system and as one of a number of states in the world with some of which, but only some of which, Russia had to maintain formal relations, and then "only at the top." However, he did not believe Russia should participate actively in world affairs. Indeed, there is some evidence that he resented and opposed all foreign alliances.

In other words, Pobedonostsev was an isolationist. The only exception to this stand helped prove the rule, for in 1876 and through much of 1877 he was an ardent advocate and later supporter of war with Turkey to free the Balkan Slavs and to unite them with Russia in a Slavic federation. However, as the war progressed, Pobedonostsev reversed his opinion. From that time forward, he turned Russian power inside, not outside. He did support Russian expansion after 1878, but he opposed entangling alliances or collisions with other states. He assigned to the Orthodox church and to economic imperialism whatever strength and influence Russia was to have beyond its borders. However, he continued to believe that it was impossible and dangerous for one society to attempt to borrow ideas and institutions from another or to impose its customs and system upon another. Each society was an independent organism.

Both the Slavophiles and the Panslavs thought Russia was unique in having a Messianic role to play in the history of Europe and the world - a different role was envisaged by each group - but Pobedonostsev and many of his generation after 1880 believed that Russia's destiny was simply to preserve and save the territory, institutions, and beliefs which he then cherished.

Turning from Pobedonostsev's conception of Russia to his definition of "the West," one finds him no more clear or consistent than we are today. Generally, though, for him and his contemporaries, from Chernyshevskii to Dostoevskii, the West meant that part of Europe west of Vienna and Berlin. Geographically and culturally, the West did not include the Balkans or any territories inhabited by Poles. Scandinavia was a part of Europe and therefore of the West, but it was generally as neglected as it is by most Americans today. Italy and Spain were naturally Western and European geographically and culturally, but Italy smacked too strongly of the Papacy, and Spain was too forlorn and backward to deserve serious consideration.

The West clearly did not include the Americas, although Pobedonostsev and his generation, of all political groupings, had much interest in American politics, economic development, and literature. Indeed, during the last decade of his life he often referred to Anglo-Saxon (English-American) ideas and institutions, just as Khrushchev refers to the United States and England as close allies and the core of a bloc today. In fact, although he did not make it explicit, by 1900 or so Pobedonostsev was beginning to consider the United States a part of Europe or the West.

However, Pobedonostsev defined the West not in terms of geography, but in terms of institutions and values. He believed that each society or state possessed distinctive political and social beliefs and institutions which helped to shape its character. Each nation's development represented an organic process based on immutable laws. Each state was thus a prisoner of its past. Thus he explained that some states, such as Russia, had centralized, authoritarian governments because in their distant past the emphasis had been upon communal life and upon firm control over the family by the father or by the patriarch; consequently, each person remained dependent, political power was highly concentrated, and strong central government developed. On the other hand, the Anglo-Saxon and Scandinavian states had decentralized democratic governments because in their distant past the emphasis had been upon individualism, and the father did not acquire absolute power in the family; consequently, democratic local government developed, and the central authority remained comparatively weak.

To Pobedonostsev, the West meant that part of Western Europe, including the British Isles, where four significant ideas were widely accepted: the concept of the excellence of natural man and the belief that man was a rational being, which he thought fundamental to Catholicism and to Protestantism and which he considered the basis of Western political institutions; the idea that the individual was important, perhaps even more important than the state or society; the belief in the effectiveness and propriety of government by law and parliamentary democracy; and the emphasis upon freedom and diversity. Pobedonostsev believed that none of these ideas and values could or should be adopted in Russia. Indeed, borrowing in this case could only be destructive, perhaps fatal. Man was not by nature good, and the idea of progress was an eighteenth-century delusion. Indeed, history is but a variation on one theme, and the "rational fanatic" threatens the unity and existence of any society.

Pobedonostsev could not have agreed with Chaadaev, or with the Westernizers in general, that "not one useful thought has germinated on the barren soil of our country; not one great truth has sprung up in our midst." He would have disagreed strongly with Nicholas Turgenev, who wrote in 1847: "In Europe, in most civilized countries, institutions have developed by stages; everything that exists there has its source and roots in the past; the Middle Ages still serve, more or less, as the basis for everything that constitutes the social, civic and political life of the European States. Russia has had no Middle Ages; everything that is to prosper there must be borrowed from Europe; Russia cannot graft it on her own ancient institutions."[7]

In other words, Pobedonostsev did not have the Westernizers' view of Russia and of the West. He did not consider the West to be the cradle of a superior universal civilization which could flourish anywhere. He did think Russia had a national culture with its own distinct personality. At the same time, he was neither a Slavophile nor a Eurasian: he could not have said that "Russia has preserved the childhood of Europe" nor that it is "a world apart." Russia to him was simply another one of the world's societies or civilizations. It had been heavily influenced by the West since Peter and Catherine, but these influences had been limited to the structure and operation of the central government and to the process of industrialization. The effort to maintain the old system, especially the old values, in the face of economic change and the rise of liberal and radical political ideas which flourished in part because of these changes, was extremely difficult for Pobedonostsev and others like him. Indeed, this was largely responsible for his pessimistic assumption that a revolution would sweep away the Russia he knew and bring in European ideas and institutions.[8]

II

Pobedonostsev, like many of the members of his class and generation, was given a European education in a Slavophile home in Moscow. He had a remarkable range of knowledge concerning Europe. He read and wrote seven European languages before he went to St. Petersburg to attend the School of Jurisprudence from 1841 to 1846. There, his knowledge of European culture was nourished by courses on Roman law, the French civil code, and German legal theory. Paul de Kock was his favorite light reading at the time. By 1848, when he sympathized with the French revolutionaries, he had read Girardin, Louis Blanc, Fourier, and Lamartine, whom he was fond of reciting.

Throughout his life, he read consistently and widely in European literature of all kinds. Carlyle, Gladstone, Seeley, Morley, Stephens, Mill,

Spencer, Darwin, and Maine were among his English favorites, and Hawthorne, Lowell, Emerson, and Cooper his American. He studied the French sociologist LePlay, Marx, Emile Zola, Max Nordau, and Ibsen. The London *Times* and the *Review des Deux Mondes* were among the publications he consumed carefully, and his knowledge of the foreign press in general was very high. In addition, he traveled widely and constantly. He visited England for long summer vacations in 1869 and 1873, he traveled in northern Italy in 1896, he visited Prague and Vienna a number of times, and he spent most of his summers after 1875 in Salzburg and Marienbad. Finally, he was well acquainted with foreign ambassadors, such as General Hans von Schweinitz, Maurice Bompard, and Andrew White. He knew well many foreign journalists and observers of Russian affairs, such as Dillon and Eugene Schuyler, and he was always eager to meet foreign visitors, such as Senator Beveridge. In other words, Pobedonostsev's knowledge of Europe was most impressive. He was obviously a highly cultured European gentleman, as much a European in many ways as Gladstone, Bismarck, Pius IX, or Andrassy.

Pobedonostsev, however, was not exceptional for his class and generation. Dostoevskii, Tolstoi, and Turgenev each in his own way was as interested in and knowledgeable about Europe as he was. Indeed, most Russian writers in the nineteenth century knew well the languages and literatures of France, England, and Germany, and many had learned Latin and Greek in school. The Panslav poet, Tiutchev, wrote violent denunciations of the Papacy and of the West in general - in good French. Even the Slavophiles were European in education and outlook. All had traveled in the West, and some had studied in England, France, and Germany. Samarin wrote in French and German, and called Montalembert and De Tocqueville "Western Slavophiles." Khomiakov wrote in French and English, and had an especial admiration and affection for England. He had a strong acquaintance with English history and literature, his works are full of references to England, and he could quote Shakespeare and Byron in particular at great length.[9]

The Slavophiles were especially attracted to and knowledgeable concerning England, for whose history they had a natural sympathy. The Westernizers, on the other hand, were especially informed about and influenced by the French and Germans, particularly the French of the Enlightenment and the Germans of the quarter-century after 1815. The royal family and the court were much influenced by German experience and thought, especially after Frederick the Great. The upbringing and character of the court after Peter were largely German, and dynastic and family considerations then played a most important part in determining Russian foreign policy. Sumner has pointed out that four of the nine Russian ambassadors to the Court of St. James between 1812 and 1917 were Baltic Germans and that these four men served Russia in London for a total of eighty-three of the one hundred and five years.[10]

It would be difficult, if not impossible, to demonstrate a connection between the sway of French or English or German culture among educated Russians, even in Russian government circles, and Russian foreign policy. Indeed, the eighteenth century, when French culture generally occupied a supreme position, was generally one of coldness or hostility between the French and Russian Governments. Both before, during, and after Napoleon's invasion in 1812, French culture retained its grip on Russian society. However, German social thought appears to have attained greater influence than French social thought after 1830. By and large, liberals and conservatives tended to look to England throughout the nineteenth century, and radicals to France and Germany. In addition, those who were most influenced by England tended to be most interested in political ideas, those who turned to France and Germany in social philosophy and in socialism. Government circles were most influenced by Germany - Samarin, for example, made a study of the Prussian administrative system - but by the German system of rule, rather than by German political and social philosophy.

Late in the nineteenth century, men such as Witte began to appear in the Russian state apparatus, by character, training, and experience affected by Western values and by Western concentrated interest in efficiency and economic progress. In fact, many Russians after the Crimean War began to acquire a new kind of knowledge from Europe, as Russia carried out its reforms and imported capital and technique, especially for industry and transportation. This view of the West came from no one country, though England and Germany were probably the most important single sources, and it had a powerful influence on Russian action and thought.[11]

The West each Russian knew was different from that of every other Russian, and this naturally much affected their separate attitudes toward the West. The Slavophile West, for example, reflected a high concentration of interest upon German romantic philosophy and upon English country life, not the life of the gentry Macaulay described in the third chapter of his *History of England* but the life of the educated country squire who had graduated from Oxford or Cambridge.

This was quite a different Europe from that of Dostoevskii or Pobedonostsev or Witte or Lenin. During the 1870s, Dostoevskii and Pobedonostsev were close friends and collaborators. They were both then conservatives and Panslavs. Both were bitterly hostile to Catholicism, to the Jews as dissolvents of Russian qualities, and to the Poles as bearers of various kinds of Western infections, but each had a different West in mind when he sought to shield Russia from its influences. Dostoevskii was profoundly affected by his years of residence in the West, especially among the Germans. He was powerfully influenced by the slums in which he had lived, and by the selfishness and money-grubbing he saw and from which he to some degree suffered. On the other hand, for Pobedonostsev the West consisted of publications and ideas. Pobedonostsev enjoyed what he saw of the West and had an especial affection for England. He was convinced that the greatest menace to Russian stability and survival came from Western ideas, particularly those deriving from the French Revolution and those which exalted individualism and constitutional government. He barely recognized the socialists, who Dostoevskii thought were the enemy.[12]

III

Generally, most informed Russians and most informed Europeans throughout the nineteenth century assumed that Russia was one of the European national states, a part of the European state system, and a leading figure in the Concert of Europe. This had probably been so since the time of Catherine the Great, and the role of Russia in the Napoleonic wars, in the peace settlement after 1815, and in international affairs in general made this most obvious. Indeed, Russia became a world power during the nineteenth century, because of its powerful position in Europe and conquests or gains during the century in the Caucasus, Central Asia, and the Pacific Far East.

At the same time, there was a serious gap between Russia's position and the foundation on which it rested. During the first half of the nineteenth century, Russia's reputation rested in a sense on its massive size and its large parade-ground army. This reputation was pricked by the Crimean War, and the new economic foundations that underlay British and German power as the century progressed exposed Russia further. Moreover, the growing dichotomy between the congealed political system of Russia and the changing forms of Western Europe also contributed to the gap between Russia and the West. Finally, of course, as more and more Russians appreciated the significant differences between Russia and the West, they became critical of their own government and society. In other words, Russia in the nineteenth century was in the West but not of it. Even those Russians who believed that Russia was and ought to remain distinct borrowed from the West and recognized its superiority in some fields.

The transformation of Russia after the Crimean War brought the West into Russia in a new form. The abolition of serfdom and the accompanying reforms, the rapid construction of railroads, massive foreign investments in Russian mining and industry, the development of modern banking and credit arrangements, and the appearance of the other economic and social institutions connected with industrialization profoundly affected Russian attitudes toward the West. Gradually, secular Western values permeated parts of Russian society. By the last decade of the century, Russia had as a leading statesman Witte, the archetype state capitalist, who sought to prod Russia into the technical West. Witte wanted to make Russia, economically at least, a Western state. The shift his rise symbolizes can best be understood by comparing Witte's stand with that of one of Nicholas I's chief ministers, Uvarov, who was even more European in culture than Witte but who sought to preserve the old Europe and keep away from Russia what he considered the new Europe, the Europe of the French Revolution, liberalism, and secularism.

There was naturally an enormous range of attitudes toward the West in the half-century or so before the 1917 revolutions. The great mass of the population was self-sufficient materially and spiritually and had little or no knowledge of the West. Generally, however, it had a strong antiforeign bias, reflecting the long and bitter struggle against the Poles and Turks in particular. This resentment and fear of foreigners were reflected in the last half of the nineteenth century in the popular expressions of feeling directed against Poles and Jews.

The antiforeign feeling among the upper class was probably less strong than among the populace at large, but it was still powerful. Thus, Professor Riasanovsky found the Slavophiles very critical of all Westerners except the English: the French were artificial, rational, abstract, depraved, and cruel; the Spanish fanatic, superstitious, aristocratic, individualistic, and proud; the Germans dull, plodding, rationalistic; and the Americans legalistic, rationalistic and grossly materialistic. These Slavophile attitudes were carried over to the Populist and Social Revolutionaries later in the nineteenth century. They reflected the conviction that Russia was a unique and worthy society with an important world mission. They reflected also a felt Russian need for recognition, which underlay much of the nationalistic and Panslav movement of the last third of the nineteenth century.

Pobedonostsev is a good example of the anti-Western attitude that developed after the Crimean War. A liberal through the revolution of 1848, a critic of the old Russian legal system, and one of the architects of the court reform of 1864, he turned against the West, its agents, and its influences. He became determined to crush the influence of Western religious groups in Russia. He was especially resolute and uncompromising in his attitude toward Catholicism and Judaism. While he was frank and even eager in the use of "firm power" to crush the "mad dream" of national independence held by some minorities, he hoped above all to convert them to Orthodoxy.

Pobedonostsev did accept the European past, as did Uvarov. Indeed, he had a great admiration and fondness for the Europe of 1788, and he also praised the Greek republics, particularly because of the role religion played, the influence of custom, the priority given local government, and the emphasis on demonstrated merit and ability for governors.

The Europe of the second half of the nineteenth century, however, he rejected, just as Pius IX did in the Syllabus of Errors. He was contemptuous of the idea that an individual had sacred rights and that all should participate in government: the rights of the state and society must always prevail over those of the individual. He saw constitutional government as "the tyranny of the mass" and the "weapon of the unrighteous." Parliamentary government and democracy to him meant party rule, and that meant the division and weakening of the state, rule by party ministries dominated by eloquent and ambitious party scoundrels, the predominance in society of party machines and corruption, the triumph of general ideas, meaningless and destructive but attractive to ambitious and unscrupulous politicians and to the ignorant masses. He was opposed even to advisory councils, such as the *Zemskii sobor*.

Pobedonostsev believed that the representative institutions of the Western continental European countries were crumbling, but he did not have this attitude toward the history and future development of England and the United States. On many occasions, most notably in a section he inserted into the fifth edition of *Moskovskii Sbornik* in 1901, he revealed a conviction that representative and democratic government, particularly in what he called the Anglo-Saxon and Scandinavian countries, developed from historical traditions in those countries and could be expected to flourish there.[13]

Pobedonostsev believed that the great dangers to Russia derived from intellectuals and the ideas they produced and carried. He considered freedom of the press a Western device for inundating Russia with lies, and he hoped to isolate Russian intellectuals from the West.

The final Western agent in Russia, for Pobedonostsev, was the judicial system created by the great reform of 1864, particularly trial by jury. He had been a prominent supporter of reform of Russia's judicial system. Indeed, his master's thesis in 1859 was a critique of the established system and an analysis of the principles on which he believed Russia's judicial institutions should be based; he denounced those who opposed reform as "legal Old Believers." He was an important member of the committee that drafted the judicial reform of 1864; some advisory members of the committee even considered him radical.[14]

However, by 1870 Pobedonostsev was a severe critic of the court system, as was his close friend, Dostoevskii. This is shown by their articles in *Grazhdanin,* by their letters, and by the general critique of the courts in Dostoevskii's novels. Pobedonostsev directly attacked the jury trial system in Russia, which he charged worked effectively only in England, where it had a long and popular tradition. Dostoevskii was just as critical. He believed that most Russian lawyers were unscrupulous and dishonest, he ridiculed distinguished lawyers for particular defense pleas, and he attacked the courts for their leniency.[15]

There were naturally many other forms of reaction to the West than those reflected by Pobedonostsev and Dostoevskii, but it is illuminating to note how the views of many Russian radicals were quite similar to those of these two extreme conservatives. As Professor Venturi's masterful study of the Populists shows, the attitudes of these Russians toward prominent Western ideas and institutions - constitutional government, political democracy, the party system, Western judicial procedures, Darwinism, Spencer, capitalism, etc. - were quite similar to those of Pobedonostsev and Dostoevskii.[16]

One finds other powerful threads running through various other parts of Russian society. Herzen's disillusion with the West and his conviction that Russia benefited from not possessing basic European ideas and institutions is one important sample. Tolstoi's philosophy of history in *War and Peace,* his exaltation of the Russian peasant, his repudiation of most European art, and his political anarchism constitute another reaction. The nihilists' critique of European culture is still another reflection. The gentry and professional-class liberals were charmed by Western political institutions and ideas. Many nationalists developed policies or attitudes that were not consistent or coherent, except for their emphasis upon things Russian. Finally, the Panslavs, such as Danilevskii, Fadeev, and Ignat'ev, developed an aggressive anti-Western attitude and policy which reflected a craving for national recognition and the reaction to the European claim that its civilization was the only true one and should serve as a model for all others. Fadeev saw the key to the Eastern Question in Vienna and wrote, "Russia's chief enemy is by no means Western Europe but the German race in its enormous pretensions."

Both he and Danilevskii, and indeed all the Panslavs, emphasized the antagonism of Russia to the West.[17]

IV

The communist definition of both Russia and the West reflects the communist view of the world, of the inevitable course of history, and of relations among states and peoples. The communists have a fervent and blind confidence in their analysis of world affairs. As the famous *Short Course* put it: "The power of the Marxist-Leninist theory lies in the fact that it enables the party to find the right orientation in any situation, to understand the inner connection of current events, to foresee their course and to perceive not only how and in what direction they are developing in the present, but how and in what direction they are bound to develop in the future."

The communists, of course, believe that relentless forces of history have produced capitalism and will in turn lead to socialism and then to communism. Capitalism is doomed by history and will collapse because it produces class conflict and war. Socialism will prevail, on the other hand, because history has fated it so and because it represents peace, democracy, social harmony, and the highest attainable general culture. Conflict at every level of society is the inevitable substance of all human relations, and the communists view the world as one in which class is hostile to class and state to state.

Marx's analysis of the course of world history, especially his analysis of the capitalist era, was written within a framework of national states and specifically in terms of the industrial development of Western Europe. In effect, he was especially informed about and interested in Europe, and he assumed the continued superiority of European civilization. Lenin, on the other hand, considered capitalism a global development. *Imperialism: The Highest Stage of Capitalism* extended the Marxist concept of the class struggle to the world stage, with the capitalist states struggling for raw materials and markets. The highest tension or conflict which the communists had previously associated with domestic politics were thus transferred to international relations throughout the world.[18]

Thus Lenin told the Ninth Congress of the Communist Party in March 1919: "We are living not merely in a state but in a system of states, and the existence of the Soviet Republic side by side with imperialist states for a long time is unthinkable. One or the other must triumph in the end. And before this end supervenes, a series of frightful collisions between the Soviet Republic and the bourgeois states will be inevitable."

By 1920, Lenin was using Russian experience to provide detailed instructions to foreign communist parties. His new definition of Russia and of the world was contained clearly in the preamble to the Soviet Constitution of 1923:

> Since the time of the formation of the Soviet republics, the states of the world have divided into two camps: the camp of capitalism and the camp of socialism. There - in the camp of

capitalism - national enmity and inequality, colonial slavery and chauvinism, national oppression and pogroms, imperialist brutalities and wars. Here - in the camp of socialism - mutual confidence and peace and the brotherly collaboration of peoples.

In 1925, Stalin was able to tell the Fourteenth Congress of the Soviet Communist Party, "Two chief but opposed centers of attraction are being formed, and, in conformity with this, two directions of gravity toward these centers throughout the world: Anglo-America ... and the Soviet Union." The world was later divided in different ways at different times by the communists, but division into hostile, armed camps, with no prospect of permanent peace between them or among them, was the central part of what Professor Barghoorn has properly labeled "The Manichean view" of world politics. Even Khrushchev's views on peaceful coexistence and on war as no longer inevitable reflect the Manichean view. Moreover, the communists in the recent past have usually found no distinction between various forms of state organization, such as the Nazi or the democratic.

Within this large frame, the communist view of the Soviet Union is rather clear. Indeed, the rhetoric used by communist leaders probably reflects their genuine beliefs. To them, the Soviet Union represents a unique and superior civilization, the establishment of which marks an historical epoch. This new society - socialist, democratic, peaceful - sets the pattern for future developments throughout the world. It is surrounded by hostile capitalist states, not so strong now as before. It therefore must remain powerful in every way, alert to any move of its enemies, and resolute and vigorous in its policy of expanding. The Soviet vocabulary frequently uses words related to conflict and struggle, and the Soviet view of the Soviet state also emphasizes military virtues.[19]

Convinced of the implacable hostility of the outside world, the Soviet leaders therefore place heavy emphasis on isolating their state and peoples from the infection of other cultures. The belief that the Soviet Union is threatened by foreign or cultural infection was most manifest during the period from 1946 until Stalin's death. Thus, Zhdanov at the September 1947 meeting which established the Cominform saw the Soviet Union and the "new democracies" as leaders of the "anti-imperialist and anti-fascist forces" against the imperialist states led by the United States and its "satellites," Britain and France. The "American imperialists" thus replaced the Nazi and Japanese militarist as the enemy camp. This campaign was accompanied by a severely repressive domestic policy, directed against "rootless cosmopolitans" and by a "gigantic ideological reconversion operation" designed to destroy the "survivals of capitalism in the consciousness of the people." Even marriage to foreign citizens was forbidden.

V

The changing Soviet definition of the West would make a fascinating project for research. The research has not yet been done, but the main outlines are clear. Lenin and the Old Bolsheviks before 1917 no doubt used the Russian geographical definition of the last third of the nineteenth century: i.e., the West referred to Western Europe, or Europe west of Berlin and Vienna, with Italy, Spain and Scandinavia not really included. For the Old Bolsheviks, the West basically meant industrial or capitalist Europe, but they were men of such wide culture that their definition extended far beyond the cold Marxist frame. For them Germany, the core of classical capitalism and of classical socialism as well, was the heart of the West. By 1925, Lenin's concept of imperialism and the situation after the First World War had created a change, and the world itself, not just Europe, was then divided into two camps. The Nazi eruption led the communists to fluctuate wildly in their definition of the West, as in their foreign policy.[20]

Since 1947, the West has meant the imperialistic United States and its allies or "satellites" throughout the world, engaged in conflict with Soviet socialism. Thus, Khrushchev in his article in the October 1959 issue of *Foreign Affairs* would apparently include Australia, Turkey, Pakistan, socialist Sweden and authoritarian Spain in his definition, with the center already removed from Europe to North America, with Eastern Europe as part of "the East," and with the economic factor only one of a series of factors involved in total power. Indeed, the Soviet leaders now probably assume that the essential factor in any country is not the organization of its economy or the size of its armed forces but the kind of political system it possesses. Thus, Western Germany must be made fit for "democracy" by the elimination of "monopoly capitalists, bankers, landowners, and militarists" and all others who might be called "anti-Soviet enemies of peace."

In addition, the Soviet communist view of the West emphasizes the so-called great powers: those states that possess relatively little economic and military strength fall on the periphery of the Soviet view. Finally, the Soviet view emphasizes significant individuals. While Marxism-Leninism emphasizes the role played by economic forces the Soviet communists, when they look at the West, probably see not only capitalistic great powers but also great men, who stand for or represent these states.

The West has several notable characteristics from the Soviet point of view. First, it is relentlessly hostile. It is doomed to collapse. It is divided class by class and state by state. It is ill and unsound, undisciplined, and in disarray. It lacks a sense of will and purpose. It is clearly not able to match the rate of growth of the Soviet economy: this and other "facts" are understood by the "broad masses," who will not forever be thwarted. It is incapable of resolving its own problems, to contribute to the solution of the underdeveloped countries' principal difficulties, and to create a supra-national system which will end present tensions and establish a secure peace.

The United States as the leader of the anti-Soviet forces has probably come to represent the West for the Soviet leaders. As Professor Barghoorn has shown, in the Soviet image the United States seeks desperately to resolve its internal problems by dominating foreign markets. It attempts at the same time to isolate and encircle the Soviet

Union, with NATO its chief instrument and with the destruction of the national sovereignty and independence of its allies one of its main techniques. Fatally stricken as a capitalist state, afflicted at the same time with mortal social and ethnic problems, burdened with a stagnant culture, the United States reels from one disaster to another, the great danger being that it will destroy the world in its own collapse.

VI

It is clearly impossible to compare with any certainty the knowledge of the West general among the ruling group in Russia in the second half of the nineteenth century with that of the rulers of Russia since 1917, since 1934, or even since 1953. One might be able to compare Pobedonostsev's information with that of Zhdanov or of Stalin, but even reducing the Soviet scene to one leader does not resolve the problem, because of the nature of the evidence, or, more accurately, the lack of evidence.

The Old Bolsheviks had a sound general knowledge of Western Europe, even though they had a distorted view. Lenin, whose mother spoke German, French, and English, spoke several European languages fluently and was at home in Capri, Berlin, Paris, London, or Brussels. Trotsky, Litvinov, Chicherin, Rakovskii, Bukharin - many of that generation were European or Western in knowledge and outlook. The generation that has risen to the top in the last twenty-five years, however, includes many Gletkins as well as many highly trained scientists and bureaucrats whose education is so highly specialized that they are what one American educator has called "rudderless rabbits."

In other words, Zhdanov's knowledge of Europe and America cannot rank with Pobedonostsev's, nor can that of Molotov or Shepilov compare with that of Giers or Lobanov. The Soviet Union has become a society with remarkable coverage of Western scientific and technical data and one in which a political attack on an American graduate student can cite a Waco, Texas newspaper. At the same time, it trains thousands of engineers with no knowledge of the rest of the world and produces English-speaking guides who have never read a page of English printed outside the Soviet Union.

Most Soviet citizens, including even highly trained men and women in professions, have little access to information about the West. In some ways, they are as ignorant as the poor, illiterate peasants of the nineteenth century. Indeed, they may truly be more ignorant because of the misinformation concerning the outer world which they are fed and because of the myths which thrive in the Soviet Union. Some individuals, of course, especially scientists and technicians, are remarkably well informed concerning developments outside Russia in their special fields of interest. On occasion, this professional knowledge expands beyond suspected limits. For example, the knowledge that a consistent Soviet student of European and American literature on petroleum engineering acquires concerning the West is almost certainly not restricted to petroleum engineering.

Soviet citizens are not only denied access to information about the West and misinformed in many ways; they also live in a particular form of society and develop a particular point of view which much affects whatever information they do acquire. The spectacles with which Soviet communists look at the world produce particularly distorted visions, and all Soviet citizens are affected by the color of the glasses through which the world is shown to them. This ideological screen is even more serious as a limitation on Soviet understanding of the outer world than are the withholding of information and the deliberate manipulation and distortion of facts.

The distortion produced by the ideological spectacles has not been a constant in Soviet history. For example, the Old Bolsheviks probably were able to modify the distortion because of their own education and personal residence abroad. However, the new generation who have predominated in the last quarter-century have lacked the knowledge and sophistication of their predecessors, have had little personal contact with foreigners and foreign societies, and have lived in a most rigidly controlled community, so that the vision they have is quite distorted. The relaxation and thaw of the last few years may have introduced some modification into this scheme, but the flood of grotesquely inaccurate propaganda continues.

We must assume that Soviet missions abroad, Soviet intelligence agencies, and foreign communists forward immense amounts of material to Moscow and that Soviet leaders have full access to the literature and other cultural products of the West, although these types of publications are denied the Soviet public in general. However, because of the nature of the Soviet system, it is quite likely that Soviet agents both select materials they believe their leaders wish to see and prepare their reports to conform to whatever the line is at the moment. Indeed, at all levels of the Soviet Government facts are probably marshaled according to a "rigidly enforced philosophy, adherence to which is the password to authority and responsibility within the Soviet system." The Soviet leaders may thus be blinding themselves about the West and the outer world in general. This factor, plus the years during which the communists' activities have been "characterized by their extraordinary ability to cultivate falsehood as a deliberate weapon of policy," has corrupted the communist mentality. Indeed, this may be at the center of the most serious problem the world now faces.[21]

As Professor Barghoorn's studies have shown, Soviet isolation, indoctrination, and doctrinal distortion have not only seriously distorted the Soviet view of the world but have contributed to the Soviet habit of projecting their own designs into the motives and plans of others. The abstract and schematic approach of the Soviet communists to human problems, their fear of aggression from others in part because of their own designs upon the rest of the world, and their desire to reduce domestic discontent and to create foreign scapegoats have all led to massive discoloring of the West.

Soviet knowledge of the West is therefore especially difficult to define. The ordinary Soviet citizen probably has little definite information: what he does know or believe is a mixture of fact and fantasy. However, in spite of all the propaganda directed against Soviet citizens, all probably suspect that life is richer, freer, and more humane in Western Europe and the United States than in the Soviet Union. In fact, the Soviet man in the street is quite susceptible to foreign influence, from jazz to pocket books.

The intellectuals or highly skilled group probably have more and better knowledge and are more friendly and envious, but on the other hand they are the more direct targets for the consistent anti-Western campaign. Recent Soviet achievements in science and technology have probably increased their pride in Soviet culture and reduced the West's fascination. The elite group almost certainly is most affected by doctrinal rigidity and wears the strongest colored glasses for viewing the world. At the same time, in recent years in particular, it has had some opportunity to travel, to meet foreigners, and to have access to foreign literature and art and information.[22]

Even when they have ample opportunity to obtain knowledge, all groups probably lack the ability to understand the constitutional and democratic states of the West, the political and spiritual values upon which they rest, and the motives that inspire their policies. B.H. Sumner's comment on Peter the Great probably applies equally well to Soviet citizens today:

> He did not explore the springs and motive forces of this western achievement; he did not seek to understand the workings of financial, political, or administrative institutions; and he had little or no conception of the slow and varied stages by which England or Holland had grown to be what they were. What never left his mind was the forest of masts on the watersides of Amsterdam and London, symbols of enriching trade reaching out to the Indies and all parts of the world; the clusters of busy towns, the creation of that independent, middle class, rich in invention, industry, and initiative, which his own country so much lacked.[23]

VII

The official communist attitude toward the West reflects the basic communist philosophy on the nature of man and the course of history. Since the mid-1930s, when most of the old Bolsheviks were eliminated, the attitude toward European politics and culture has been particularly rigid and doctrinaire. Bukharin and some of the other Old Bolsheviks saw the Nazis in the early thirties as a threat to European civilization as well as to the Soviet Union. They wanted to cooperate with the German social democrats and other moderates to prevent the Nazis from seizing power. However, the Soviet communist decision was that "the establishment of an open Fascist dictatorship ... accelerates the rate of Germany's development towards proletarian revolution." As late as December 1933, *Bolshevik* proclaimed, "In Germany, the proletarian revolution is nearer to realization than in any other country; and victory of the proletariat in Germany means victory of the proletarian revolution throughout Europe." The "petty bourgeois move at the service of the German bourgeoisie" produced more than a "temporary triumph," Bukharin and many of his supporters were executed later, and the official Soviet attitude toward the West has since lacked the understanding of Europe it once had, while at the same time it has placed more emphasis on the native Russian heritage.[24]

If Russian leaders in the nineteenth century thought Russia was in the West but not of it, the Soviet leaders believe they are a part of the West but opposed to it. The Soviet Union is a part of the European state system, and it also plays a major role in the United Nations. The Soviet Government acts on one level as though it were an ordinary nation-state, and its diplomats use the traditional and established forms and concepts. At the same time, the Soviet leaders seek a world system of their own and to break whatever unity the West possesses. The threats they have used in recent years reveal a consciousness of power and a contempt for "passive majorities without a faith and without organization."

The clearest, most fundamental, and most pervasive characteristic of the official Soviet attitude toward the West is "unrelenting hostility." This helps account for the grudging and inadequate credit given the West for its military activities during the Second World War. It helps explain the remarkable folly with which the Soviet leaders in 1945 deliberately destroyed the immense fund of good will that had accumulated in the West, as well as the implacable campaign launched in 1947 against Western influence within the Soviet Union.

The communists also fear the West, both its infectious ideas and its economic and military power, although this fear is apparently not as great as it was only a decade ago. The virulent and sustained anticosmopolitan campaign, the propaganda attacks launched upon "the decadent West," the efficiency of the censor and the police in isolating the Soviet population from Westerners and Western influence, and the way in which the Soviet leaders have projected their methods and plotting into the minds of their opponents all reflect fear. This now centers on the United States, the great imperialist dragon since 1946, but the German menace is inflated also.

Soviet fear of the West, now declining, is matched by Soviet scorn and arrogance. During the last decade in particular, developments in Soviet science and technology, Soviet success in negotiating the succession crisis after the death of Stalin, the continuing rapid growth of the Soviet economy, the frequent skill and daring of Soviet foreign policy, the frequent disarray, confusion, and lack of will demonstrated by the West, and the immense opportunities that have unfolded in Asia and Africa have all contributed to the confident and brash air with which Soviet communists view the world. The slogan to "overtake and surpass" is still a significant one, but a confident and even arrogant spirit has developed because of the considerable triumphs already achieved. Indeed, today one might ask, "who is encircling whom?"

The Soviet Union still borrows extensively from the West. It has not only adopted Western industrial techniques, but it has also brazenly stolen and misused the Western vocabulary. However, the Soviet leaders now surely see the Soviet Union as a philosophical and economic magnet for the world. In fact, having "defended Western culture" against the Nazis during the Second World War, they now have acquired a Messianic spirit for the world at large. They see the Soviet Union, on balance, as an exporter of institutions and ideas, not an importer. They are beginning to feel equal, if not superior, to the West and to believe that the wave of the future is indeed a communist one. Russian culture is already of "world significance." The West, in fact, is doomed.[25]

Alas, the communist attitude cannot be this clear and optimistic. The party leaders and those who are blinded by their philosophy and their own interpretation of the course of events probably do accept this view. The privileged elite group who profit from the Soviet system may also share this optimism, although the forbidden fruits of the West do tempt, and doubt raises its ugly head even among privileged artists and political leaders.

Moreover, the Russian populace, while probably strongly affected by Soviet pride and by resurgent Russian nationalism, also sees the West in different colors from those in which the regime paints it. The party fears greatly lest the Soviet people be corrupted by alien doctrines, although it proudly claims their enthusiastic support. This helps explain the massive campaign to show the Russian workers that people in other parts of the world do not live so well as they, the general effort to blacken Western life and culture (especially American), the use of stolen Western political symbols and terms, and the glorification of all things Soviet. In spite of the censorship, the terror, the isolation, and the propaganda, the mass of the Soviet population has genuine good will and admiration for Westerners, especially Americans, and there is a serious gap between the attitude of the regime and that of the populace. The Soviet peoples, indeed, may exaggerate the material wealth of the West. They envy these material achievements, but even more they desire the simple human liberties generally possessed in the West.[26]

Finally, the peoples of Eastern Europe, now ruled by Moscow in its "controlled neighbor policy," significantly influence Soviet attitudes toward the West. Control of Eastern Europe has moved the boundary line between Russia and the West to the Oder-Neisse, which is approximately where many Russians would have placed it a century ago. This position helps assure the frontiers of the Soviet Union against attack; it gives the Soviet Union a powerful advance base against the West; It has divided the great continent of Europe and placed a gun at the forehead of the West; It has given the Soviet Union a veto on any solution to the unification of Germany; and it has strengthened the confidence of the communists, and the fear of the neutralists, that these increments to Soviet power prove that communism represents the wave of the future. However, the extensive disintegration of Moscow's authority within the Soviet orbit in 1956, and the revelations the 1956 revolutions provided have complicated the Soviet vision of the Soviet empire and of the West. The darlings of the Soviet regime - the workers, the intellectuals, and the students - led the rebellions and thereby shook the confidence of the communists in themselves and their peoples. Moreover, the Soviet rulers have rediscovered that the Poles are Western and carry Western ideas directly into the heart of the empire. The

West, in other words, is still a dangerous carrier of infectious political diseases.

VIII

There are many enlightening comparisons and contrasts between the attitude of nineteenth-century Russian statesmen toward the West, and the foundations on which it was based, and the attitude of the leaders of the Soviet Communist Party during the recent past. For example, the generally accepted definition of the West held in Russia has changed considerably. In particular, Western Europe no longer constitutes the West, as it did a century ago and even sixty years ago; for both Soviet leaders and almost certainly the populace at large, the West now includes the United States and indeed most of the states allied with or associated with the United States throughout the world.

The West is defined differently in other ways as well. During the second half of the nineteenth century, those Russians who had any knowledge of the outside world saw the West as the hub of the world, whether they believed Russia should become increasingly a part of this cultural core or believed instead that Russia possessed a unique and superior culture of its own, which should remain unaffected by outside influence. In effect, most informed Russians almost instinctively looked to the West for ideas and inspiration. The West's pre-eminent position has clearly been shaken to some degree, although admiration and resentment both affect the Soviet view of the West, from the Kremlin to the collective farmer.

It is difficult to compare the knowledge of the West available in the second half of the nineteenth century and that available since the end of the Second World War. Generally, those who were privileged and who assisted in governing Russia before the revolutions had quite free access to the West. Many Russians were extremely well informed, whether or not they were sympathetic. For those educated Russians who were critical of the old regime, the flow of information of all kinds was restricted, but not consistently or efficiently. Indeed, compared to practices common in recent history, the policies of Tsarist Russia were liberal and enlightened.

Under Soviet rule, especially since the mid-1930s, the Russian people have lived under the most totalitarian government known to man. Data from the West are carefully controlled; in effect, access to information from the West has been denied the population of the Soviet Union. However, the loopholes in even the rigid Soviet system are large. Careful study of the Western economy and Western technology has brought into the Soviet Union masses of material about everything Western. The "thaw" since 1953, like that which followed 1856, has allowed considerable light into the old dark room.

Soviet knowledge of the West, however, is hideously distorted by the screen through which the Soviet rulers seek to filter all information from abroad. It is always difficult to understand another society, but the cliche-ridden view of the "capitalist" world gives Soviet understanding of the West an Alice-in-Wonderland quality. The Soviet rulers not only deceive their populations, but themselves as well. Indeed, "if the Soviet leaders really think us to be as evil as they depict us to their own people, how can they seriously believe in the possibility of coexisting peacefully with us? If, on the other hand, they are misleading their own people, how can we, on our side, have confidence in them?"[27]

Quite clearly, the Marxist-Leninist injunction that the socialist world overcome and destroy the "capitalist" world constitutes the most significant change that has occurred in the Russian view of the West. The population of the Soviet Union, deprived of accurate information, especially on many distant areas now in contest, and naturally inclined to support their government in crisis, almost certainly accepts the communist two-camp definition of the world, with its implicit abandonment of the balance of power and of the traditional manner of conducting international relations. However, some aspects of Soviet foreign policy may have very shallow popular support because of the gap between official and popular attitudes.

The West still represents the goal, the standard of excellence for the Soviet Union. For the intelligentsia, the populace at large, and even many of the party elite, the West offers the lure of freedoms, diversity, and a high and carefree standard of living. Consequently, fear of the West remains powerful in Russia: the Iron Curtain of today is only higher and tighter than that of a century ago. The treatment granted Chaadaev, Tolstoi, and Pasternak reflects similar governmental policies.

While the Soviet leaders are almost as suspicious and fearful of the West as was Pobedonostsev, they and their people, especially the intelligentsia, have a pride that amounts on occasion to blind arrogance. Perhaps the sputniks' greatest effect in the long run will be on the Soviet peoples, now more confident of their nation's place in the sun because of the achievements in outer space. The Soviet Union now exports ideas and values, where before it was only an importer. In the long run, the assurance this provides may make the Soviet Union a more comfortable neighbor.

There is no necessary or logical connection between the attitude of a government or people toward another people or culture and the government's foreign policies. National interest, in the long run, will prevail over attitudes, however powerful they may be. Russia's relations with Germany and France, for example, have not been a careful reflection of governmental or popular attitudes. Some of America's current allies were its recent enemies, and the policies changed before the various components of national attitude did.

Even so, the Russian attitude toward the West has had and will continue to have a profound impact on foreign policy. The Soviet view of the world and of the role the West should play in it is the most impressive illustration. Soviet policy toward the European Defense Community and other steps toward European unity and toward NATO reflects this view. Similarly, the Soviet assumption that the capitalistic West seeks to expand and to destroy the Soviet empire has a powerful impact on Soviet policy and on world affairs. Finally, and just as important, Soviet fear and unease because of the West and of what it represents contribute significantly to the pressures for a revolution from above and for an aggressive foreign policy.

In other words, some of the main features of the Soviet system have developed because of the official attitude toward the West.

Other preliminary conclusions of some general significance emerge. The impact of Western ideas obviously helped to undermine the old regime in Russia. The Soviet Union is in the curious position of borrowing heavily but selectively from the West, with a most rigid screening of infectious subversive ideas. However, it is quite likely that the Soviet rulers will not succeed in borrowing only what they wish. It may, in fact, be impossible for any society to borrow selectively from another society. Thus, this most intensely anti-Western regime may be undermining its own conservative position in a most paradoxical manner.

Secondly, the West will continue to influence Russia and the Russians just by its existence. Even the most efficient and ruthless censorship and propaganda system will not be able to blot out the West; as long as the West exists the Soviet Government will feel unsure. Curiously, the expansion of the Soviet empire into Eastern Europe has increased the hazard, for the Poles, Hungarians, and the Czechs in particular, deeply influenced on one side by Soviet rule, at the same time are carriers of Western influence into the heart of the Soviet empire.

Finally, Russian attitudes toward the West serve as a mirror, if a grotesque one, of the West. The period during which Russia's relations with the West have been closest and most fruitful has been the most revolutionary, violent, and disorganized period in Western history. The West has been going through the most dramatic, complicated, and dangerous transformation in its history at just the time when Russia was thrown most closely against it and sought to learn most rapidly from it. When one reviews Russian attitudes toward the West, one must remember that "the West" includes the Nazis as well as John Stuart Mill. Russia's attitudes toward the West therefore mirror this transformation within the West itself.

NOTES

1. More complete information concerning Pobedonostsev than is here provided can be found in "Pobedonostsev's Conception of the Good Society," *Review of Politics,* XIII (1951), 169-90; "Pobedonostsev as an Historian," in H. Stuart Hughes, ed., *Teachers of History: Essays in Honor of Laurence Bradford Packard* (Ithaca, N.Y., 1954), 105-21; "Pobedonostsev on the Instruments of Russian Government," in Ernest J. Simmons, ed., *Continuity and Change in Russian and Soviet Thought* (Cambridge, Mass., 1955), 113-28; "The Pobedonostsev Family," *Indiana Slavic Studies,* II (1958), 63-78.

2. I.S. Aksakov, *Biografiia Fedora Ivanovicha Tiutcheva* (Moscow, 1886), 240-45; E.N. Medynskii, *Istoriia russkoi pedagogiki do velikoi oktiabr'skoi sotsialisticheskoi revoliutsii* (Moscow, 1938), 168-70; Albert Gratieux, *A.S. Khomiakhov et le mouvement slavophile* (Paris, 1939), 2, 3; Nicholas Riasanovsky, *Russia and the West in the Teaching of the Slavophiles* (Cambridge, 1952), 14-33; Alexander von Schelting, *Russland und Europa im Russischen Geschichtsdenken* (Bern, 1948), 147-49, 162-66.

3. Medynskii, *Istoriia,* 165-70; Riasanovsky, *Russia and the West,* 62, 77, 120-25, 141-43, 149-52, 206-07.
4. Konstantin P. Pobedonostsev, "Gosudar' Imperator Aleksandr Aleksandrovich," *Russkii Arkhiv, I* (1906), 619-24; Pobedonostsev, *Pis'ma Pobedonostseva k Aleksandru III* (Moscow, 1925-1926), I, 170-71; II, 3-4, 46-47, 115; Pobedonostsev, *K.P. Pobedonostsev i ego korrespondenty: pis'ma i zapiski. Novum Regnum* (Moscow, 1923), 2, 832-35, 1004-06.
5. Konstantin P. Pobedonostsev, "Iz chernovykh bumag K.P. Pobedonostseva," *Krasnyi Arkhiv, XVIII* (1926), 205; Pobedonostsev, *Moskovskii Sbornik* (Moscow, 1896), 3-9, 12-16, 20-23, 154-56, 216-21; Pobedonostsev, *Pis'ma, II,* 79-82, 102-04, 108-10, 191-92, 259-60, 308-09; Hans Lothar von Schweinitz, *Denkwürdigkeiten des Botschafters General v. Schweinitz* (Berlin, 1927), *II,* 243-44, 275, 302, 388, 395-96.
6. Konstantin P. Pobedonostsev, *Prazdniki gospodni,* 7th ed. (Moscow, 1905), 14; Pobedonostsev, *Moskovskii Sbornik* (Moscow, 1897), 33-34, 183-95, 258-65; Maurice Bompard, *Mon Ambassade en Russie, 1903-1908* (Paris, 1937), 257-58.
7. Quoted by E.H. Carr, " 'Russia and Europe' as a Theme of Russian History," in Richard Pares and A.J.P. Taylor, eds., *Essays Presented to Sir Lewis Namier* (London, 1956), 362.
8. Wladimir Weidlé, *Russia: Absent and Present* (New York, 1952), 2; Benedict H. Sumner, "Russia and Europe," *Oxford Slavonic Papers,* II (1951), 1-3; Frederick C. Barghoorn, "Some Russian Images of the West," in Cyril E. Black, ed., *The Transformation of Russian Society* (Cambridge, 1960), 575-78; Riasanovsky, *Russia and the West,* 78-80.
9. Benedict H. Sumner, *A Short History of Russia* (New York, 1943), 308.
10. Ibid., 331.
11. Benedict H. Sumner, *Peter the Great and the Emergence of Russia* (New York, 1951), 84, 190-92; Sumner, "Russia and Europe," 4; Weidlé, *Russia,* 48-49; Riasanovsky, *Russia and the West,* 32-42.
12. Ernest J. Simmons, *Dostoevsky* (London, 1950), 219-32.
13. Pobedonostsev , *Moskovskii Sbornik* (Moscow, 1896), 25-52; Pobedonostsev, *Moskovskii Sbornik* (Moscow, 1901), 30-37, 54-57; Pobedonostsev, *Pis'ma, I,* 379-81; Iurii V. Got'e, "Bor'ba pravitel'stvennykh gruppirovok i manifest 29 aprelia 1881 g.," *Istoricheskie Zapiski,* (1938), 259; Evgenii Feoktistov, *Vospominaniia* (Leningrad, 1929), 206-12.
14. Konstantin P. Pobedonostsev, *Vechnaia pamiat'* (Moscow, 1896), 56-62; Pobedonostsev, *K.P. Pobedonostsev i ego korrespondenty, I,* Pt. I, 68-69; A.F. Koni, *Na zhiznennom puti* (Moscow, 1914-29), *III,* 191-92; Grigorii A. Dzhanshiev, *Epokha Velikikh Reform,* 2nd ed. (Moscow, 1900), 365-67, 552.
15. F.M. Dostoevskii, *Sobranie Sochinenii* (Paris, 1945-46), *IV,* 194-208; *V,* 71-73, 78-101; Dostoievsky, *The Diary of a Writer* (New York, 1949), *I,* 16-22, 30, 213-38; Samuel Kucherov, *Courts, Lawyers and Trials under the Last Three Tsars* (New York, 1953), 169-71; *Grazhdanin,* October 29, 1873, 1173-75; *Grazhdanin,* December 22, 1873, 1371-72; *Grazhdanin,* December 29, 1873, 1380.
16. Franco Venturi, *Roots of Revolution* (New York, 1960).
17. Benedict H. Sumner, *Russia and the Balkans, 1870-1880* (Oxford, 1937), 36, 43, 72, 80; Sumner, *A Short History,* 309-11; Barghoorn, "Some Russian Images," 576-77.
18. Frederick C. Barghoorn, *The Soviet Image of the United States* (New York, 1950), 125; Barghoorn, *Soviet Russian Nationalism* (New York, 1956), 187-94.
19. Max Beloff, *The Foreign Policy of Soviet Russia, 1929-1941* (New York, 1947-49), *I,* 2; Leonard Schapiro, *The Communist Party of the Soviet Union* (New York, 1960), 196-97; Barghoorn, *The Soviet Image,* 16; Barghoorn, "Some Russian Images," 578-84.

20. Barghoorn, *The Soviet Image,* 16, 103-04, 265-75.

21. Merle Fainsod, *How Russia Is Ruled* (Cambridge, 1953), 283-84, 538-39; Philip E. Mosely, *The Kremlin and World Politics* (New York, 1960), 5-6, 307-08; George Kennan, *Russia, the Atom and the West* (New York, 1957), 21-24; Kennan, "Peaceful Coexistence: A Western View," *Foreign Affairs,* XLVIII (1960), 171-90; Marshall D. Shulman, "Changing Appreciation of the Soviet Problem," *World Politics,* X (1958), 507-08.

22. Barghoorn, *The Soviet Image,* 117-23, 230-65.

23. Sumner, *Peter the Great,* 41.

24. Elliot Goodman, *The Soviet Design for a World State* (New York, 1960), 380-82, 420-21; Beloff, *Foreign Policy, I,* 56-65; Schapiro, *The Communist Party,* 481.

25. Raymond Aron, *The Century of Total War* (Boston, 1955), 150, 215; Mosely, *The Kremlin,* 468-69; Frederick C. Barghoorn, "Great Russian Messianism in Postwar Soviet Ideology," in Ernest J. Simmons, ed., *Continuity and Change in Russian and Soviet Thought* (Cambridge, 1955), 541-48.

26. Barghoorn, *The Soviet Image,* 21-37.

27. Kennan, "Peaceful Coexistence," 189.

7

Soviet Policy Toward Western Europe Since Stalin

Stalin's successors inherited a policy which was global and which reflected Stalin's personal ambitions, the accumulated baggage of Russian history and of the Marxist-Leninist-Stalinist philosophy, domestic problems and pressures, and critical situations around the world, such as stalled armistice negotiations in Korea, a new administration in Washington which talked of liberation, and a divided France wrestling with the problems posed by West German economic recovery and with plans for bringing Western Germany into the Western community. Both Stalin and his successors considered Western Europe their primary political target, but they defined Soviet policy toward this crucial area with other world problems in mind. Moreover, Stalin's successors must have been at least as impressed as some Western observers by the magnitude of the succession problem and by the growing demands of the new Soviet elite.

STAGES OF SOVIET POLICY

The history of Soviet foreign policy has been marked by extraordinary tactical switches, most notably by the sudden reversal in policy toward Nazi Germany in August 1939. This history and the great vacuum left by the charismatic Stalin have naturally increased the attentiveness with which Western observers have searched for sharp changes. Fundamentally, there has been no great change in Soviet policy toward Western Europe since Stalin's death. There has been little change in Soviet tactics, although the apparent variations have been numerous and sometimes spectacular. However, in its general emphasis, Soviet policy toward Western Europe has increasingly favored the carrot more and the stick less. In addition, the general line has been softer, subtler, and more persuasive than it was under Stalin.

During the twenty-three months in which Malenkov was Premier, there were no concessions to the West, although the tone of the Soviet Union was more mild than it had been under Stalin. The Korean armistice negotiations were finally concluded on July 27, 1953, reducing the divisive

Reprinted with permission from "The Soviet Union since the Death of Stalin," Philip E. Mosely, ed., in *The Annals of the American Academy of Political and Social Science*, CCCIII (January, 1956), 166-178.

issues affecting relations between the United States and its European allies, but these conflicts were soon replaced by problems deriving from Indochina and Formosa. The Berlin and Geneva conferences early in 1954 demonstrated that Molotov still deserved his reputation and his nickname.

With the demotion of Malenkov, in February 1955, some Western observers, who had been impressed by his apparent reasonableness and occasional civilities, feared that the "final" opportunity to negotiate with the Soviet Union had been lost. However, the regime led by Khrushchev and Bulganin has maintained the principal lines of Soviet foreign policy as well as the little amenities. The most coarse anti-American propaganda has disappeared, and Soviet policy toward the West has been more flexible, moderate, and skillful. The Soviet Union in the spring of 1955 finally accepted the Austrian State Treaty, and the Soviet leaders in June 1955 made a sensational pilgrimage to a Yugoslav Canossa to admit error in past Soviet policy toward Tito. At the Geneva conference, in July 1955, they exuded friendliness and good fellowship in a meeting designed to take advantage of and to extend the new "atmosphere" so that negotiations on the basic issues might be undertaken in a friendly spirit. In September 1955, after a Soviet initiative, diplomatic relations were opened between Moscow and Bonn, which the Russians had previously denounced as a Nazi stooge of the United States.

The recent changes do emphasize the eternal problem: Is there now a genuine shift in Soviet policy toward Western Europe? Do the recent reversals on details conceal a genuine change on matters of substance or are they merely skillful tactical maneuvers? Are we at least witnessing a gradual trend which will ultimately produce a basic modification? Available evidence suggests that there has been no basic change in Soviet policy or goals, although the tactics used are now different. The Soviet rulers are simply adjusting to life without Stalin and to a new phase in post-war relations, one which assumes a temporary political and military stalemate, avoidance of war between the great powers, and continuation of the cold war by political and economic means which do not involve increasing the likelihood of general war.

SOVIET GOALS

The primary aim of Soviet policy, of course, is the defense of the Soviet Union and of the Soviet empire. With regard to Western Europe, the unspoken Soviet goal is Soviet control, which would swing the world balance of power clearly to the advantage of the Soviet Union. To attain this goal, the Soviet leaders seek to oust United States forces and bases and to destroy all the organizations and institutions established to promote Western unity. They seek to destroy the North Atlantic Treaty Organization, to dissolve the ties between Western Germany and its allies, and to incorporate Western Germany into a unified Germany under Soviet rule, which would enable the Soviet Union to control all of Europe. The Soviet leaders have a keen appreciation of the crucial significance of Germany and of the role of Western Germany in the West European

Union. They also have understood more clearly than most West Europeans the political importance of the European Defense Community and of the European Political Community as means of damping and extinguishing the Franco-German conflict, directing the spiritual, economic, and military forces of Western Europe into new channels, and creating a political unity which could resist Soviet influence, pull Britain, Canada, and the United States more firmly into European affairs, and serve as a magnet to draw satellite Europe from the Soviet grip.

BASE OF SOVIET POLICY

The principal Soviet means to attain these great goals are sometimes not noticed and usually not mentioned, because at the same time they constitute the bases of Soviet power. The basic Soviet weapon is the industrial and military power of the Soviet Union, which Stalin's successors have been just as assiduous as he to strengthen. The Soviet rulers denounce others for seeking to negotiate from a "position of force," but Soviet industrial and military power provides the base from which Soviet policy operates. The impressive growth of the Soviet economy has had a noticeable impact upon the underdeveloped countries, some of which consider the Soviet rise to power a model. However, its effect has been just as powerful upon the governments and peoples of Western Europe, which has lost to the United States and the Soviet Union its role as world leader and which in its relative weakness and decline feels naked and defenseless before growing Soviet power and Soviet ruthlessness in the use of that power. Indeed, if the Soviet economic program is successful, within a generation or so Western Europe may be forced "irrevocably into a position of complete dependence" upon either the Soviet or the American industrial and power complex.[1]

Since the death of Stalin, several waves of Soviet speeches and decrees have signaled an apparent reversal of established policy and a heavy increase in capital investment for the production of consumers' goods. However, the industries producing capital goods and military equipment have retained their priority and still receive the lion's share of capital investment. Indeed, in the budget announced on February 3, 1955, by Minister of Finance Zverev, the funds allotted to heavy industry were more than double those assigned to agriculture and light industry combined. Expenditures for defense in 1955 were increased by almost twelve percent over those of 1954, and the Soviet military capability continues to grow. The hearty but false emphasis on consumers' goods was designed to ease the transition from Stalin to the new regime, to placate the Soviet upper classes, and to persuade the non-communist world, especially Western Europe, of the peaceful intentions of the Soviet rulers.

Soviet control over East Central Europe and the gradual but inexorable reshaping of this critical area along Soviet lines constitute the second fixed base for Soviet policy toward Western Europe. The brutal division of Europe and the presence of Soviet and satellite forces at the waist of Europe have placed Western Europe in jeopardy and form the core of the threat under which it lives. Moreover, Soviet control of Eastern Germany and Soviet ability to prevent the unification of Germany block the Western program for unity and grant the Soviet Union a disruptive weapon of enormous power in Germany and in all of Western Europe.

The third established base of Soviet power is the international communist movement, which controls hundreds of thousands of communists and which leads millions of dupes around the world in support of Soviet policies. Every government in Western Europe, particularly the weak and unstable governments of France and Italy, is sensitive to the various forms of pressure which the Soviet Government generates through its network of organizations and its vast propaganda system. These also exploit the philosophical vacuums which exist in many parts of the world by peddling the Soviet philosophy, one of the Soviet Union's most potent weapons. The Soviet rulers almost certainly believe that the road to Paris lies through Hanoi and that the channel to power in Western Europe runs through the Sea of Confusion and Despair. Consequently, the international communist movement exerts pressures in manifold ways, from colonial revolution to incessant propaganda for "peace," and its instruments include civil war in Indochina and Malaya, the World Peace Council, Soviet Friendship Societies, the French Communist Party, and the World Federation of Trade Unions.

GENERAL RELAXATION OF TENSION

Western success in rebuilding the economic, political, and military power and unity of Western Europe and the containment of Soviet expansion in Western Europe have forced the Soviet Union to revise its tactics. Even before Stalin's death, greater emphasis was being placed upon political warfare in all its forms and upon softening resistance to expansion. The new Soviet leaders emphasize those actions in Soviet domestic policy which may help persuade the Western observer in particular that the Soviet system is thawing. At the same time, in their policies toward foreign governments and peoples, they have introduced civilities and amenities to obtain a relaxation of Western vigilance.

Domestic policy

Within the Soviet Union, these steps have been restricted to a major amnesty shortly after Stalin's death, another amnesty in September 1955, occasional emphasis upon the rights of Soviet citizens, a small, gradual increase in the production of consumers' goods, and increased access to the products of foreign culture. This approach became most marked in the summer of 1955, when tourist traffic into and out of the Soviet Union widened to a trickle. All of these steps, plus the so-called "New Course" in East Central Europe, were designed to convince West Europeans that the Soviet menace had evaporated and that the Western program for military strength and unity should be abandoned.

The amenities

With regard to Soviet policy toward Western Europe itself, the steps taken have generally been small. Indeed, most of them have been simple conciliatory gestures and have merely marked Soviet adoption of the minimum standards of civilized life. They included allowing Russian wives of foreigners to leave the Soviet Union to join their husbands, allowing Swedish and Danish trawlers to fish within twelve miles of the Baltic states coast, and returning some prisoners of war. The Soviet Union "interceded" with its Far Eastern allies on behalf of civilian prisoners, and it helped to make possible the conclusion of the Korean truce. On May 30, 1953, in a note published July 19, 1953, the Soviet Union renounced its claims to Turkish territory and to special privileges in the Dardanelles. It has also resumed "normal" diplomatic relations with Greece, Israel, and Yugoslavia. The norm of Soviet practice and the eagerness with which the West hopes for change were both illustrated by the wild flurry of speculation concerning Soviet policy when Malenkov, in August 1954, picked a bouquet of flowers for a member of a visiting British Labor delegation. As someone remarked, Western observers often seem to believe that the appearance of *petits pois à la française* on a Kremlin menu marks a new policy toward France.

Current Soviet tactics are well illustrated by the action of the Supreme Soviet during the last year or so in encouraging representatives of various parliamentary bodies to exchange visits with "the Soviet parliament." In February 1955, it voted to join the Interparliamentary Union, and delegates of the Supreme Soviet attended the forty-fourth annual conference of the Union at Helsinki in August. Official delegations of the parliaments of Britain, Finland, Sweden, India, Syria, Yugoslavia, and Japan have already visited Moscow, and the parliaments of Belgium, France, Austria, Italy, and Canada have accepted invitations. While this procedure exposes some of the Soviet elite to the wholesome influence of Western parliamentary tradition, it also opens up an important new propaganda avenue for the Soviet Union. Above all, it enables the Supreme Soviet to pose as a genuine parliament, thus helping to persuade West Europeans that the Soviet Union is governed by law and that there is no Soviet menace.

Peace campaign

This approach is a fundamental part of the Soviet campaign for "peace" and for "peaceful coexistence." The Soviet rulers remember clearly the immense advantage Lenin obtained in 1917 by his campaign for immediate peace, and they appreciate that an opponent of this campaign is easily labeled a warmonger. Moreover, their approach to "all men of good will" for peace and "friendship among nations," their emphasis upon noble emotions and high principles, and their attacks upon Western alliances and bases and upon alleged barbarous American practices have a strong appeal in this nuclear age not only to neutralists, but even to strong anti-communists affected by fear of nuclear war. The Soviet demands for immediate prohibition of the use and manufacture of nuclear weapons, for a reduction in conventional arms and effectives to agreed levels, and for control machinery to be created at a later date have had little effect upon *informed* opinion throughout the world but have been important propaganda weapons for weakening *popular* resistance to Soviet policy. As such, the spurious Soviet "peace" campaign constitutes a deadly threat to Western unity and vigilance.

Trade

In its efforts to convince the world that it wants peace and wishes to strengthen peaceful relationships, the Soviet Union has sought to break Western controls over the export of strategic goods, to persuade Western Europeans that the Soviet empire constitutes a vast untapped market, and to create divisions within Western Europe over trade policy. This Soviet program has been waged on several levels - the completion of short-term bilateral trade agreements, political campaigning within the United Nations Economic Commission for Europe, and general propaganda. For example, the trade agreement signed with France in July 1953 was negotiated more quickly than the one signed with Italy in November of that year, and the Soviet Union purchased some items from France rather than Italy because France and the French vote on the European Defense Community were important Soviet political targets.

The Soviet Union has been especially skillful in dangling lucrative orders before Western businessmen. For example, Kabanov, the Minister of Foreign Trade, in February 1954 told a group of British businessmen visiting Moscow that the Soviet Union was prepared to place orders in Britain for more than a billion dollars between 1955 and 1957. About half of the goods he listed were under strategic controls, but this appeal for "normalization of Anglo-Soviet trade" stimulated British industrial and commercial appetites and strengthened criticism of Western controls. Moreover, such promises created a sensation in Western Germany, where fear is strong that Britain may gain a lead in Soviet trade. Dangling the same lure before West Germans, especially after the visit of Adenauer to Moscow, will worry the British and increase competition for Soviet markets.

The Russians had shown an interest in ECE even before Stalin's death, and on January 30, 1953, the ECE announced that the Soviet Union had agreed to participate in a conference on East-West trade, although in September 1952 it had refused a similar invitation. In the various ECE conferences the Soviet representatives have given especial priority to "removal of obstacles to foreign trade" and to denunciation of the United States as the power responsible for the COCOM (Consultative Group Coordinating Committee) strategic controls.

This theme has been a favorite one for Soviet political warriors, and they have declared Western strategic controls responsible for the decline after 1949 in trade between Western Europe and the Soviet empire. This campaign ignores the facts of this trade, which had declined before strategic controls were established. The Soviet Union has reorganized the economic structures of the countries of East Central Europe and has tied their trade strings to Moscow. Moreover, these states now lack supplies of grain and timber for export to the West. Indeed, on balance the Soviet Union and its satellite states even imported foodstuffs in 1954. In addition, while the COCOM states pruned the strategic list in August 1954, exports from the Soviet empire remain under complete control. Finally, Soviet abrogation of trade with Yugoslavia in 1948 and with Australia in 1954 demonstrated that Soviet trade controls are used for political reasons in a way which is not possible in the West.

Western communist parties

Western communist parties as instruments of the Soviet Union are used to support the impression that the Soviet Union is not a threat and that each national communist party is just another political party. Thus, in 1953 the French party abandoned the forceful program which had led to incidents such as the Ridgeway riots in May 1952, and began to work for a "patriotic national front." Jacques Duclos on October 22, 1953, indicated that the party was prepared to join with any other Frenchmen in a national campaign to end the war in Indochina, to prevent German rearmament, and to hasten general disarmament. The communists have cooperated closely with the radical socialists and the Gaullists, especially against EDC. On June 8, 1954, Thorez proclaimed that it was "orthodox communist doctrine" to accept allies wherever they could be found, and persistent efforts have been made for a united front with the socialists or a popular front with other political groups. The communist effort to infiltrate political, religious, educational, and labor organizations in particular has been quite successful, especially in France, where the use of *la douce parole* works as effectively for the communists as it did for Philip the Fair centuries ago.

International organizations

The new Soviet leaders use international organizations to carry political warfare against Western Europe. The primary forum since 1945 has been the United Nations. In addition, the Soviet Union joined the United Nations Educational, Scientific and Cultural Organization in April 1954. In July 1955 it announced it would resume active participation in the World Health Organization, from which it had withdrawn in 1949, that it would become a member of the International Bureau of Education, and that it would contribute two million rubles in kind and services to the United Nations Children's Fund. These steps, and the participation of the Soviet Union and some of its satellites in the International Labor Organization, not only provide new forums but also help convince other states and peoples that the Soviet Union is a normal state seeking to attain its goals in normal ways.

DIPLOMACY: AUSTRIA

The principal Soviet weapon against Western Europe during the past thirty months has been Soviet diplomacy, which has been generally used with great effectiveness to attain Soviet goals or to prevent the United States and the Western European states from attaining their aims. This can be seen most clearly in the long Western struggle to obtain freedom and independence for Austria and unification for Germany. In the case of Austria, the Soviet Union in the spring of 1955 finally yielded, at a high price and in return for other advantages which it estimated then outweighed the benefits to be derived from continuing to block the treaty.

At the close of the Moscow Conference on November 1, 1943, the United States, the United Kingdom and the Soviet Union had issued a joint declaration pledging the re-establishment of "a free and independent Austria." All but five articles of the Austrian State Treaty had been agreed to by 1949. However, Austria was not freed until the spring of 1955, even though the foreign ministers dealt with the Austrian State Treaty in six conferences between 1947 and 1953 while over the same years their deputies had held more than 260 meetings. The Soviet policy was clearly based on the desire to retain troops in Austria, to prevent Austria from joining the West, to obtain economic profit from the Soviet zone, and to use Austria as a bargaining counter on the German and other issues.

The long period of Soviet recalcitrance reached its depths at the Berlin conference of the foreign ministers, in February 1954, when Molotov proposed that the Austrian treaty be linked to an agreement on German unification and that the withdrawal of foreign troops from Austria be postponed until a peace treaty with Germany had been concluded. He even refused to sign the Austrian State Treaty when the three Western powers agreed to accept the Soviet version of the five articles which had been in dispute since 1949.

The Berlin conference of 1954 was preceded and followed by minor concessions to the Austrian Government, such as the note on June 30, 1953, announcing that the Soviet Union would assume all Soviet occupation costs as of September 1. However, the pressures on Austrian government and police officials remained sharp and strong, and the Soviet Union refused to discuss reducing its heavy claims upon the Austrian economy.

Signature of Austrian treaty

However, the Soviet policy toward Austria was suddenly reversed in March 1955, when Molotov announced that the Austrian treaty was not dependent upon a German treaty. He also proposed preliminary negotiations between Austria and the Soviet Union on the basis of withdrawal of all foreign troops from Austria and an Austrian undertaking not to join any military alliance or to allow military bases on Austrian territory. With this Soviet reversal, the way was opened to the signature of the Austrian treaty, on May 15, 1955. This treaty gave Austria its freedom and independence; prohibited *Anschluss* with Germany, foreign alliances, and foreign bases; provided for the withdrawal of foreign troops within ninety days of ratification; and provided for substantial payments by Austria to the Soviet Union as the price of its freedom. These payments include delivery of $150,000,000 in Austrian goods over six years, in return for handing back the ex-German assets seized by the Soviet Union; the delivery of 1,000,000 tons of crude oil a year for ten years from the oil fields and refineries of eastern Austria; and purchase of the Soviet-controlled Danube Shipping Company for $2,000,000

Signature of the Austrian State Treaty removed the Soviet grip from Austria and marks a step backward for the Soviet forces in Central Europe. However, Western troops have also left Austria, and Austria has now been neutralized. The Soviet Union added to its laurels as a peacemaker, since the final initiative came from Molotov and the treaty was concluded after a visit of Chancellor Raab in Moscow. Moreover, Austria will remain in economic bondage to Moscow for a full decade. The Kremlin obviously hopes to draw Austria into its orbit through trade bonds and to make of Austria a kind of Central European Finland. Finally, the Soviet leaders obviously hope that this will serve as a precedent for achieving a united neutralized Germany and for forcing the withdrawal of American troops from Europe.

Diplomacy: Germany

The Soviet leaders recognize Germany as the key to Europe, and they intend in one way or another, sooner or later, to bring all of Germany under Soviet control. In this, they are simply continuing a policy which Stalin set in motion. Soviet control over Eastern Germany has given the Soviet Union the power to veto any program for the unification of Germany which it does not find acceptable. It has been clear since the end of the Second World War, and the Soviet leaders made it brutally plain to Adenauer and the West in Moscow in September 1955, that the Soviet Union intends to retain control over Eastern Germany and to force Western Germany and the West ultimately to sue for unification on Soviet terms. To attain this great goal, the Soviet Union has used both pressure and guile, varying its tactics and its themes as circumstances required but always keeping the main goal in view and utilizing simultaneously every type of technique.

The extraordinary reconstruction and economic recovery of Western Germany, since 1949 in particular, its rapid rise to political respectability, and the program for a European Defense Community incorporating Western Germany led the Soviet Union until September 6, 1953, to concentrate upon defeating Adenauer. After his victory in the election, the Soviet Union concentrated until late summer 1954 upon influencing the French vote on EDC. The French failure to ratify EDC was only a brief victory, because the London and Paris agreements provided a substitute which was weaker, but still too strong from the Soviet point of view, in the form of West European union, West German sovereignty, and West German membership in NATO. After these agreements had been ratified, the Soviet leaders again shifted gears, widened their smiles, opened diplomatic relations with the West German government, and inaugurated another period in Soviet European policy.

Eastern Germany

Eastern Germany is an important pawn in Soviet policy toward Western Europe, and the Soviet leaders like to believe that the existence of a "socialist" state in Eastern Germany exerts a magnetic influence upon

Western Germany. However, Soviet control, the vast economic and political contrasts between Eastern and Western Germany, and the fraudulent elections, especially those of October 17, 1954, handicap the Soviet Union. The steady flow of refugees from Eastern Germany - over two million have "voted with their feet" by fleeing to West Berlin and Western Germany - daily indicts Soviet rule and cripples the Soviet effort to make Eastern Germany a magnet.

In the spring of 1953, following the decision of the Soviet leaders that the puppet state needed more attractive window dressing, the Pankow government announced a series of minor reform measures, such as returning confiscated waste land to farmers, increasing the production of consumers' goods, reducing labor controls, relaxing the drive for collectivization, and correcting tax collection methods. This program was upset by the June riots, which weakened the Soviet line for the September elections in Western Germany and which underlined the basic Soviet dilemma. The June riots in the East and the continued economic and political progress in Western Germany have led the Soviet leaders to increase their efforts to reward, strengthen, and dignify the German Democratic Republic. Thus, during the last few months of 1953 the Soviet Union returned about 10,000 prisoners of war to Eastern Germany. As of January 1, 1954, reparations payments to the Soviet Union ceased, firms taken over by the Soviet Union were returned to German control, and occupation costs were limited to not more than five percent of the East German national income. On March 25, 1954, the Soviet Government announced that it would henceforth treat Eastern Germany as a sovereign state, with "freedom to make decisions according to its own views in domestic and foreign affairs." Following the Adenauer trip to Moscow and the opening of diplomatic relations between Moscow and Bonn, the Soviet Government, on September 20, 1955, granted full sovereignty to the German Democratic Republic, including control of civilian traffic between Western Germany and West Berlin and the right to rearm and to play a full role in the Warsaw Pact.

As the campaign to whitewash and dignify the government of the German Democratic Republic progressed, Eastern Germany began to play a more prominent role in the Soviet plan. Its leaders frequently appealed to the French Government and to groups of Frenchmen to defeat EDC and WEU. Intensive efforts were made to increase the range of contacts with West German technicians and officials on matters concerning trade, transport, sport, and cultural affairs. The program for "all Germans around one table" sought to bring workers, churchmen, athletes, newsmen, women, and above all elected representatives together for friendly discussions. Threats to force West German officials and representatives to meet with communists were also used, most notably in the spring of 1955, when the German Democratic Republic levied enormous increases in dues on West German vehicles using Soviet-zone roads.

France

Soviet policy toward Western Germany and the Soviet design for neutralizing Western Europe are generally defined with one eye on France.

Soviet policy toward France has emphasized both Soviet economic and military power and Soviet "peace" proposals. At the same time, the Soviet Union has exerted pressure on France through Indochina. It has appealed to the traditional French fear of Germany and to the old French policy of cooperating with Germany's eastern neighbors to prevent German revival and expansion.

Thus, Soviet propaganda in France through all of its outlets emphasized the dangers courted by Western policy toward Germany and the great virtues of the Franco-Soviet treaty of alliance of 1944. Great efforts were made to improve relations between France and the communist governments of Poland and Czechoslovakia. For example, just before the final debate on EDC, Poland offered France a treaty of alliance and mutual assistance. The legislatures of Poland, Czechoslovakia, and Eastern Germany in December 1954 appealed to the French National Assembly not to ratify the Paris agreement on West German rearmament. At the same time, the Soviet Government several times warned both France and the United Kingdom that the London and Paris agreements flagrantly violated the Franco-Soviet and Anglo-Soviet treaties and that ratification would lead the Soviet Union to annul the treaties. When this threat did not succeed, the treaties were annulled by the Presidium of the Supreme Soviet on May 7, 1955. Only one month later, the carrot reappeared, when Molotov at a luncheon in Paris referred to the need to forget the past, expressed a wish for more frequent and direct contacts with French leaders, and invited Pinay and Faure to Moscow.

German unification

The Western powers have sought to rebuild Western economic and political strength and to create a new unity to resist Soviet pressure and to lead toward a stable and peaceful future. General Western success and the recovery of Western Germany have thus raised to a new level questions concerning German unification and the position of a united Germany in Europe. The Western states propose free elections throughout Germany under a law drafted and promulgated by the four occupying powers and supervised by them; the convocation of a national assembly; the drafting of a constitution and the preparation of peace treaty negotiations by this assembly; the adoption of the constitution and the formation of an all-German government; and the signature and entry into force of the peace treaty. The heart of the Western position lies in free elections. As Bidault pointed out to Molotov at Berlin, "From a democratic point of view, it seems obvious that it is elections which create governments and not governments which create elections."

To counter the Western program, the Soviet Union has stood fast behind a policy which seeks controlled elections and communist control over all of Germany. This position has been stated quite clearly a number of times, notably in a Soviet note to France, Britain, and the United States on August 16, 1953, again at the Berlin conference in January and February 1954, and during and after the Geneva conference in July 1955. Fundamentally, although this is always concealed and denied, the Soviet

Union has no intention of accepting free elections. Soviet policy on German unification emphasizes the following: representatives of the governments of both Eastern and Western Germany should participate in any conference discussing German unification and a German peace treaty; an all-German provisional government, created by the parliaments of the two Germanies with the cooperation of "democratic parties and organizations," should draft an electoral law and prepare "free and secret elections" for a national assembly and should help prepare and sign a German peace treaty; all occupation forces should leave Germany after the signature of the peace treaty; German armed forces should be limited to those required for internal security and frontier patrol; and no foreign bases should be allowed. The heart of the Soviet position lies in the precedence granted to the formation of a German government over elections, which would be rigged by the government.

European "security"

The bald Soviet program for controlled elections leading to German unity under communism has been both sweetened and concealed by Soviet proposals for the withdrawal of all occupation forces and for the establishment of a European "security" system. Soviet suggestions that occupation forces be withdrawn are frequently reiterated, but this campaign for a neutralized Germany and an exposed Europe has generally had little effect.

The proposal for a European "security" system first appeared in January 1953, but it was presented in more elaborate form at the Berlin conference early in 1954 and has since become a standard Soviet prop. Fundamentally, this proposal is a device for removing American influence and power from Europe and for providing an ostensible substitute to NATO. In effect, it constitutes a system of "Europe for the Europeans," with the Soviet Union of course counted as a European state and with the United States belatedly recognized as one also. The pact is open to all European states "without regard to their social systems," to both German governments, and later to a reunified Germany. It specifically binds its members "not to enter any coalition or alliance." When these proposals were rejected as a plan to divide Germany for fifty years and to neutralize Western Europe, Molotov on March 31, 1954, proposed that the Soviet Union and "other European countries" join NATO to give it "a really defensive character" and to preclude Germany's being drawn into military groupings.

Soviet policy since WEU

During the past nine months or so, Soviet policy has paid particular attention to four simultaneous lines. The first of these has emphasized Soviet power and resolution and the consequences of Western refusal to abandon NATO and WEU. The Soviet Union has not threatened war - indeed, it has prated of peace - but it has reiterated that ratification of WEU would lead to the annulment of the Franco-Soviet and Anglo-Soviet treaties, to the creation of an East European parallel to NATO, and to the "permanent" division of Germany. When the threats failed, the treaties were annulled. The Soviet Union and its satellites, in May 1955 at Warsaw, then "formed" a military organization under Soviet command. Finally, the opening of diplomatic relations with Western Germany and the grant of full "sovereignty" to Eastern Germany in September underlined that the West had reached a stone wall on German unification, unless it surrendered to Soviet terms.

The second emphasis has been upon the proposed Soviet European "security" system. This is offered as a substitute for NATO and WEU, as a device for bringing the two Germanies into one organization, and as a means of obtaining Western recognition of the Soviet position in East Central Europe. It has little appeal, except to communists, but there is some danger that it will be confused with Western plans being developed to win Soviet approval to German unity within Western union.

The third accent, and currently the most noticeable one, is upon the general relaxation of tensions. While the Soviet leaders have not concealed their goals, they have at the same time adopted a friendly, cheerful, benevolent pose to lull their opponents into carelessness and slumber. This tactic was most marked at the Geneva "summit" conference, where all of the ideas came from the West and where the Soviet leaders concentrated upon spreading an atmosphere of cordiality and friendliness.

Finally, Soviet policy stresses relations with Western Germany. The establishment of diplomatic relations between Moscow and Bonn was foreshadowed by a Moscow radio broadcast on January 15, 1955. It sent a shiver of fear through the West, which remembers August 1939, which notes with apprehension the age and importance of Adenauer, and which worries over the power of German nationalism as unification is delayed and as the two Germanies are driven into closer relationships with each other.

In other words, with regard to Germany, the Soviet leaders apparently have settled down for the long haul. While exuding good cheer and cordiality, broadcasting the virtues of peaceful coexistence, and buying apparent virtue at little price through ceding their Porkkala base to Finland, they will seek to isolate and overthrow Adenauer or to wait until his death or retirement creates a new political situation in Western Germany. In the meantime, they will strive in every way to push the two Germanies into closer contact. As these relationships improve, the structure of the East German state will probably be revised along ostensibly federal lines, and Soviet policy will concentrate upon weakening the center parties in Western Germany, strengthening the left-wing Socialists, the neo-Nazis, and the nationalists, and working for a National Front in both Germanies. In short, the Soviet leaders will probably rely upon this approach, as well as on increased trade between Western Germany and the Soviet empire under a new Rapallo, a Western economic and political crisis, the desire for "peace," and the carelessness or impatience of the West, to bring about German unification on Soviet terms.

OUTLOOK

Soviet policy toward Western Europe since the death of Stalin has been marked by the same failures which attended Stalin's efforts. The communists have failed to prevent or even seriously to hinder the economic and political recovery of Western Europe from the depths of 1945 and 1947. NATO continues to thrive, though its foundations seem perilously military and fragile and though it is wracked by occasional conflicts between members and by growing reluctance to meet its high annual costs. The Western European Union has been established, with Western Germany a member. Above all, the United States has maintained its forces and its commitments in Western Europe.

While the Soviet leaders have failed to attain their goals, they have achieved some successes and they have made some progress toward undermining Western unity and resolution. The Soviet Union contributed heavily to the French refusal to ratify EDC through its skillful political warfare in France and through the continuing influence of the French communist party. While the size of the communist parties and of communist-controlled organizations in Western Europe has continued to decline steadily, neutralism, pacifism, and nationalism, stimulated by the communists, have grown, undermining the foundations of Western resolution and strength. The skillful Soviet effort to persuade Western Europe that the Soviet Union is not a threat and that the high costs of defense are not necessary has softened the Western program and made the great alliance hesitate. The Geneva conference in particular has influenced popular opinion, and the smiles and bouquets of Khrushchev and Bulganin are weakening Western persistence far more than did the arrogance and ruthlessness of Stalin. In this general approach toward relaxation, the Soviet leaders have clearly inherited Stalin's great ability to create a success out of a series of failures.

Problems on both sides

Both Western Europe and the Soviet Union face serious problems. The West suffers now from its own achievements, and its prosperity and security seem so solid that vigilance slackens. Western stability and unity depend to a large degree on the solidity of economic foundations, and the economies of several of the key states and of the area in general are somewhat vulnerable. In addition, Western recovery depends to a great degree upon the survival of democracy in Western Germany, still naturally a suspect neighbor. Finally, in its present moods, Western Europe is increasingly vulnerable to the current Soviet political warfare tune. There is some danger that the populace in one of the links which make up Western Europe will succumb to the lure of neutralism or even to a Soviet European "security" pact which would relax the vigilance of the West, lead to a serious reduction in forces, and divide the allies as they were divided during the 1930s by the Nazis. Indeed, there is some likelihood that those who stand for strength and vigilance will be hounded as was Churchill in the 1930s.

In other words, the West provides vulnerabilities and opportunities to the Soviet leaders for exploitation. However, at the same time Soviet policy must continue to operate under serious handicaps. To begin with, the Soviet record cannot be erased. In addition, while Soviet control over Eastern Europe provides a great addition to Soviet power, a strategic area of great value, and a prime source of Soviet political influence in Western Europe, at the same time it constitutes a disadvantage. This is particularly so in the case of Eastern Germany, whose true status is exposed daily by a flood of refugees and which falls ever further behind Western Germany in every index.

Moreover, while the Soviet Union can play one tune in France and another in Germany, it cannot forever be all things to all people without paying a penalty. Finally, while the current policy of smiles and cooperation helps to undermine Western vigilance, at the same time it corrodes the vitals of communist political power. A system which is based on conflict and war requires tension and feeds on struggle. No system is more vulnerable to relaxation than a totalitarian state.

NOTE

1. Philip E. Mosely, "Can Moscow Match Us Industrially?" *Harvard Business Review*, *XXXV* (1955), 103.

8

Exchanges of Scholars with the Soviet Union: Advantages and Dilemmas

INTRODUCTION

During the last quarter century, the role of the American university and of the American scholar have quietly and gradually changed almost beyond the comprehension of even those who have participated actively in the revolution. Expansion of higher education and of access to it in every part of the country has brought more than seven million students to American campuses in the fall of 1969. These students, their faculties, the libraries which serve them both, and the entire college and university complex all face a continuing "knowledge explosion," an increase of information in most fields of study so rapid that most of what is now taught in some fields was not known as recently as ten years ago.

The role of the university in American life has so changed that the ivory tower has been demolished. Many Americans instead believe that the university, while continuing its usual functions for the rapidly growing student body, should also be the principal instrument for resolving our social problems. Indeed, many are now convinced that new knowledge generated and spread by the university is the most important factor in social and economic change.

The appearance of new fields of study, of new knowledge, especially in the sciences, and of new responsibilities is matched by growing interest in the rest of the world, especially the so-called non-Western areas, which were neglected before the Second World War. The technical revolutions in communication and in transportation, the growing appreciation by Americans of the position their country occupies in international affairs, and the general shrinking of the world have all contributed to an increase of research and instruction in areas as different as the Soviet Union and Africa. This revolution in our view of the rest of the world has been especially reflected in the increased emphasis devoted by the American educational system to the Soviet Union, largely because of the growth and outward thrust of Soviet power. As a consequence, thousands of Americans have learned Russian, have become interested in Russian history, literature and

Reprinted with permission from *Memorandum for the Senate Subcommittee on National Security and International Operations* (Washington, DC: US Government Printing Office, 1969) 19 pp.

government, and have sought to analyze Soviet power and policy. Inevitably, just as American libraries have increased their resources to enable all to study the newly-discovered universe, so American universities have attempted to enable those interested in the Soviet Union to study there. This effort to encourage study within the Soviet Union has directly involved American universities and scholars in official exchange programs with the Soviet Government and has therefore created both problems and dilemmas.

Participation by American universities in formal exchange programs with a country as ideologically and politically different from ours as the Soviet Union is only one of the ways through which they have developed close relationships with agencies of our own government and with other governments as well. This position of the universities is, of course, not new, because the state universities in particular, and American colleges and universities in general, have never separated themselves from the concerns of the people and their government at the local, state, and national level. However, the ties with our national government in particular have changed since the Second World War to such a degree that a quiet revolution has taken place, and few American universities dealt with even friendly foreign governments before the Second World War. In recent years, most American universities have done extensive work overseas through organizations such as AID, largely to help universities and other educational organizations in underdeveloped countries. They have also helped to train young men and women for work in organizations such as the Peace Corps, and many of our large universities have as many as a thousand foreign students on campus, many on grants from their governments or from the American Government. Scientists on campuses throughout the United States have undertaken research projects for agencies such as the Atomic Energy Commission, NASA, and the National Institute of Health. Many institutions maintain study centers or student centers abroad, and many have direct exchange relationships with colleges and universities in other parts of the world.

In short, the role of the American university within our society and the relationships the university has with other parts of the world have both changed rapidly. The participation of American universities and their scholars in academic exchanges with countries like the Soviet Union fits into this framework, one in which the university serves its own purposes and at the same time participates in international activities which directly involve the national interest. The university's role in cultural exchanges with countries like the Soviet Union is simply more complicated and more difficult than the other kinds of work for or with governments in which many educational institutions are now engaged.

The phrase "cultural exchanges" is difficult to define. It means "an exchange of accumulated knowledge and methods which forms the present outlook of mankind and reflects best on the problems of the past, the present, and the future." Ordinarily, of course, scholars and students travel freely without any concept or framework of reciprocal giving and receiving, with an American scholar going to an institution in France about as easily as he would to one in this country, and with a French scholar coming to the

United States or going to Japan with no special formalities or difficulties and with neither government involved or even informed.

Research for foreigners in the Soviet Union, however, is quite a different matter, because opportunities for Americans to study there, or for Soviet scholars to continue their work in the United States are possible, at Soviet insistence, only as part of an official cultural exchange agreement negotiated between the two governments. Under this agreement, specified numbers of artists, dancers, bands, athletes, delegations of specified types, movies, special publications (such as *Amerika*), and exhibitions are exchanged between the two countries, who also agree on specific forms of scientific cooperation and on participation in congresses held in the two countries. The number of men and women involved in these exchanges is small, only a few hundred each way each year, and the number of dollars or rubles involved also is not large. (In fact, the total cost [including actual cost of instruction for Soviet graduate students and scholars in American universities] of all the *academic* exchange programs with the Soviet Union since 1958 probably does not exceed $20,000,000.) However, the importance of these developments for the scholars and the universities, and for the national interest, far outweighs their apparent insignificance in numbers and in funds.

The fall of 1969 provides an especially appropriate time to review exchanges of scholars with the Soviet Union because American universities have just completed their first decade of such exchanges and because ominous repression in the Soviet Union and the uneasy situation in Czechoslovakia and in Eastern Europe may raise questions in the near future about whether and how these relations can be continued.

Moreover, in the summer of 1969, the Inter-University Committee, a private organization founded by seven universities in 1956 which grew to fifty-five institutions in 1969, presented its responsibilities for exchanges with the Soviet Union and some of the countries in Eastern Europe to a new organization, the International Research and Exchange Board, which also assumed authority for the Ford Foundation programs in Eastern Europe and for the small American Council of Learned Societies senior scholar exchange programs. The experience of the Inter-University Committee provides a fine opportunity for review, since the Committee was the earliest, the largest, and most important private organization involved in academic exchanges with any communist country. Financed originally by the Carnegie Corporation and then supported in approximately equal parts by the Ford Foundation, the Bureau of Educational and Cultural Affairs of the Department of State, and the participating universities themselves, the Committee has helped to bring about an extraordinary improvement and expansion in American research and instruction concerning the Soviet Union, which was precisely its goal. Moreover, the experiences which the Committee enjoyed were not notably different from those of other private organizations, such as the American Friends Service Committee, semi-public organizations, such as the National Academy of Sciences, or government agencies, such as the Public Health Service and the Atomic Energy Commission.

The year 1969 is an appropriate time for a review also because we have apparently reached a plateau in our exchanges with the Soviet Union and some of the countries of communist Europe, after a peak of interest in 1963 and 1964. In fact, the invasion of Czechoslovakia in August 1968, which crushed high hopes for expanding exchanges with that country and with some of the other countries of Eastern Europe, may instead mark a sharp demarcation of possibilities for peaceful exchanges of all kinds with the Soviet Union and its associated states.

At the same time, while no one can estimate the time or the circumstances, we will certainly one day establish exchanges of scholars with Mainland China. Official Chinese suspicion and hostility towards the United States are similar to those in the Soviet Union, so the circumstances under which any exchange program will be established and conducted will probably resemble those which have prevailed in the last few years. However, Chinese history and tradition, and Chinese interests, are somewhat different from those of the Soviet Union, and American attitudes are even more confused, so some differences in the attitudes and arrangements on both sides will surely appear. In any case, those in the universities and in government who will be responsible for cultural exchanges with Mainland China can clearly benefit substantially from analysis of the principles and problems involved in our exchanges with the Soviet Union.

Finally, our review of exchanges of scholars with the Soviet Union should illuminate the relationships between the two countries during a very critical and dangerous period because the exchange is both a model and a symbol of the difficulties we have in dealing with each other. It helps to explain some of the criticism from the New Left of the universities for their relationship, or even partnership, with the government in Washington. It also helps illuminate the curious drift towards isolationism which has been a prominent feature of the last few years of our political life, as the American people have shown increasing resentment over the war in Viet Nam and increasing weariness over the long burden of high taxation, assistance to foreign countries, and constant international tension.

THE ADVANTAGES

Scholars and their universities

American universities and their scholars would naturally prefer that those interested in continuing their study in the Soviet Union be as free to travel there as they are to France or Mexico, just as they would prefer that Soviet scholars be able freely to come to this country. In fact, during the 1930s, a small number of men, including John Curtiss, John Hazard, Calvin Hoover, Philip Mosely, G.T. Robinson, and Ernest J. Simmons, were able to study in this way in the Soviet Union. Indeed, the inability of our scholars to continue their work in the Soviet Union as they did thirty years ago under Stalin is one evidence of an increase in restrictions, and in isolation, introduced there since even the grim 1930s. Because of Soviet insistence, the only way in which Soviet and American scholars can study in the other country is under a formal exchange agreement, the first of which was signed on January 27, 1958, and others of which have been signed in succeeding years after increasingly prolonged negotiations. Consequently, while these agreements do provide some protection or security for Americans studying in the Soviet Union, they are directly responsible for bringing American universities into close relations with their own government and with the Soviet Government as well.

Our academic institutions and their scholars have agreed to participate in the exchange agreement because of the significant advantages they offer, the primary one, of course, the opportunity for American scholars to increase their knowledge and understanding of Russia. In 1956, the United States had less than ten scholars who had spent an appreciable period of time in the Soviet Union. In 1969, while many scholars whose professional interest is the Soviet Union have not visited that country, approximately a thousand have spent from a month to two years studying in the country in which they are professionally interested. We have not yet produced a de Tocqueville, but our research and instruction have improved considerably because of the opportunities our scholars have had to work in Soviet libraries, to become acquainted with Soviet students and scholars, and to get some taste of the spirit and quality of Soviet society. In fact, the exchange program is now far less important to the American academic community than it was in 1958, a fact which should be made clear to the Soviet authorities.

This improved understanding of the Soviet Union has been spread throughout American society through teaching and publications, which have contributed an increasingly realistic appraisal of Soviet life and Soviet policy, one quite remote from that produced by the glories of Russian literature of the nineteenth century or by the extraordinary heroism of the Soviet soldier and Soviet citizen during the Second World War. Those who have studied in Russia have a confidence about their work from having seen and felt the element about which they teach. In the universities in particular, they have also participated in educating many of those who constitute the core of our specialists on the Soviet Union in the various branches of our government. When one considers that the military intelligence staff concerned with Russia in the summer of 1939 consisted of a colonel and a sergeant, neither of whom knew Russian and both of whom relied substantially upon the American press for information, one can appreciate the progress made.

A subsidiary benefit has been an increased understanding of American history, tradition, values, and shortcomings. This improved understanding of other cultures and of ourselves has helped American universities to contribute more effectively to help educate minorities who in the past have been denied equal opportunities. In sum, the exchange programs have helped us to provide a new definition of a liberal education and to widen educational opportunities here at home.

In an age afflicted by nationalism and by the dreadful consequences of a series of destructive wars, the exchange programs have also helped American scholars to recognize the special obligations our blessings have bestowed upon them as citizens of the world and as responsible members of a universal scholarly community. We are, in short, beginning to see the universe as a whole, as did the middle ages, when the foundations of the modern university were being laid and when the traveling scholar was even more common than today. The medieval scholar recognized and acted upon the conviction that all share the same interests and have an obligation to work together. Today, we have learned again that we have a special obligation to assist scholars in other countries who are living and working in less comfortable and free circumstances than we, a most important truth which the circumstances of our age could easily smother. In fact, the growing sense of responsibility among many of our scholars and the treatment which American universities have provided Soviet scholars in this country have constituted one of our glories.

Study in the Soviet Union has contributed in still other ways to changing American education. For example, the enthusiasm of our returning scholars, those in fields such as history as well as those who specialize in language teaching, for improving and expanding instruction in Russian has been one of the important factors in the foreign language revolution which has swept the colleges and even the high schools of the United States in the last fifteen years. Similarly, study of a society quite different in every way from ours has contributed to the expansion of area programs designed to encourage the student to study every aspect of a society, rather than just the history or the literature. This development has been one of the most important forces weakening the departmental boundaries which have traditionally separated scholars in universities. It has therefore contributed to a new, more wholesome approach toward the nature of knowledge and the field of study. In short, the openness, the excitement, and the quality of those involved in Russian studies have helped to change the nature and character of the university and to increase its involvement in world affairs.

At the same time, the organizational arrangements which American universities made to help resolve the problems which the exchange programs created have helped improve relationships among scholars and among universities. In short, bringing a number of universities together in a delicate and difficult task, with the institutions assigning administrative responsibility to one university and with the various tasks assumed by committees of scholars from many universities in different parts of the country, has helped to create new patterns of cooperation among American institutions of higher education. This has aided in breaking down the barriers which have separated American universities from one another and which had them so conscious of their sovereignty that they were self-isolated in ivory towers in an Anglo-Saxon world. Since the educational revolution has placed heavy strains upon even our resources and since American universities must learn to cooperate more, both within the United States and abroad, the experiences of this exchange program have been of considerable significance, affecting the development of joint programs toward improving libraries, administering overseas centers, and selecting and educating scholars and students from foreign countries.

American scholars who have participated in the exchange program have also increased their understanding of the Soviet system and of Soviet foreign policy, whether their main concern has been linguistics or history or government. A happy consequence of this knowledge and understanding of Soviet totalitarianism is the growing appreciation among specialists of the problems which the Department of State faces in dealing with the Soviet Union. This may in fact be one of the most important national benefits from the exchange program, because it has reduced the likelihood that unknowing scholars, operating only on what they read and typical of American "transcendental populism" and of American suspicion of our own government, would heavily criticize officials engaged in negotiations with the Soviet Government in circumstances which scholars who had not left the library or the "Intourist world" could not understand.

The national interest

From the point of view of the American Government and of the American public, perhaps the greatest contribution of the academic exchange programs has been their success in maintaining a tie with a group of important Soviet citizens at a time of high tension and great hazard. In fact, the great paradox of the exchange programs has been that the universities and the scholars, by seeking primarily to advance knowledge and their own special interests, have in fact served the national interest supremely well by the effectiveness with which they have maintained this narrow bridge between the two countries. This opportunity for dialogue reinforces the tendency within the higher levels of the Soviet Government towards peaceful relations with the United States and provides whatever influence we have "towards rationality, permissiveness, and openness." One should not overestimate the impact of programs such as this, but they do constitute a positive addition to the containment policy. They do to some degree soften the Soviet Union by opening a window in that closed society to the rest of the world. They do persuade the Soviet Government to engage in relationships with the United States on peaceful grounds under conditions which are of mutual advantage, a practice which is regularly condemned in the Soviet Union as "ideological coexistence."

The academic exchange programs also contribute to the national interest by increasing Soviet understanding of the United States. The handful of Americans who live in Soviet dormitories and who come to know well Soviet scholars and Soviet students, the future elite of their society, inevitably provide them some understanding of the quality and of the friendliness of our society. Similarly, those Soviet scholars who work in the United States must acquire an increased understanding of the nature of our society and must have the Marxist-Leninist glasses with which they view the rest of the world to some degree cleaned. In fact, in 1964, seven Soviet alumni of the program who had each spent an academic year in an American university were serving their government in the United States, in their embassies in Washington or at the United Nations or in organizations such as TASS. This will in the long run contribute to reducing misunderstanding and fears on both sides and will help the Soviet elite to see more clearly the wider one world in which we all live. In fact, as Mr. Toynbee long ago recognized, the Soviet Union may now be learning that it is impossible to borrow Western efficiency without borrowing Western values, that it is impossible to import only a part of the West.

Finally, the exchange program provides a kind of index or barometer of the atmosphere in which Soviet decisions are made. Identifying or defining Soviet policies and the considerations underlying these positions is a difficult task complicated by lack of information and the problems we face in penetrating the Soviet mind. The exchange program, one of the few direct, constant, measurable ties we have with the Soviet Government, therefore serves as an effective touchstone of larger Soviet policies. Thus, recent increased harassment of American scholars by the Soviet KGB reveals a change in the temperature or atmosphere within which all Soviet policies are decided. Moreover, the established history and the symbolic importance of the exchanges are such that a Soviet decision to reduce them sharply or end them would constitute a most important signal about basic Soviet goals and policies.

THE PROBLEMS AND DILEMMAS

Like any complicated new program, the academic exchange is an expensive one in the time and intellectual energy of scholars and administrators it consumes. Soviet administrative rigidity and inefficiency are so vast, and Soviet ability to create and to magnify problems so great that the exchange programs probably devour more administrative time and energy per individual involved than any other academic enterprise in which an American university has ever engaged. Only intense interest and resolute good will have triumphed over these Soviet qualities, which are apparently eternal and which deserve a new Gogol.

Great universities have been especially hampered because they are not properly organized to identify their own interests in such a program or to work effectively with other universities in a national organization. Thus, it is easy to identify the specialists in Russian history or literature or government who should be encouraged to study in the Soviet Union, but few universities have recognized the other fields of study which would offer benefits for Americans.

However, the university's principal problem has clearly been its transformation into an action agency, and the main dilemma is a simple one. Should the university accept a share of responsibility for exchanges of scholars with communist countries and in so doing defend its integrity as a free institution, while at the same time developing close relations with agencies of our own government and of the foreign government, and exposing itself to domestic and foreign criticism and to the whims of international politics? Or should it instead allow our government to conduct the programs, with the great likelihood that inroads upon the university's integrity would occur? Or should the university declare that the problems are so complicated and so alien to its experience that it should not participate in any way?

The university's decision to accept responsibility has helped break down and destroy the ivory tower and bring it into the middle of public life, and even into international politics, positions which the university and scholar have not sought and which it is hazardous for them to share. Work for the Peace Corps, for AID, and for other government agencies, and especially programs involving foreign governments, has drastically changed the nature and character of the relationship between the university and the government. Thus far, the principles and procedures established have recognized the special role free universities must always play, and the main hazards have been avoided. Moreover, everyone agrees, first, that the university today cannot be removed from the society in which it functions and which it serves, and second, that the university in a free country must remain true to its primary educational goals if it is to serve society effectively and remain truly independent.

In the exchange programs, for example, even though the university often plays an important political role in a front line capacity, it must at all times remain a privileged sanctuary of freedom. Our educational institutions are free and independent, suspicious of government, and accustomed to their own ways in their assigned areas of responsibility. They must remain sovereign, conduct their work of research and instruction as they see best, and have a large share in the direction of cultural relations, in which they have always had an abiding interest. In brief, "political warfare" use of the universities and of the arts is useless and in the long run destructive, even though universities, artists, and scientists operating independently, doing their own work in their own best way, do have a very powerful impact.

Relations between the Department of State and the universities have been remarkably effective and amicable because the men and women involved have so well understood the others' purposes, qualities, and problems. However, tension between American universities and the Department of State over exchange programs is natural, because the State Department has the primary responsibility for critical, delicate, and highly involved relations with the Soviet Union, which cannot be separated from relations with our allies and with other countries in the world. Moreover, while the universities are interested basically in only a small part of the cultural affairs agreement with the Soviet Union, the Department of State has responsibility for the entire agreement, which it naturally sees as a whole and which it wishes to administer in a coherent and coordinated way, keeping in mind our total foreign policy towards the Soviet Union and with other countries as well.

The particular issues of disagreement are obvious and will continue. Thus, the Department controls admission to the United States and has on occasion denied visas to Soviet scholars nominated in fields which have military significance, such as microelectronics or new types of computers, or in subjects in which the Soviet Union has refused to accept American scholars. In addition, in retaliation for travel restrictions imposed on all Americans in the Soviet Union, Soviet participants in the United States must inform the Department of State of intended travel four days before they can leave their home campus. In cases such as this, American scholars who are not informed concerning Soviet policies or concerning the larger framework in which the academic exchange resides, or who have a special personal interest in one person or one aspect of the program, frequently denounce the Department for policies which seem to them petty or senseless.

The Department of State is also vulnerable to domestic political pressures and critics, some of whom denounce the Department because "the Soviets send scientists to work on important problems in American laboratories while we send scholars to work in ancient Russian history in Soviet libraries." Some Americans and their representatives believe that the programs should be curtailed or abolished because they are convinced that the Soviet Union obtains a significantly greater advantage from them than we do. Others on occasion believe we can and should send ten thousand each year, bringing the walls of Moscow down by turning pages. The State Department, in short, is constantly vulnerable to critics and serves as a perpetual target for all Americans, some of whom have some influence on the annual appropriations for the Department and therefore for exchange programs. These pressures often cause disagreements between the Department and the universities, which resent any apparent Departmental weakening before popular pressures and who resist suggestions from the Department which would help satisfy the most responsible of the public criticisms.

Unfortunately, the Department of State is not the only American Government agency with which universities engaged in academic exchange programs have to deal. Some of these government institutions, such as the National Academy of Sciences and the Atomic Energy Commission, have exchange programs of their own, which are financed by the government but which rely on American universities to provide most of the American participants and the laboratories and libraries in which Soviet participants continue their studies. The AEC and the NAS tend to be quite independent because they are within the government, and because their programs involve scientists, in whom the Soviet Union is particularly interested and for whom, therefore, it creates more comfortable arrangements and fewer problems than it does for scholars in the ordinary academic exchange program.

However, the Central Intelligence Agency and the Federal Bureau of Investigation have raised greater problems for the American universities and their constituents, who tend to be critical of much of the government but especially critical of these two organizations. The CIA and the FBI, which have important national responsibilities, are interested in information concerning Soviet strengths and weaknesses, policies and practices. On the Soviet side, officials of the KGB almost inevitably evaluate all academic exchange programs with the Soviet Union in this context and, above all, in the perspective of their eternal suspicions and of their own extensive efforts. In fact, the universities' emphasis upon selecting young men and women of high intellectual quality with good command of Russian, considerable knowledge of the Soviet Union, and great interest in learning about Soviet society has no doubt increased Soviet suspicion.

The American scholarly organizations engaged in exchanges with the Soviet Union have done their utmost to ensure that their programs provide no grounds for suspicion, but they are essentially powerless to affect the

Soviet attitude. These organizations, such as the Inter-University Committee and the International Research and Exchanges Board, are interested exclusively in scholarly activities. They have no ties with the Central Intelligence Agency or any other intelligence organization. They receive no funds from any intelligence organization, and they provide them no information. The Inter-University Committee in addition warned every candidate for study in the Soviet Union not only to reject any approaches that might be made by intelligence or other government agencies, but to report such incidents should they occur. Finally, every participant in the Committee's exchange program signed a pledge that he would undertake no activity other than the scholarly ones for which he was selected.

Even so, the existence and the activities of these government agencies have created difficulties for the American universities in their dealings with the ever-suspicious Soviet Government. They have also created problems with the American academic community, in spite of the efforts of the academic organizations and in spite of the genuine care, discretion, and propriety with which these organizations have carried out their activities.

Another kind of dilemma which the universities and all of those concerned with the national interest face reflects the advantages which the Soviet Government derives from academic exchange programs. In fact, it has been evident throughout the discussions and bargaining over cultural exchanges, that tough-minded Soviet diplomats and officials have taken advantage of the abiding American concern about the international crisis and of our efforts to persuade the Soviet Union to adopt more peaceful policies. In short, they use our efforts to launch and to maintain these programs to obtain vast opportunities for themselves. American diplomats have sought not only to advance our own national interests, but have also recognized legitimate Soviet objectives, because they perceived that any agreement would have to provide benefits to both countries. However, above all, they have sought to create an international framework and atmosphere in which the two countries together could reduce the tensions which afflict us both. Basically, the Soviet leaders have taken advantage of this spirit and approach and have concentrated on their own restricted interests, while seeking to minimize our benefits and to prevent our joint escape from the present hazardous situation into a new structure and a new atmosphere. For every apparent step towards a freer world and greater international amity, they have insisted upon a parochial Soviet advantage which has not affected the commonweal, except in a divisive way, and which has indeed exposed the Americans involved to substantial criticism.

Here one must recognize that Soviet scholars, artists, and intellectuals have almost no influence on Soviet policy or on Soviet administration of exchange programs. These men and women share many of our scholars' interests. They seek to increase their knowledge within their own special field. They are eager to cooperate with other scholars. They seek the recognition and respect of other members of the international community of scholars. Above all, they look forward to opportunities to leave the Soviet Union, to go "out," for a few months or a year.

Those of the party and the government who make the decisions are different people and have different goals. Basically, they seek to strengthen the Soviet system and to weaken ours. Their primary concern has been to obtain scientific, technical, and military information from the United States. They have, in short, sought to use the exchange programs to strengthen their economy and to obtain important information and techniques from a more advanced country. Almost eighty percent of the Soviet participants in the basic program administered by the Inter-University Committee have been scientists or engineers, while somewhat less than ten percent of the Americans have been in science or technology. Thus, the Soviet Union has obtained a significant increment to its scientific and technical knowledge from these programs, from basic knowledge concerning polio vaccines to training in econometrics and new systems of business management to the latest work in biochemistry.

In addition, the Soviet Government has acquired a kind of respectability both at home and abroad, especially among the large and important class of intellectuals or intelligentsia, who have been persuaded in part by these programs that the Soviet Union is a peaceful and responsible member of the family of nations. It also believes it derives recognition, prestige, and propaganda advantages from the presence of carefully selected Soviet scholars in American universities, and the impact which life in the Soviet Union presumably has on American scholars. Finally, it utilizes the exchange program to train specialists on the United States for work in various parts of the Soviet Government.

The difference between our goals and the Soviet goals is at the root of our problems, but there are even more essential factors involved. The principal one is the Soviet system, which differs in almost every way from ours, particularly in its values and in its political organization. Recognizing and accepting this system in the atmosphere of the 1960s apparently reflects the willingness of many Americans also to accept Soviet control of Eastern Europe and the permanence of communist control wherever it exists. In addition, we have difficulty dealing with the Soviet Union, because the economic and political levels of the two countries are different, one an advanced industrial society with a political and social democracy, and the other basically an underdeveloped society under authoritarian rule, with a highly developed military system, and motivated by suspicion and hostility toward the rest of the world.

Relations with the Soviet Government and with its controlled universities therefore create a series of problems for American institutions, which are participating in formal, highly organized and even sanitized exchange arrangements with a totalitarian government, which naturally takes advantage of its negotiating position. One of the dangers is that we accept this primitive system of barter as a permanent practice, in violation of the ways in which we live and believe scholars ought to work. Moreover, the constant compromises which we have to make with the Soviet Union concerning the status of the participants, fields of study, travel opportunities, and essentials of life may weary the Americans responsible to the point that they will accept these temporary compromises as permanent. In short, it will be very difficult in the long run for Americans to be firm towards the Soviet Government but gentle and humane towards the Soviet scholars, and we may drift into a type of moral demobilization.

Another great hazard for American universities is the degree of influence they surrender to the Soviet Government over the direction of American scholarship. Thus, the Soviet Ministry of Higher and Specialized Education, and other Soviet officials, have denied the opportunity for study in the Soviet Union to Americans highly qualified for study there, on the ground that the subject, such as the allocation of labor resources, is not one studied in Soviet universities, or that political theory in the sixteenth century is a religious issue and therefore unworthy of study, or that everything important in Soviet agricultural problems and policies had already been enunciated by Khrushchev, whose speeches the interested American scholar could examine in the United States. In other words, the Soviet Ministry has denied admission to most Americans who wish to study the Soviet economy, modern or recent history, Soviet politics, Soviet foreign policy, and many scientific fields, while American universities through 1968 placed every Soviet scholar nominated in a field in which he could work in an American university and for which he could obtain a visa.

This Soviet practice has also led American scholars, who are mainly interested in seeing the Soviet Union, to change their research projects so that they might obtain admission under conditions dictated by the Soviet Government. This has helped create an imbalance among the fields of study within American universities which may become permanent. Thus, we have sent eighty-three historians to study Russian history, but no Americans have been admitted to analyze Soviet foreign policy or the relations between the party and the government. The Soviet Government has therefore been able to have a profound influence in fields which are important to it and has succeeded at the same time in deflecting the direction of American scholarship.

The Soviet Government may also have some influence over Americans who have studied in the Soviet Union and who wish to return to the country of their special professional interest as scholars in Russian history, literature, or government. Soviet denials to some scholars of the opportunity to return for further study because of their publications or speeches can induce cautious behavior both within the Soviet Union and within the United States by American scholars. This may tend to restrict the freedoms of Americans, and it will also assist the Soviet Government to keep its scholars and other intellectuals isolated and under control, which is one of its main concerns.

Another serious problem has been what one American has called the "eternal indecencies and inequities" of dealing with the Soviet Union. American scholars in most programs are not allowed to bring their children, which naturally reduces the number interested, and the Soviet Government even has a quota for the number of wives allowed each year. Almost all of the Americans (295 of the first 300) who went to the Soviet Union were placed in Moscow State and Leningrad State Universities and were denied opportunities to study in research institutes of the Academy of Sciences, while at the same time, Soviet scholars have been placed in that American institution most qualified to serve them, wherever in the United States that institution might be. Thus, the great majority of American scholars have been restricted to two universities, while Soviet scholars have worked in fifty-two different American institutions.

In the largest and most important exchange program, that for graduate students and young scholars, each American participant has been treated as an *aspirant stazhor,* or probationary graduate student, regardless of his qualifications, achievements, and age. He is therefore directly subject to his Soviet professor and needs his approval for his program, for access to libraries and archives, and for study-related travel. One associate professor from the University of California who had already produced an excellent book was thus denied the right to study in Leningrad State University and to work in the Leningrad libraries on the grounds that the Soviet specialist in that field in Leningrad was too busy to direct his work.

American scholars also have great difficulties obtaining access to archives, to living sources, and to some kinds of publications in Soviet libraries, such as doctoral theses. At the same time, Soviet scholars have the same access to information in this country that any American scholar does. Americans are seriously restricted in their opportunities to travel for study or study-related purposes from Moscow and Leningrad, and they ordinarily travel only in groups and accompanied by Soviet "guides," when they do travel. One young American spent forty hours obtaining permission to go to Leningrad from Moscow to work in Leningrad libraries, even though the Soviet Ministry of Education in admitting him to the Soviet Union had assured him of this opportunity. At the same time, Soviet scholars are allowed to travel freely throughout the United States, although they do have to inform the Department of State four days in advance of leaving their campus.

Life in the Soviet Union itself constitutes a kind of permanent inequity, because of the living conditions, the frustrations, annoyances, indignities, and inefficiency, the assessment of discriminatory prices for microfilming research materials and for hotel rooms, the effort in recent years to segregate Americans from Soviet scholars and students, and the harassment to which Americans are subject.

Americans have come to consider the Soviet postal system as "the opened mail" and to realize that diaries have official readers. They are never certain who their Soviet friends are and which are involuntary informers or *agents provocateurs.* Some had close friends regretfully discontinue relationships because the friends were frightened by police interrogation, and all have learned never to mention one Soviet friend to another. Some were followed frequently, particularly just before they left the Soviet Union or during trips, and all of them, and their Soviet friends, came to believe that the rooms in which they lived, which often were rooms in which other Americans had lived in previous years, had listening devices installed in the walls, and that their telephone conversations were monitored. Many became justifiably suspicious of officials in the university foreign study offices, some of whom they came to know had responsibilities to the KGB, the Soviet Secret Police, as well as to the university. In addition, a small percentage of the American participants had direct and unpleasant experiences with the KGB. Seven were expelled from the Soviet Union, so far as we can determine without cause and also without consultation or advance notice to the participant's American university or to the Committee. Eighteen left early because of fear caused by Secret Police interest in their work or were urged to leave by the American Embassy because KGB interest in them had been so visibly expressed. More than twenty other participants in our major program have been criticized crudely, viciously, and without foundation in the Soviet press as spies or "ideological saboteurs."

There is no dignified or proper response to these Soviet policies and practices, which create a serious dilemma and which have been accepted in part because they do educate American scholars concerning the nature of the Soviet system. All of the Soviet actions have been annoying and irritating, and some of them have been hazardous. However, they have all been spaced in time and in quality in such a way that neither the American universities nor the Department of State considered that the threshold point had been passed.

THE SOVIET DILEMMA

The responsible Soviet officials who have decided that the Soviet Union should participate in exchange programs with the United States and who have determined to continue them are thoroughly aware of the advantages we obtain and of the challenges which exchange programs pose for them. They obviously recognize the significant advantages which accrue to the Soviet Union, and they must believe that these advantages outweigh those we gain and the hazards to them. At the same time, there is an eternal "great debate" within the Soviet ruling group about the utility and wisdom of continuing academic exchanges. In this discussion, clearly those who decide have concluded that the benefits to the Soviet Union justify the risks taken; they would otherwise have ended the exchange program. However, this discussion continues on almost a daily basis, the "score" changes often, and those who favor exchanges may not always triumph and may not control actions taken at every policy level.

The main problem for the Soviet leadership is the challenge this new "window to the West" poses for the Soviet political system, especially the communist emphasis on a political monopoly, on absolute control, and on carefully monitored relationships with other parts of the world. This system rests not only on communist suspicion of others, but also on the suspicion which is a traditional and even inherent part of the Russian view of the rest of the world. The police and other members of the ruling class have become increasingly fearful of Soviet intellectuals and of Western influences upon them. Indeed, the Soviet rulers apparently believe the greatest internal threat to their system is from the intelligentsia and those most highly trained. They seem to agree with Louis XIV that "nations touch only at the top" and that outside influences, which can penetrate the Soviet system best at its upper level, must be contained and destroyed. They are convinced that "we are betrayed by what is false within." The government now headed by Brezhnev and Kosygin very much resembles that of Nicholas I in the suspicion with which it views all peoples, including its own, and in the "plot mentality" which corrodes its approach towards everyone, native or foreign, in the Soviet Union.

These beliefs and Soviet "ideological sensitivity" are reflected in the constant vigilance campaigns and in press attacks upon Soviet intellectuals, especially writers, for their alleged vulnerability to foreign ideas and influences. The communist political system and philosophy, and the suspicion with which they view even the most loyal servitors - and the Soviet intellectuals are by and large loyal - therefore help explain the Soviet dilemma and resultant Soviet policies. The presence of Americans and other foreigners in Soviet universities, where the future elite are being trained; the published materials which they bring with them and on occasion share with their Soviet fellows; the conversations they have in their dormitories and in class; everything which Americans and others do in the Soviet Union is considered a threat. As one American expressed it: "We *are* propaganda, simply because of our presence here." In short, the very nature of the exchange program raises very difficult problems for the Soviet Union and places it on the horns of a fearful and continual dilemma. To obtain gains which it thinks important, even crucial, it must risk contamination of its intellectual elite and of the ideological future of the country. To obtain the advantages it seeks in the West, it must open up the Soviet Union to some degree to foreign scholars. To obtain scientific and technical and military information, and some political advantages, it must expose itself to criticism from Chinese communists and at the same time tolerate similar policies from the East European governments, which are even more interested than the Soviet Union in exchanges with the United States. In summary, just as the Department of State and the universities ever ponder the wisdom of continuing to endure the inequities and hazards created by the Soviet Government, so the Soviet rulers constantly discuss the balance between the advantages they acquire and the "infections" which may constitute the price.

CONCLUSIONS

Most of the advantages and the disadvantages academic exchanges provide are clear, but perhaps some of the achievements of the past twelve or fifteen years should be emphasized because they are not visible. One important accomplishment is the simple survival of programs between two suspicious and hostile states, through a series of international crises, at a time when failure, cancellation, or a breach of one kind or another might have produced a great crisis. American institutions involved have demonstrated great skill and wisdom in the selection of mature and able young men and women and have ignored the occasional dramatic calls for sending massive numbers. The universities have retained their responsibility and control in a program which must be of, by, and for the universities if it is to be successful and if they are to survive as free institutions. They have honored themselves and their traditions in the way in which they have treated all Soviet scholars on their campuses. At the same time, they have successfully avoided any taint of relationships with the Central Intelligence Agency or any other intelligence organization, they have skillfully avoided taking direct part in political warfare between the two countries, and they have escaped such tragic affairs as that of Camelot. The Department of State has shown the same degree of wisdom, restraint, and skill in its work with the universities and scholars, who are acutely sensitive concerning their rights and responsibilities, and with the Soviet Ministry of Foreign Affairs and other Soviet Government agencies, which have been vigorous and demanding in pursuit of what they consider Soviet interests.

At the same time, the exchange programs in many ways have been a failure. We are following the principles and working within the framework established in 1958 and are now more than ever committed to a program which is the antithesis of the way in which Americans believe research in other countries should be arranged. Soviet scholars and other Soviet citizens are no more free to obtain American and other Western publications than they were when the exchanges began. In fact, we have made no progress towards the hopes which Ambassador Lacy expressed in 1947 for "removing barriers currently obstructing the free flow of information and ideas" and providing benefit to both people "of free discussion, criticism, and debate on the vital issues of the day." We have not succeeded in exchanging teachers, even teachers of language; there are no joint research projects, even on subjects of common concern, such as air pollution; the exchange of radio and television programs is extremely limited and directly controlled by the Soviet Government; and all American proposals for expanding the exchange program even in the present framework, such as through summer study and summer seminars, have been brusquely rejected by the Soviet Government. Indeed, the programs in progress in 1969-1970 are just half as large as those the American universities anticipated when they made their budget estimates for 1965-1970 in the spring of 1964.

In short, there has been more continuity than change in Soviet policy and practice. The stone wall of the closed society still exists, even though the powerful magnet of Western ideas and Western progress still attracts, perhaps more strongly than ever, the Soviet intellectuals still isolated behind those barriers.

Even so, the exchanges on balance have been an advantage to us, and we should continue them. In fact, both we and the Soviet Union have little choice but to continue, because ending them now would be such a dreadful blow at a time of high crisis. They constitute, in fact, a valuable opportunity to continue to work with the Soviet Government and to reach Soviet citizens. We should rejoice over this opportunity, particularly because the exchange involves ideas and information, and therefore a kind of competition with the Soviet Union on grounds congenial or favorable to us in areas where freedom has given us great advantages in cultural vitality.

However, we should also appreciate the new and to some degree dangerous role the American university and scholars now occupy. For those who believe that the work of the college should be "relevant," American educational institutions in this case at least have placed themselves on the firing line. This shift places a very heavy responsibility on the universities and on all those who wish them to accept such a role.

The experience of the past fifteen years suggests that the American universities and the American Government together have identified the correct principles for administering scholarly exchange programs with governments which have different ideologies and philosophies. Administrators and scholars in particular must ensure that universities remain centers of free inquiry; that they maintain the clear distinction between scholarship and political warfare and espionage; and that they be eternally vigilant in their relations with our government and with other governments as well. Above all, they should insist that our scholars are treated with the decency and dignity all men and women deserve, especially when they are guests in another country. We can achieve no great purpose by tolerating procedures which undermine the principles for which we stand.

Moreover, the role of the university, and of the scholars, scientists and artists, should be pre-eminent in those fields in which they have particular concern and responsibility; academic quality should be the primary factor in the selection process; the Americans selected for study in a communist country should be men and women of maturity and stability; the selection process should be on a national basis, with recognized and competent scholars making the decisions and with scholars and graduate students in all fields of knowledge encouraged to participate.

At the same time, we have learned that academic exchange programs of this kind require reorganization of individual universities and increased cooperative efforts among educational institutions. University administrators and scholars must maintain a high degree of sophistication if programs like this are to be successful. We must pay more attention to educating the American public concerning the significance of academic exchanges and the problems which they inevitably raise, if the public is to understand them and provide the necessary support in the long future.

Above all, we should have learned that the universities, the other scholarly organizations involved, and the government should work together to create a new kind of organization of public and private institutions, including the foundations, to coordinate the work involved. Our resources for exchange programs with communist countries are too scarce to allow us to continue on a kind of free-for-all, highly competitive, and dangerous basis. Ideally, this "American Council" should be a semi-public organization, with the Board of Directors composed of private citizens nominated by the President and approved by the Senate, and with funds contributed in part by the federal government and in part by private organizations, such as foundations, universities, business and labor groups, and organizations especially interested in the arts and sciences. It should possess full authority for all cultural exchange programs with all countries ruled by communists, and it should speak for the universities and other cultural organizations in its dealings with the Department of State and with foreign governments.

If it should prove impossible to establish such an organization - and recent unsuccessful efforts have identified a number of complications - the organizations involved in and responsible for such exchange programs should at least form a loose federal organization to pool information, to consult concerning plans and programs, and to coordinate activities. After they have learned to cooperate and to work together, they should consider combining their operations and then coordinating American programs with those of other countries in an open way so as to persuade the Soviet Union that no conspiracy was being directed against it.

Such an organization and such a program should reduce the invisible costs which academic exchanges involve, eliminate some of the friction and tension among American organizations, and reflect the pluralistic approach which Americans traditionally adopt. At the same time, they should guarantee the necessary political sensitivity. Such an organization should also serve as a shock absorber, on one side for the universities, and on the other side for the federal government, reducing the pressures to which both are now subject.

The long term goal for everyone involved in academic exchanges with the Soviet Union and with other communist countries should remain, of course, the free movement of people and materials. In fact, the new coordinating organization should be established with the expressed hope and goal that it wither away when free movement becomes possible.

China has isolated itself, and has in general been isolated from, the rest of the world for the twenty years during which communists have had control over that enormous country. This isolation will end one day, with new problems and new opportunities for the Chinese and for the rest of the world. Clearly, American scholars and American Government officials should begin to plan now for that day, benefiting from the experiences provided by our exchanges with the Soviet Union. In particular, we should recognize that the first steps will be decisive, as they have been in our arrangements with the Soviet Union, because they will establish the structure, principles, and procedures which communist rulers will be most reluctant to change.

We should, therefore, seek to ensure that all institutions and all fields of study be open to scholars of both countries, and that the entire areas of both countries should be freely accessible. We should seek equity, not reciprocity. We should insist upon, or at least always retain the opportunity for, arrangements for exchanges of all kinds, short and long-term, of specialists and of teachers, of senior scholars and of graduate students. We should guarantee that scholars from both countries receive appropriate status and recognition, possess the right for study-related travel, and have the same access to research materials in libraries and laboratories as do natives. Finally, we should ensure that the academic exchanges not be restricted to men and women; the free flow of published materials between the two countries should be an integral part of the agreement.

The nature of the world in which the Americans, the Chinese, and the Russians live suggests that relations among these states and their peoples will remain delicate and hazardous. We shall no doubt remain locked in a shrinking world, suspicious of and hostile toward each other, unable on one hand to conquer or overthrow the other but equally unable to disengage and flee into some kind of armed security. Cultural relations in this situation will remain of considerable importance, but can never be decisive. In such a position, we in the United States should maintain our economic, political, and spiritual vitality and our military strength, cooperate with other peoples who share our general goals and who are committed to peaceful progress, and continue to demonstrate that we are as resolute as in 1776 or in 1942 to defend our interests. At the same time, we should try further to define and understand the nature of the political and economic systems with which we are engaged, to persuade them of our goals and of the kind of world we seek, and to make effective use of cultural exchange, of trade, and of other peaceful instruments to bring these goals within reach.

The situation we face is very much like the Eastern Question, devilishly complicated, deeply rooted in the past, involving numbers of peoples, and beyond easy or quick solution. Intellect and strength, grace and perseverance will both be required and expected of us. Scholarly exchanges in these circumstances provide us an opportunity to use some of our enduring strengths to assist our rivals and ourselves together to make a step towards peace.

9

Cultural Exchange and Competition Between Societies: An American View

The peoples and governments of all signatories of the Final Act, and indeed of the world, enjoy common benefits from the movement toward increased cultural exchange and other forms of peaceful relationships between East and West. At the same time, however, the individual states seek different national interests in these exchanges. Moreover, the concerns of the scholars, intellectuals, and artists who participate often differ in some degree from the interests of their governments. Consequently, increasing cultural exchange and competition raises complicated issues for the governments and societies involved.

The nature of thermo-nuclear war would be such that everyone in the world profits from efforts to reduce the likelihood of conflict. In fact, the prospect of nuclear war is so terrifying that most governments are interested in reducing strains and eliminating crises which might lead to annihilation. Moreover, the nature of the world in the fourth quarter of the twentieth century is such that all free governments, and those of many authoritarian states as well, recognize the advantages of cultural ties, particularly in reducing age-old cultural barriers, increasing knowledge and understanding of other peoples, and beginning the long, vital process toward cooperation in resolving common, indeed universal problems. The most effective expressions of such universal cooperation are those toward developing new strains of rice, grain and maize and spreading knowledge of these discoveries into every interested country. In relations between the West, the states of Eastern Europe, and the Soviet Union, such cooperative enterprises are not yet possible. However, the bilateral research cooperation agreements signed by the United States and the Soviet Union between 1972 and 1974 for eleven different fields of study (such as agriculture, atomic energy, environmental protection, and medical sciences and public health), and similar agreements other Western states have with the Soviet Union, are at least a beginning toward peaceful cooperation between hostile states and may constitute a step toward a universal approach, which would benefit all.

Reprinted with permission from *Uncertain Detente: A Pre-Belgrade Evaluation of Post-Helsinki Developments,* Frans Alting van Geusau, ed. (Alphen aan den Ryn, The Netherlands, 1979), 231-249.

ADVANTAGES OF EXCHANGE AND COMPETITION

American benefits

The initial steps which led to the cultural exchange agreement between the United States and the Soviet Union in March 1958 were taken by American scholars particularly interested in Soviet studies who wished to visit the country about which they were teaching and to carry on research in Soviet libraries. At that time, and still today, these scholars, and the intellectuals and artists who have participated in the exchange programmes, have sought principally to increase their knowledge and understanding of a different culture and political system, to learn from others who have the same scholarly and intellectual interests, and to obtain the advantages any educated person derives from widened horizons and access to new points of view. These aims are not unique to those interested in the Soviet Union and Eastern Europe, for they are only a part of the vast American effort since the Second World War to increase knowledge and understanding of the so-called non-Western countries and cultures, which American education had virtually ignored.

The American people support and assist these efforts to improve research and instruction throughout the educational system because they appreciate the importance of knowledge and understanding of others in this ever-shrinking world. Indeed, almost all Americans now understand, as almost none did in the 1940s, that they live in a small world in which all must cooperate to survive. In addition, Americans support closer cultural relations because they consider peaceful competition in intellectual fields more "safe and sane" than rivalry in arms or constant confrontations. Americans, and of course other Western peoples, are accustomed to cooperation and peaceful competition in ideas, as well as in trade. Expanding cultural relations with a rival, hostile state such as the Soviet Union therefore seems both natural and sensible. Above all, most Americans recognize the extraordinary advantages the United States and the West acquire in diverting competition from political warfare, an arms race, and endless crises to one in which the West is invincibly strong. Americans not only prefer transferring the competition to the safer cultural field, but were, are, and will remain confident that the United States and the West will emerge stronger and the world safer from such a test. The freedom and the intellectual vitality, effervescence, and openness of the United States and its allies and friends are the principal weapons of the West in peaceful intellectual competition. Indeed, Americans are delighted to participate in this test at every level, from jazz to computers, against what Sir Isaiah Berlin has called "the silence of Soviet culture."[1]

The American Government from the beginning has endorsed this position of the scholars and the public because it shares the same values and views. Indeed, as time has passed, the government has come to appreciate the growing importance of this once "neglected aspect" of American foreign policy. Moreover, from the point of view of American national interest, increased cultural exchange and competition have brought at least a few Soviet and American citizens into contact and enabled those in an elite group on each side to demonstrate the interests of their governments and to learn about the other system, a process in which Americans believe both sides gain. These relations also provide the American Government an opportunity to influence the Soviet political elite, a critical group, because in the last third of the twentieth century, as in the age of Louis XIV, "nations touch most at the top." In short, expanding cultural relations has not only brought the Soviet Union into the world from the isolation and ignorance which Stalin had imposed on it, but has also given the United States and other Western countries increased knowledge of Soviet policy and some slight leverage to use in the total Soviet-American relationship.

Over the years, some changes have occurred in popular and national American positions with regard to cultural exchange, and the relationships are somewhat larger and more significant than twenty years ago. However, the fundamental positions remain the same, just more deeply appreciated, understood, and supported.

Soviet benefits

The Soviet Union also obtains concrete advantages from cultural exchanges, which Soviet leaders declare an essential part of their doctrine of "peaceful coexistence." Americans cannot be certain of the meaning of this phrase, which remains "the general guideline of Soviet foreign policy," and which Soviet leaders have defined as "class war on the international level" and "the highest form of class struggle."[2] Cultural exchanges support the Soviet effort to persuade other governments and peoples that the Soviet Union has no aggressive designs or ambitions, that placid normalcy has returned, and that the Western states need not rearm or unite in defense. They also provide the Soviet Union respectability, still greatly needed after Stalin's twenty-five years of rule and its continuation by other leaders, and the opportunity to reward loyal Soviet scholars and cultural leaders. Finally, such relationships provide a fine opportunity to acquire access to the science and technology of Western societies. In the exchanges with the United States, more than eighty percent of the Soviet participants in the last fifteen years were scientists or engineers. In recent years, that percentage has risen to more than ninety percent of the total, thus demonstrating a powerful Soviet interest and advantage.

East European benefits

The peoples of Eastern Europe and their governments share many of the same interests as the American and Western peoples and their governments. In addition, they seek access to the wealth of the Western economies and to their scientific and technical achievements. They also seek to end the isolation long imposed on them during and after the Second World War and to return to their traditional relationships with Western Europe and its culture, which they share. This applies in particular to the peoples of Poland, Czechoslovakia, and Hungary, who have for centuries had powerful ties with the West. The peoples of Eastern Europe, in short, have an interest in overcoming the division of Europe at least as strong as that of the peoples of Western Europe.

PERSPECTIVES SINCE STALIN'S DEATH

During the time when Stalin ruled, and today as well, the basic elements in international politics remain economic and military power, vitality and stability, resolution, and skill in diplomacy. In 1977, even more than twenty-five years ago, reaching agreements on disarmament and on crisis management remain more important than expanding cultural relationships. In short, SALT and MBFR are far more vital in the short run than is any mustard seed.

However, in the long run, the role played by economic and intellectual relationships will acquire ever greater significance, not only in the reality of international politics but also in public understanding of those relations. In the long run, the competition of ideas may prove the decisive factor in the contest between two powerful systems.

During the last years of Stalin's life, no Western scholars were allowed to study in the Soviet Union, Soviet intellectuals (and other citizens as well) were prohibited from visiting even neighboring states ruled by communists, and control over access to information within the Soviet Union, and from outside, was as tight as any government has ever managed. Not even a socialist state was allowed to send a commercial aeroplane into the air space of the Soviet Union so long as Stalin lived.

1977 is somewhat different, although many commentators have compared the gradual, slow opening of the Soviet Union and increased contact with the West to moving "the massive groaning gate of a medieval castle" and have described it as "the beginning of a beginning."[3]

In spite of the progress made in the past two decades, the patterns remain substantially the same. The divisions within Europe are much greater than they were a hundred years ago or even forty years ago, when Nazi Germany was ready to launch attacks upon its neighbors. Even the Final Act in Helsinki was signed only after more than two years of negotiations by 492 diplomats from thirty-five countries.

Progress since the mid-fifties

An American can best obtain perspective concerning these changes by reviewing the discussions which led to the March 1958 Soviet-American cultural exchange agreement. Ambassador William S.B. Lacy defined American goals as "removing barriers currently obstructing the free flow of information and debate on the vital issues of the day."[4] In his opening talk, he urged the Soviet Union as a great step toward peace to end censorship, to cease jamming Western radio broadcasts, and to abolish all controls over access to information and to travel. We have made perilously little progress toward those aims.

The Soviet Ambassador, Georgii Zarubin, on the other hand, described Soviet goals as "normalization of Soviet-American relations and the relaxation of international tensions." No one has agreed yet on the meaning of "normalization." Ambassador Zarubin also suggested the immediate exchange of fifty-six delegations in important fields of science and technology, a position which underlines one of the main purposes of cultural exchange for the Soviet Union.

The Soviet Union allowed twelve foreign correspondents to work in Moscow in 1953, compared with about 250 in 1977, twenty-five of whom are American (the Soviet Union has thirty-six correspondents in the United States). The direct flights between New York and Moscow approved in the March 1958 agreement began eight years later. The exchange of classroom teachers accepted in 1958 began in 1974, with fewer than ten teachers each way. The Soviet Union signed the International Copyright Convention in February 1973. Forty-three Americans visited the Soviet Union as tourists the year in which Stalin died, and about 100,000 a quarter-century later. In this period, the largest number of Soviet tourists who visited the United States in any one year has never exceeded 600. The total number of participants in the cultural exchange agreement between 1958 and 1973 included 13,178 Soviet and 17,071 American citizens. In other words, some improvement has occurred.

For the Americans who launched these programs, the academic exchanges remain the most significant symbol or touchstone. Between 1958 and 1975, about a thousand American senior graduate students and scholars spent from two months to two years in the Soviet Union, and approximately the same number of Soviet scholars and graduate students spent the same periods of time in the United States. During that period, 3,000 scholars and students from all the Western states studied in the Soviet Union. However, one must put these figures into perspective. For example, in 1976, 150,000 foreign students continued their studies in the United States and 25,000 in the Soviet Union. In each year since 1963, more scholars from Iceland have studied in the United States than have scholars from the Soviet Union.

Eastern Europe, in contrast, has been far more free, and exchanges have expanded far more rapidly than they have with the Soviet Union, although they usually began later. For example, a total of 1,000 Polish scholars studied in the United States between 1956 and 1960. 422 Czechoslovak scholars studied in the United States in 1967 and 1,000 in 1969 alone. 154 Rumanian scholars were in the United States in 1970. The University of Warsaw in 1976 launched an American Studies Center, with American faculty members in important instructional roles and a fine, open American library.[5]

Progress in recent years

Cultural exchanges have continued in a slightly different spirit and tempo since 1969 or 1970, although the pattern remains basically as established twenty years ago. It is difficult to determine the reasons for this Soviet relaxation: perhaps Soviet appreciation of the achievements of the previous years, the strain in Soviet-Chinese relations and the need to reduce pressures in the West, the "spring" in Czechoslovakia in 1968 and Soviet realization that Eastern Europe remains in disarray, and the Soviet discovery at about the same time of a growing gap in science, technology, and agriculture between the Soviet Union and the West. In any case, during the years in which the Western states and the Soviet Union were preparing for the Helsinki discussions, during the talks themselves, and since the signing of the Final Act on August 1, 1975, some improvements have occurred. These limited and uneven changes give some hope that other modifications will occur and that the Soviet system may mellow and adopt different foreign policies.

Thus, during these years, especially after the signing of the agreement, the Soviet Union has adopted a somewhat less rigorous attitude toward allowing emigration, particularly of members of divided families. It has at the same time forced some of its most distinguished dissidents to leave the Soviet Union, a barbarous practice but one which most Westerners consider an advance upon labor camps or psychiatric treatment. Travel by foreigners within the Soviet Union is under somewhat less constraint, but the right of Soviet citizens to travel abroad has remained unaffected.

With regard to access to information, progress has occurred. Thus, the Soviet Union ceased jamming such national government stations as the BBC and the Voice of America in 1974. Since the signing of the Final Act, it has allowed some Western journalists multiple entry visas and has given them the same travel opportunities as it provides diplomats. The Soviet Government at Helsinki agreed "gradually to increase the quantities and number of titles of newspapers and publications imported," and has made some slight improvement in the number of Western newspapers available in hotels to which Western tourists are assigned. In academic exchanges, some slight improvement has occurred in admitting a higher percentage of Americans nominated who are interested in contemporary issues, in access to libraries and archives, and in travel for study-related purposes. In areas such as medical research and public health, less political than most, satisfaction is greater on both sides than it is, for example, in the exchange of publications.

The East European states were far more free and less restrictive than the Soviet Union, but, even so, the changes there have been more visible and significant. In academic exchanges, for example, neither the United States nor its Western allies suffer the problems in admission or placement which they have in the Soviet Union. Western scholars travel freely within the East European countries, libraries and archives are open, and establishment of direct exchanges between institutions and even individuals has been easy. As one British observer described, cultural relationships with the Soviet Union involve climbing a wall and crossing a moat, while those with Eastern Europe involve going through a complicated turnstile.[6]

At the same time, the Soviet Union maintains a massive capacity for jamming foreign radio broadcasts and continues vigorously to jam Radio Liberty, Kol Israel, Radio Peking and Radio Tirana. Soviet hours of broadcasting to Western Europe and North America remain approximately fifty percent higher than those from Western Europe and North America directed to the Soviet Union. Yet, illogically but in accordance with the doctrine of peaceful coexistence and the simultaneous denial of ideological coexistence, the Soviet Government continues both its intensive jamming and its vigorous campaign to close down Radio Free Europe and Radio Liberty. In addition, it has made a sustained effort since 1972 in UNESCO, in the General Assembly of the United Nations, and in the International Telecommunications Union to prevent radio and television broadcasts from artificial earth satellites into a country without that country's permission, activities not yet technically possible but which will one day raise critical problems for all governments which seek to control the flow of information.

Some of the conditions under which Western journalists work in the Soviet Union have improved, but they continue to live in ghettos. Soviet agents follow them. The Soviet press has launched vicious and utterly unwarranted attacks upon some as spies. In February 1977, the Soviet Government expelled a responsible American journalist, George Krimsky, apparently because Krimsky was maintaining contact with Soviet dissidents. This first expulsion since 1970 was followed by American retaliation against a TASS reporter in Washington. The Soviet Union continues to deny Western states the right to open reading rooms. It even censors Western publications which it imports under the International Copyright Convention for its research institutions. For example, the editors of *Science* discovered that Soviet officials are violating the contract under which they purchase and reproduce a number of copies of *Science,* by blotting out some articles, news items, editorials and letters to the editor before they distribute the issues.

Travel remains tightly controlled. For instance, American soil scientists in 1976 were not allowed to travel to areas which the Soviet Government had previously agreed would be opened to them, and Western scholars encounter difficulties in obtaining research travel. Indeed, the scholars responsible for administering the academic exchange programs note that the fundamental problems which appeared in 1958 still exist. Many Soviet citizens who have relatives abroad are denied the opportunity to leave the Soviet Union, even to visit. The Western press is full of information concerning Soviet citizens, especially Jews, who are not only not allowed to emigrate but are severely penalized for seeking exit visas. The Soviet Government, and the East European states subsequently, even denied visas to the Commission on Security and Cooperation in Europe of the American Congress, which visited Europe in November 1976 as part of a fact-finding and review process of developments since Helsinki.

Above all, Soviet, Czechoslovak, East German, and to some degree Polish and Rumanian treatment of dissidents in the past two years has raised a great threat to cultural exchange and competition. The arrest of a number of prominent Soviet dissidents, such as Andrei Tvordokhlebov of Amnesty International, Yuri Orlov of the Public Group to promote the Observance of the Helsinki Agreement in the USSR, and Alexander Ginsburg, a leading advocate of human rights, all darken the scene because of the dramatic character of these assaults on human rights, which are fundamental to any honorable intellectual exchange.

Similarly, the East German Government's banning of Wolf Biermann, an utterly loyal communist, for his songs in Hamburg, the house arrest of Robert Havermann, and the modulated pressures against West Berlin because about 100,000 East Germans have requested exit visas all remind Americans that the Berlin Wall and the death strips survive as denials of the qualities on which cultural exchange, indeed any kind of peaceful relations, rest. The ferocious attacks upon those who signed Charter 77 in Czechoslovakia and the arrest of some of those most prominent in the request that the Czechoslovak Government honor its own constitution, a number of other agreements, and the Final Act, also indicate that failure to honor the promises of Helsinki is not confined to the Soviet Union and East Germany.

THE PARADOXICAL REVERSALS OF POSITION ON HELSINKI

The long negotiations about security and cooperation in Europe and the Final Act itself have proved far more significant than most Western observers thought likely. In fact, by the spring of 1977, both the Soviet Union and the United States had reversed the positions they had adopted eighteen months earlier, in one of the most striking paradoxes of recent international politics. At the time of the signing and for several months afterwards, the Soviet Union in particular praised the Helsinki Pact as a great achievement, one which marked the end of the Second World War and ensured stability in Eastern Europe through exchanged pledges of the inviolability of frontiers. In short, the Soviet view of the pact emphasized the past, and the Final Act is an important element in a Soviet defensive position.

On the other hand, most Western leaders signed the Final Act with reluctance. Most Western peoples, as well as dissidents in the Soviet Union and Eastern Europe, were deeply critical of the West for "sanctifying" the Soviet position in Eastern Europe and the Soviet Union's acquisition of 114,000 square miles of territory, in return for more Soviet promises of greater freedoms in the future. However, most Westerners now see some progress toward accepted Western standards and toward Helsinki commitments. Above all, they now believe that the Final Act offers dynamic possibilities for peaceful change within the conservative Soviet system.

Helsinki offers some promise for widening cultural exchange and competition, in part because the issue of human rights in the states which communists rule has emerged as a dramatic symbol, recognized as central for every person and every society, by those who restrict these rights and by those who struggle that they be honored. These rights, which are an essential part of Basket Three, are also included as Principle Seven of Basket One, which provides for "respect for human rights and fundamental freedoms, including the freedom of thought, conscience, religion, or belief." Discussion of their significance during the negotiations, the long and successful struggle to include them, and then, ironically, the Soviet acclaim of the Final Act all combined to raise this issue to an important position in international politics.

Moreover, the Final Act has provided a constitution or foundation which has legitimated and greatly encouraged the hopes of thousands of men and women in the Soviet Union and Eastern Europe that they will be able to enjoy a better and freer life. This reaction to the Final Act shows that hope springs eternal, that the desire for liberty never dies, even among privileged generations who had never known it. Those who have witnessed several times the "death" of the dissident movement have seen the civic courage and thrust for greater freedom rise again, this time based on an international agreement which the Soviet Government has lauded. The personal character and courage, the good sense and restraint, and the civilized way in which the dissidents have responded to their governments' often vicious reactions have contributed greatly to Western comprehension of the human rights issue within each state, of the differences which exist among societies, and of both the necessity for and the difficulties in cultural relations and competition.

Indeed, this issue has dramatized the central difference which divides East and West, one on which scholars and workers, Frenchmen and Swedes, radicals and conservatives, are united. While most people cannot understand the complicated equations which enter the SALT for both sides, everyone can understand human rights, their central importance, and the hazards raised when governments deny them. This knowledge and understanding is especially great because developments in Greece, Portugal and Spain during the Helsinki negotiations and since August 1975 have underlined the contrast between East and West and encouraged the hope that other states will follow the path which the Spain once ruled by Franco has taken.

Fortunately for the West, the changes in the Mediterranean authoritarian states have occurred at the same time as the leadership of the Spanish and Italian Communist Parties have apparently revised some central ideological positions. These men and their organizations, which have considerable influence in parts of Eastern Europe and occupy an important position in the international grouping of communist parties, for reasons of principle or political expediency also support the Western position on human rights and on relaxation of controls in general. This helps strengthen the Western position, sustain the East European dissidents in particular, and exert a restraining influence upon regimes sorely tempted to throttle those who seek their constitutional rights, to repress all who question such actions, and to restrict the free movement essential for cultural exchange and competition.

The inclusion of the profound statement concerning human rights in a document thirty-five governments signed has also made this issue as legitimate a part of the agenda concerning relations between East and West as trade relations and threats to security. The Final Act provides diplomats of all countries an opportunity for making enquiries and for pressing other governments to meet approved standards of behavior. It therefore acts as a deterrent to the Soviet and East European governments. At the same time, and perhaps more important because treaties have not always deterred governments, it reminds the Soviet Government that it will pay a heavy price, including within many communist parties, if it violates agreements it sought so desperately and signed so enthusiastically.

Helsinki has excited profound scholarly, popular, and official support in the United States for these reasons and others. First, it represents both the culmination and the consequences of two decades of American experience in cultural exchange with the Soviet Union. As I indicated earlier, American scholars, the public, and the government support cultural exchange with the Soviet Union and Eastern Europe. Both sides have benefited; if they had not, the exchanges would not have survived. At the same time, American dissatisfaction has always been great and has increased over the years, in part because hopes were so high that conditions would improve. Moreover, continuation of the same pattern of problems and limitations has strained the attitudes of a people who consider change and improvement natural laws and who do not have the same sense of time and patience as some others, especially Russians. The period of exotic interest in the Soviet Union long ago ended. After twenty years, most scholars and artists want "to end scholarly tourism" and establish the kind of free movement with which all within Western society is familiar.

Developments which have occurred under detente have profoundly influenced these developments. Rightly or wrongly, most Americans believe that the Soviet Union has benefited significantly more than the United States from detente. The failure to make progress on MBFR, which was originally tied to Helsinki; "the great grain robbery;" disappointment concerning the absence of improvement in East German policies after *Ostpolitik;* the presence of thousands of Cuban troops in an Angola which had just liberated itself from Portuguese rule - factors such as these deeply influence the American view of Helsinki and American determination that its terms be honored.[7]

Helsinki has drawn increasing attention from Americans for other reasons as well. The principles Basket Two and Three emphasize are central in American history and tradition. The return of American interest to Europe after a decade of involvement in Southeast Asia has contributed. Moreover, a period marked by the effort to end discrimination and to increase opportunity for blacks, women's liberation, the movement against the war in Viet Nam, Watergate, and the exposure of improper CIA and FBI activities, would almost inevitably produce concentrated interest upon the free movement of men and ideas and upon human rights in world politics.

In addition, the growing interest of scientists in international politics has become an important factor. Scientists have acquired a new concern in politics because of their appreciation of the role science and scientists play in modern technology, in national and international environment issues, in the exchange programs with the Soviet Union, in Pugwash and other international conferences, and, above all, in war itself. This interest has been a most important element stimulating their work for peaceful relations with the Soviet Union and increasing their understanding of the Soviet system and policy. The prestigious National Academy of Sciences and the large Federation of American Scientists have both become active in shaping American positions toward Helsinki. The National Academy of Sciences' cable to the Soviet Academy of Sciences in the fall of 1973 that any action depriving Sakharov of his rights would end scientific exchanges not only helped to preserve Sakharov's freedom, but illustrated dramatically the issue Sakharov raised and the power scientists wield. Indeed, the participation of American scientists over the past two decades in the Soviet-American cultural exchange has helped educate them concerning the ethics of science itself, the right of scientists to travel, and the need to protect freedom of inquiry and expression everywhere.

The threat to Sakharov in 1973 and to Solzhenitsyn in February 1974 and Soviet refusal to permit Sakharov to visit Oslo to accept the Nobel Prize in December 1975 helped to stimulate still another significant American response, the decision of the Congress early in the summer of 1976 to establish a joint Commission on Security and Cooperation in Europe to monitor observance of Helsinki and to advocate new steps toward security and peace. The election of Carter in November 1976 in a sense culminated the process of this approach toward Helsinki, especially human rights. In short, the Carter letter to Sakharov in February 1977 is part of a pattern which was developing throughout the 1970s, and will continue throughout the foreseeable future.

This escalation coincides with, and has been enlivened and strengthened by the dissident movements in the Soviet Union, Poland, Czechoslovakia, and East Germany. Pasternak, Sakharov, Solzhenitsyn, Amalrik, Bukovsky, and their courageous friends have helped educate millions. At the same time, Western knowledge of and interest in dissatisfactions and the dissident movements have helped both to stimulate and protect critics within the Soviet systems.

THE SIGNIFICANCE OF HELSINKI

On the American side, the reversal of position constitutes one of the most important consequences of Helsinki. This American view of Helsinki, particularly of the civil rights factor, makes the Final Act and its fulfilment burning symbols at a time when no other understandable issue dominates relations between the Soviet Union and the United States. It unites opinion in the United States, and it also brings the United States, its European allies, and even its most bitter critics among the neutral states together, not only with regard to the Soviet Union but also with regard to justice, human dignity, and the precedence of human rights in South Africa and Chile. At the same time, it has revived discussion concerning the nature of communism in a world-wide debate involving socialists and communists outside the Soviet Union. The remarkable evolution of Spain towards democracy and of Portugal to free its empire and to begin its own transformation, at a time when the Soviet Union remains frozen, dramatizes the issue and deeply affects views and policies of communists everywhere, notably in Italy and Spain. The new attitudes toward pluralism and peaceful change by these parties, the criticisms of the Soviet Union by even the most staunch defenders of Stalinism, and the discussions which led to the East Berlin conference of communist parties in the summer of 1976 all demonstrate that the impact of Helsinki has spread far beyond its anticipated limits.

THE DILEMMAS

The basic difficulty between the Soviet Union and the United States reflects the eternal contest between authority and freedom, between the state established on Lenin's ideas and that on those of Jefferson. The concentration camp and the Berlin Wall, the open library and the travelling scholar, are its appropriate symbols.

In addition, unrelated to any philosophical or ideological difference, the Soviet Union and the United States are suspicious rival powers, sparring against each other, consciously measuring advantages and disadvantages in every relationship. Their national interests differ. Moreover, the two states and societies differ greatly from each other, with some in each society convinced that that society is morally superior, stronger, and sure to triumph. One state is an open, pluralistic political and social democracy with an advanced industrial economy, and the other is a closed, unitarian, proudly authoritarian state which has been trying to catch up with, or overtake and surpass the West since the time of Peter the Great. Cooperation between states is always difficult, but it is especially complicated when the states are sensitive, are not entirely equal, and view the world through different sets of glasses.

The Soviet dilemma

The Soviet leaders clearly believe that the Final Act achieved great advantages for the Soviet Union. However, it has also led to an ever-increasing price, not only in stimulating and to some degree legalizing dissidence but also in exposing the system's major flaws and opening the character of the system to question. Soviet diplomats have sought to restrict these impacts by emphasizing "strict observance of the laws, customs, and traditions of each other" and "respect for the principles of sovereignty and noninterference." Insistence that coexistence does not apply to ideology or that the two systems can compete in every way except ideas is much like Nicholas I's search for a fire that would not burn. Cultural exchanges, trade, construction of factories in remote Soviet areas by Italian workers, importation of Western computers, the signature of agreements assuring human rights - all these introduce outside ideas into a previously closed system. The Soviet Union cannot be in the world, but not of it. It cannot join the world in every aspect but one, that of ideas, which inevitably enter along with the scientists, artists, and machinery it welcomes in order to strengthen the system and its economy. Moreover, the relaxation of controls within Eastern Europe, which is far more vulnerable than the Soviet Union to Western ideas, helps introduce these same virulent concepts into the Soviet Union. Intellectually, or ideologically, Eastern Europe is a carrier, not a barrier. How long can the Soviet Union tolerate the infections, the defectors, the dissidents, the clamour? What price must it pay to close the Pandora's box loosed by detente and the Final Act. Will hope in fact return submissively to the box?

The American dilemma

The American dilemma is as acute. At the moment, the West has an apparent advantage in the eternal struggle with authoritarianism, aided in good part by the cultural exchange agreements, increased trade, and the Final Act, all of which serve to loosen the Soviet system somewhat. However, the exchange agreements themselves are a violation of the Western view that information and men should move freely among societies, without restraints of any kind. The agreements are like reciprocal tariff treaties. They provide for barter and horse-trading of artists, basketball players, language teachers, and scholars, just as though these men and women were bales of cotton. They also make cultural exchange and scholarly cooperation an essential element of foreign policy, subject therefore to restrictions imposed by two governments and dependent on diplomatic priorities unrelated to intellectual life. In fact, this kind of arrangement, which puts governments and their bureaucracies in control of cultural exchange, is an extension of Soviet practice into the glades of Western intellectual freedom.

Moreover, many Americans, particularly those who reflect upon the progress of the last twenty years, are convinced that the United States should not have cultural agreements with countries which are repressive, which censor information, harass and imprison critical scholars and other citizens, license and reward subservient intellectuals, and in general violate the precepts which are vital for civilized life. Indeed, they criticize agreements or other formal arrangements with such governments, because they are morally demobilizing and intellectually corrupting. They give respectability, dignity, and legitimacy to systems which openly flout their constitutions and charters which they sign.

In short, Americans face the dilemma which dealing with authoritarian regimes creates for democratic societies. They have begun to learn to live with totalitarian states, but their appreciation of the dilemma divides them on one hand, unites them on the other, and persuades the great majority that the way out of the dilemma is to press ever more resolutely and skillfully for the end of restraints, wherever they may be.

THE FUTURE

No one can predict with any confidence the future of this competition, which is part of a larger struggle and which will remain a long, gruelling contest. President Carter's vivid interest in cultural relations and human rights may assist toward joint progress in relaxing controls and expanding cooperation, as well toward concluding SALT II, ending all nuclear tests, and proceeding toward disarmament. On the other hand, American and Western determination to stand by their ancient values may lead the Soviet rulers to retreat to old fortresses and to be ever less cooperative in negotiations on disarmament and crisis management. In any case, progress will, at best, be grudging and slow.

Many observers believe that some Soviet leaders are beginning to appreciate that the old repressions will no longer work. They view the revival of the human spirit in Eastern Europe and the Soviet Union as part of an irreversible, irresistible force, as elemental as the growth of grass in the spring, which affects the advantaged third-generation communist as it does the Lithuanian Catholic or the Armenian nationalist. They see this continual "spring" as another illustration of the invincible power of ideas, flowing this time from the West to the East. They ask: can authoritarianism survive in an ever-smaller, interdependent world in which revolutions in transportation and communication are bringing about the unbinding of all customs and controls?

Other observers see cultural exchange and competition as an unimportant element in international politics, in which technology, raw power, political organization, and determined leadership will move the entire world toward a universal authoritarian system or at least a series of powerful despotic states. They suggest that plural, open, free societies cannot survive in this struggle, particularly because the West has lost its cohesion, spiritual base, and nerve. They ask: can or will the Soviet system change? Are communism and liberty irreconcilable? Can democracy survive?

Both views are no doubt too cataclysmic. Today's conflict more resembles the Eastern Question or the Reformation than the fall of the Roman Empire or 1812.

Some proposals

The process of multilateral negotiations begun with the CSCE has far more importance than anyone thought possible in August, 1975. The thought and care with which the United States and the other Western states conduct negotiations will be especially important, because their position must represent Western values and strategies, reflect and sustain public support, and help move both sides into ever more constructive and cooperative policies. The United States must assist those who share Western values and who seek to move their States towards establishing open, free, and peaceful societies. It must encourage private citizens and organizations everywhere, because reliance upon the individual is a cardinal quality of Western society and because this issue is too critical to be left solely to governments.

The United States should continue to provide a helpful, constructive critique of the achievements and failures of the Soviet Union, the East European states, and of the United States itself in honoring the Final Act. It should seek to avoid a slanging match, but should press toward its basic goals - the elimination of restraints, such as jamming and censorship, and the expansion of freedoms. Jamming and censorship are in fact the true obscenities of this era. Progress in expanding trade should be related to progress in eliminating these controls.

The United States should welcome and encourage suggestions from other participants which seek to move beyond Helsinki toward greater security and cooperation. It should also try to move the discussion to a new, cooperative level by advancing proposals, with a specific agreed target date, which will promote American interests and those of the world so far as Americans can understand them.

These might include:

(1) Re-establishing the Informational Media Guarantee Program for the East European states, assisting them to overcome hard currency shortages in the purchase of American publications and films. The West European and North American states might together sponsor such a program for all Western publications and films. By January 1, 1979.

(2) Establishing common passport and visa requirements for all signatory states. By January 1, 1980.

(3) Agreement that travel be as free among all signatory states as it is now within the West European states. By January 1, 1981.

(4) Establishment of a large international program, a combination of Rhodes Scholarship and Fulbright Fellowship, under an international selection committee, enabling a number of outstanding young men and women (the number proportionate to the size of each nation's population and the funding by contributions from each state, based on relative GNP) to travel and study freely in the other part of Europe, for two or three year periods. By January 1, 1982.

(5) Establishment of a bookstore in university territory in Moscow in which any Soviet institution or citizen may buy any Western book with Soviet currency, as Westerners can purchase Soviet and East European publications in Soviet stores in many Western cities. This store might also serve as a central purchasing center for Soviet books, magazines, newspapers and films for Western educational institutions and individuals, using the rubles obtained from sales to purchase Soviet publications and the hard currencies from Western institutions and individuals to purchase the Western volumes for the bookstore. A Swiss or Swedish university should assume administrative responsibility. By January 1, 1983.

(6) Ending all cultural agreements, enabling individuals and publications to move freely from country to country, and encouraging institutions to make their own arrangements with each other, as they did in the Middle Ages and as they do today in the West. By January 1, *1984*.

NOTES

1. Isaiah Berlin, "The Silence in Russian Culture," *Foreign Affairs*, XXXVI Number 1 (October, 1957), 1-24.

2. Georgii Zhukov, "Cultural Contacts: Two Approaches," *International Affairs* (Moscow), *V*, Number 11 (November, 1959), 19-27; *Kommunist*, September, 1973, editorial; *Pravda*, January 5, January 6, 1973.

3. Senator Lyndon B. Johnson in the *New York Times,* January 28, January 29, 1958.

4. Joseph Quinn, *The Anatomy of East-West Cooperation: U.S.-U.S.S.R., Public Health Exchange Program 1958-1967* (Washington, 1969).

5. Robert F. Byrnes, *Soviet-American Academic Exchanges, 1958-1975* (Bloomington, 1976) 276 pp., provides detailed information concerning academic exchanges, and other cultural exchanges as well.

6. Sir George Weidenfeld, *The Publisher as Internationalist* (Denver, 1971), 2.

7. Soviet participants in this conference will naturally speak concerning the Soviet view of the benefits both sides have obtained from Helsinki. The Soviet Union legitimately complains that the United States continues to delay and deny visas, a policy many Americans hope new legislation will revise, even though most trade union leaders will find it difficult to accept men like Shelepin as genuine union officials. However, legislation cannot remove the considerable difference between the number of Soviet books which Americans translate and publish and the number of American novels published in the Soviet Union because Soviet literature, and even the finest Soviet films, simply do not interest Americans (or other Westerners, for that matter). Other Soviet complaints are beyond remedy and derive from the simple fact that the United States and the West exist: Soviet ballet dancers will therefore continue to defect, emigrants will leave and be welcomed, dissidents excited and honored, gallant underdogs and rebels supported. Neither the American Government nor the Americans could or would adopt policies to help resolve these issues for the Soviet Government.

10

Influencing Soviet Policy by Western Trade Restrictions: Some Reflections

INTRODUCTION

Most informed observers throughout the world consider Soviet-American relations so crucial in this age of intercontinental nuclear ballistic missiles that they concentrate their energies on trying to identify and remove the causes of conflict and to devise ways of reducing tensions. These relations occupy a central position in the agendas of the Soviet and American people and of the Soviet and American Governments and in international politics. Each side seeks ways of increasing its own power and authority and of weakening the military power and resolution and the political stability of the other. Moreover, whenever the rival state enjoys a temporary advantage or commits an action the other considers especially damaging or outrageous, the weakened or offended state adopts measures to overcome the advantage or to penalize the offending state.

Each state naturally uses its strengths as it jockeys for power and position. The apparent relative balance of military power and the hazards of using military force to respond to offensive actions and the complications and disadvantages for ourselves and our allies at revising our political and cultural policies have led the United States to resort to using its great scientific, technical, and economic supremacy through trade restrictions and embargoes to exercise leverage on Soviet policy. Boycotting the 1980 Olympic Games, the grain embargo, and tightened restrictions on Soviet access to high-quality American industrial products, grain, and equipment of direct military use were therefore prompt and temporarily popular and effective responses to the Soviet invasion of Afghanistan, to Western annoyance at Soviet violations of human rights, even as defined in the Soviet constitution and in the Helsinki Agreement, and to various other Soviet barbarisms.

This paper examines the vulnerability of the Soviet economy to restrictive trade policies toward the Soviet Union and suggests that such policies have considerable limitations, in spite of the Soviet system's grave economic weaknesses and of the immense advantages the United States and its allies possess.

Reprinted with permission from *Annali di Dipartimento di Studi dele' Europa Orientale* (Naples), IV-V (1986), 361-365.

THE SOVIET ECONOMY

Western knowledge of developments within the Soviet Union has increased greatly in recent years. However, we still lack confident understanding of the core of men at the top who make the key decisions, of their perspectives, and of the way they react to developments beyond their boundaries.

We do know that a small, coherent group of dedicated party members use the party, the highly-centralized state apparatus, and the patriotism and passivity of the great majority of Soviet citizens to maintain effective direction throughout society. The Soviet Union has powerful military forces that continue to grow in strength and quality. It possesses the third largest economy in the world, one that from 1965 through 1980 or so grew rapidly and at the same time raised the standard of living considerably, supported a vast expansion of Soviet military strength, and extended Soviet authority into distant parts of the world.

However, foreign specialists on the Soviet economy believe that the Soviet Union faces grave economic, and therefore political problems. These problems are manageable in that they do not threaten the stability of the system, but they are the most fundamental the government has faced since the early 1920s.

The three principal economic difficulties the Soviet rulers face are the slowing of the economy's rate of growth, the growing gap in science and technology between the Soviet Union and the West in the industries at the crest of the most recent wave of the industrial revolution, and the dilemma the age of information or telematics creates for the Soviet system as knowledge becomes a vital resource essential to economic progress and competitiveness.

The Soviet economy has grown at an ever slower pace since the early 1950s. Most specialists believe it will expand in the foreseeable future at approximately two percent a year and perhaps even faces stagnation. Above all, they note that most industrial growth occurs in the old "smoke-stack" industries and that the relative absence of Soviet progress in the new series of industries responsible for much Western growth and for the renewed Western technological advance handicaps the Soviet Union in a most significant competition.

The main causes for the Soviet Union's economic problems are:

1. Long over-emphasis on rapid growth and on the expansion of military forces and of empire, the resultant neglect of economic and social infrastructures, such as housing, transportation, and public health, social problems such as low civic morale and alcoholism, and the substitution of subsidies and the import of Western science and technology in the 1970s for the economic innovations already clearly necessary. The Soviet Union must now pay a penalty for deferring economic modernization. Perhaps the most critical economic-political issue is that the Soviet Union cannot sustain past improvements in the consumer economy for the foreseeable future. The intense competition for resources because of the "deferred tasks of modernization," now becoming increasingly dysfunctional and extremely

expensive to correct, and the increasingly serious distortions in the distribution of major inputs in the Soviet economy make it difficult, if not impossible, for the leaders even to maintain present consumption levels.

2. The coming together in the 1980s of a series of converging economic issues, all inescapably related to each other and to the Soviet Union's international position and all difficult, if not impossible to solve, because of these relationships. This is especially true in the succession cycle through which the Soviet leadership is passing, a process that makes decisive action on delicate and complicated issues especially difficult. For example, accepting substantial change in Poland now would threaten the survival of the communist system there, as elsewhere in Eastern Europe, and would intensify economic-political issues within the Soviet Union.

3. The declining rate of growth of population, making impossible the traditional solution (using new labor forces) to overcome declining productivity. Moreover, the only significant demographic increase, among the Turkish Muslims in Central Asia, raises other complicated problems for economic planning and for the military forces.

4. The nature of the system itself. Soviet society has many strengths, but the enforced acceptance of authority, passivity, and inertia are handicaps in a situation that now demands innovation and change. Encouraging initiative and enterprise in an authoritarian system is a contradiction in terms, and signs of creativity from below would almost certainly lead to the same renewed control from the top that the "100 Flowers" did in China.

Second, the new industrial age, based on knowledge and the production of knowledge, requires free access to information if a society is to obtain full advantage from the new communications systems and computer technology. Nothing is more hazardous to the Soviet system than open availability of facts, because control remains the essential word.

Third, the shortened life-cycles of the new technologies, that rely heavily on the role of innovative individuals and small firms in the rapid race for new products, make it ever more difficult for the centralized economy to catch up. Paradoxically, the pressures of these rapidly-changing advances make the Soviets cling more tenaciously to centralized control in order to channel scarcer resources to high priority sectors.

Fourth, genuine economic reform, decentralization, would encounter a number of powerful obstacles: the nationality issue, because decentralization would enhance the economic autonomy of areas where minorities predominate; growing competition for regional development (older European industrial republic vs Central Asian and Siberian developments); and fierce competition for scarce resources among sectoral competitors, the military, industrial modernization, agriculture and the consumer sector, and infrastructural needs.

Above all, the Soviet system, one of the most conservative in the world and one that lacks reform mechanisms, rests on the control a small group at the center exercises over the entire country. Many Soviet economists recognize that decentralizing the established economy is essential. Almost all outside observers agree, and note as well that progress in the critical new industries rests on individual enterprise, small firms, and the easy diffusion of technology throughout the industrial system - for which decentralization is absolutely fundamental. However, decentralizing the economy would represent an abrupt reversal of Soviet policy and would constitute an ideologically unacceptable hazard to the rulers' values and authority. It would threaten the fundamental character of the system and the privileges which millions of Soviet citizens - party and state officials, managers, officers, academics, foremen, etc., - now enjoy. These men are in a position to blunt or check any changes threatening their advantages.

In short, the Soviet leaders must choose between the disagreeable and the intolerable, a choice they have confronted for a number of years and remain unable to resolve because of the character of the problems and disagreements about the best way to approach them.

The consequences these problems raise are fundamental. The slowing down or stagnant growth of the economic pie raises painful issues concerning the division of resources among the military, who have always received top priority and whose prestige and the achievements of Soviet foreign policy now constitute the bases of the system's legitimacy; investment, which more than ever needs an increase to stimulate productivity and to enable the Soviet Union to remain respectable as a world power; and the worker, who has no incentive to work harder because of the absence of adequate supplies of high quality consumer goods. In short, the economics of scarcity raise difficult political problems, compounded by the conflict among regions of the country concerning new investment.

Soviet military power will continue to grow because of internal Soviet reasons, even if the Soviet Union and the United States should complete a number of arms control agreements. In addition, increased American military power, and the almost certainty that Japan and China will also enlarge their armed strength (largely as a reaction against the growth of Soviet military power and the character of Soviet foreign policy) create a situation in which the Soviet Government will feel it imperative to give ever larger shares of Soviet economic resources to the military forces, thereby reducing the likelihood the economy can resume rapid growth and increasing the tensions within Soviet society.

Slow growth has also occurred just when the problems of maintaining the empire have become increasingly expensive, perhaps as much as forty billion dollars a year. Eastern Europe in the 1950s contributed to the economic growth of the Soviet Union: it now constitutes a heavy drain, with Poland the outstanding illustration. Thus, Eastern Europe's requirements for oil and gas grow just as the Soviet Union needs to sell increasing quantities to the West to pay for the grain and other products it imports. Allowing or encouraging the East European states to purchase oil elsewhere and therefore to become more active in the world economy would threaten Soviet control over an area its leaders consider absolutely essential to the security and stability of the Soviet Union itself. Cuba, Viet Nam, Afghanistan, and various African areas of interest also press continuous demands upon the Soviet state.

The effort of Russian leaders since Peter the Great, through Witte, Stalin, and Brezhnev, to make the country a powerful industrialized state has been one of "catching up," in Peter the Great's phrase, or "overtaking and surpassing," in Stalin's words. Unfortunately for the Soviet leaders, the West does not stand still. Throughout their history, the Russians have "caught up" with the West, only to have the outside world develop new techniques and new industries, and leap further ahead. In brief, as Masaryk once said, "Russia is what the West was." Thus, the Soviet Union began to produce more steel than any other country just when the West launched a series of fundamental changes that rest on miniature electronics, automatic machinery, robots, and millions of computers. The stretched-out Soviet economy simply lacks the resources and the organizational arrangements to enter this new competition. Soviet history reminds one of Sysyphus, almost always reaching the top, only to have the boulder roll down the hill again, leading to another painful but fruitless effort.

While it reveres science, emphasizes education and recognizes the importance of "the "scientific and technical revolution," the Soviet Union lacks a significant capacity to make new scientific and technical advances and even to adopt effectively and then to improve technical developments from other countries.

Germany, the United States, and Japan for long periods of time borrowed capital and ideas from more advanced countries, but were then able to advance independently into leadership positions. The Soviet Union, generally, has not been able to follow this pattern: since the Second World War, for example, it has not demonstrated Japan's capacity to borrow, improve upon, and export throughout the world scientific and technical discoveries of other people. Imagine the plight of the West if Soviet automobiles, television sets, motorcycles, and computers flooded the United States!

"Catching up" is both critical and perilous in the combination of technologies which are creating "the age of information." The Soviets have always recognized the perils of borrowing from others: the periods in the last three hundred years in which the Russians have borrowed most intensively from the West have also been those of the most repressive governments. The age which the West is now entering requires free access to information. The Soviet Government is therefore condemned to backwardness if it does not enter this age, as it would have been handicapped if it had rejected nuclear power or jet engines. On the other hand, the regime could hardly survive the kind of access to data which a computer-based economy requires.

WESTERN CAPACITY TO INFLUENCE
THE SOVIET UNION

The Western world should first recognize that there is no likelihood whatsoever that the Soviet Union will become a political democracy or that it will collapse in the foreseeable future, and very little likelihood that it will become a congenial or peaceful member of the international community for as far ahead as one can see.

It should also recognize that the Soviet Union is an important part of the world and participates in the world economy. The West cannot restrict that participation and it should not attempt to do so. The United States and its allies should accept this, even facilitate it, seek to obtain as many legitimate benefits as possible from Soviet participation in the world economy, and concentrate upon establishing a coherent and coordinated program of preventing the export of information and equipment that would directly help increase Soviet military strength.

The United States and its allies would violate their own national interests, prospects for peaceful change in the Soviet Union, and the likelihood of peace if they set out to strengthen the Soviet regime by assisting its rulers to resolve their economic and other problems. We would receive no benefit from contributing to the strength and stability of the Soviet state, which by denying human rights to its people, multiplying fear and suspicion by maintaining strict secrecy concerning its military forces and their operations, and remaining a threat to its neighbors constitutes a destabilizing force in the world.

Our goal should be a Soviet Government more tolerable for its citizens and less threatening to the outside world, but our capacity to change the system or to reduce its authority is limited, as are our capacities to affect greatly the nature and policies of other states, large and small.

Our capacities are limited for a number of reasons. First, the Soviet leaders are determined to increase Soviet strength and to remain independent of outside states, because their first goal is to maintain their own positions and communist rule. Second, the Soviet economy is more able than most to muddle along with even reduced economic ties with the outside world because of Soviet natural resources, Soviet emphasis on economic autarchy, and the toughness and submissiveness of its population. In addition, American embargo efforts have produced a natural Soviet shift away from trade with United States to that with other "more reliable" countries, so that earlier restrictive efforts have increased Soviet invulnerability.

Anyone who believes that communists will yield to internal or external pressures should review recent history, especially that of Poland, which illustrates the lengths to which a small group of determined leaders will go to preserve their rule. The capacity of earlier Russian governments, and of the Soviet Union since 1917, to borrow from the outside world while at the same time preserving the system also demonstrates this ability. Comparing the changes in Spain since Franco, of Portugal since Salazar, and of China since Mao with the immobility of the Soviet Union since Stalin suggests the character and durability of the Soviet system. One should note too that Soviet policies have not changed greatly - although some tinkering and shallow and temporary relaxing have impressed some foreign observers - whether Western trade with the Soviet Union were up or down, and whether relations were relaxed or cool.

Historically, trade has not affected political systems or policies. France and Germany, Germany and Russia, Nazi Germany and the Soviet Union - all were close trading partners, and all went to war against each other. Neither the use of inducements nor pressures has had productive records in this century. American aid to other underdeveloped countries in the last three decades demonstrates that creating beneficial, open change requires traditions and circumstances that are rare, and are absent totally in the Soviet Union. Western trade and credit programs in the 1970s did not modify the Soviet system or its policies. The embargoes directed against Franco's Spain, Japan in the 1930s, and South Africa in more recent times have leaked like sieves and were in fact counter-productive, as they would be if directed against the Soviet Union. Indeed, embargoes have been effective only when directed against small and weak states. Moreover, Soviet internal and external policy would almost inevitably harden in reaction to an embargo, with the likelihood of well-organized popular support from a people accustomed to hardship. The likelihood of peaceful internal change would decline and the Soviets would have at least some success in creating domestic alternatives to the products denied.

In addition, within the United States, inducements or embargoes would intensify political divisions, upon which the Soviet leaders would play with some skill. Popular annoyance or outrage because of particular Soviet policies is short-lived in democracies, and of especially brief duration among farmers, trade unionists, manufacturers of export goods, scientists, and other well-organized interest groups that restrictive policies affect directly. American farmers or machine tool makers or scientists would oppose "denial" policies that they thought directly affected their interests. European neutrals would take advantage of an embargo to supply the Soviets missing ingredients. Other countries, Argentina or Brazil or Australia or . . . would cooperate with the Soviets to undermine any effort directly to hamper the Soviet economy. Above all, our allies would resent, oppose, and frustrate an embargo, largely because of their strictly regional view of the Soviet Union and its policies, the short-term character of popular outrage, and the power of political-economic groups an embargo would affect. In short, attempting an embargo would deeply separate the allies from the United States and present the Soviet Union splendid opportunities for widening the fissures. General Marshall once noted that we should never enter a conflict we cannot win. An embargo would constitute such a situation.

Moreover, an embargo violates our own principles and interests. The United States seeks an open world, one in which ideas, information, men, and trade flow freely, not only because a democratic society can survive and grow best in such circumstances but also because free exchange of all kinds offers the best hope that other countries will become ever more open and that peaceful relations will prevail. We should not inflict injuries upon ourselves by adopting restrictive policies.

Conclusions

1. The Soviet economy, like all economies, exhibits several visible weaknesses, especially its almost stagnant rate of growth and its trailing the West in those industries at the crest of the new wave of the scientific-technical revolution.

2. Limited Soviet economic resources and the refusal of the Soviet rulers to decentralize the economy and to encourage innovation in a population inured to passivity hamper solutions of the fundamental problems and Soviet progress in the new technologies.

3. The Unites States and its allies should define an agreed set of goals, strategic concept, and policy for defense, trade, and cultural relations. These should also rest on the assumption that no likelihood exists that the Soviet Union will become a political democracy or that it will collapse and very little likelihood that it will become a congenial member of the international community in the foreseeable future.

4. Soviet economic shortcomings tempt Western publics and governments to seek influence upon Soviet policies through trade. However, trade is a delicate, two-edged instrument, especially for a democracy subject to economic-political pressures and a member of an alliance whose states' economic interests are rarely in harmony. Moreover, democracies thrive best in, indeed require, an open world in which men, information, and goods flow freely. Such circumstances also provide the best hope that other countries will become more open and that peaceful relations will prevail.

5. We, with our allies, should define an agreed set of goals, strategic concept, and policy that bring together defense, trade, cultural relations, and human rights. On trade policy, we should learn from our twenty-five years of experience with academic exchanges, on which our government, universities, and scholars (who correspond to economic interest groups that have a deep interest in trade) have defined agreed goals and procedures that reflect our principles, provide each of the two countries advantages of different kinds but of approximately equal weight, and have survived the changes in the temperature of Soviet-American relations.

6. We should encourage the Soviet Union to participate actively in the world economy. It is a part of the world. We cannot seek to exclude it from normal trade arrangements without damaging ourselves, but we should give it no special advantages. We should give high priority to obtaining agreement among all states that trade with the Soviet Union that none will offer special benefits in prices, facilities, or credit terms different from commercial arrangements available to other states.

7. Soviet access to ideas and equipment of direct military utility constitutes a distinct issue which we should separate sharply from others. We should give a high priority to a cooperative effort with our allies and friends through COCOM to define carefully that information and those technologies and equipment that we should all deny to the Soviet Union because they would directly increase Soviet military capabilities, which is clearly not in our interest. We should also establish an effective system for continuing review of ideas and information which have a dual use, i.e., can make a direct military contribution and can also strengthen the economy. This is a central issue which we should separate from other trade issues. It is so critical and complicated that avoiding futile and counterproductive

sanctions on general trade, which would impede Western cooperation on limiting Soviet access to technology with direct military applications, is particularly important.

8. All who criticize the Olympic boycott, trade embargoes, or restrictive trade amendments should recognize that the American public, and the peoples of other democratic societies as well, will on occasion properly demand some official response to outrageous Soviet domestic or foreign policies. These critics, and everyone concerned about American policy, should therefore concentrate their efforts upon designing other policies that will penalize the Soviet Union without dividing or otherwise harming the West.

9. Some actions American leaders and those of our allies should consider for joint action to respond to Soviet threats or indecencies include, in ascending order of magnitude:

(a) Reducing the size of the staff of Soviet embassies, and affiliated groups such as trade organizations and media representatives, to the same number in each Western state that that state maintains in the Soviet Union.

(b) Closing consulates, such as the Soviet consulate in San Francisco.

(c) Reducing or ending various scientific, technical, and cultural exchanges.

(d) Reducing the size of embassy staffs.

(e) Withdrawing ambassadors.

10. We should increase greatly popular knowledge and understanding of the Soviet Union and of the world in which we live. In a democratic society, policy necessarily and properly requires public support: the most sensible policies will be effective only when the public understands and endorses them.

11

The USSR in the 1980s and Beyond

INTRODUCTION

Determining accurately what has happened in another culture, especially the Soviet Union, is difficult. Analyzing today's developments is even more puzzling, and making judgments concerning the next ten or fifteen years in the Soviet Union is hazardous in the extreme. This is especially so because none of us is objective concerning that rival. Our knowledge of the society as a whole is new, rests largely on study from afar, and suffers from sharply restricted access to information. We also lack confident understanding of the relationships among the leaders of the Soviet Union and above all of the ways their minds work. Moreover, we live in a world that is changing rapidly in every way. No one can anticipate the impact of social and intellectual developments, or of economic or scientific transformations, even within his own society: no forecasters in 1945 even mentioned the computer. Finally, of course, no one can foresee catastrophes or events as influential as the escalation of oil prices in 1973 or the overthrow of the Shah in 1979.

Nevertheless, observers benefit from a vastly expanded range of knowledge and an international research base that has examined practically every aspect of Soviet society. In addition, while changes will continue to occur in the Soviet Union, the USSR is a remarkably stable and conservative system, one that not only lacks a mechanism for change but is conditioned to resist innovation.

THE GORBACHEV LEADERSHIP

The accession to leadership of Gorbachev in February 1985 and his bringing into positions of authority men from his generation does raise the possibility of changes in policy and, perhaps, ultimately in the system itself. These may sharply affect Soviet power and even more the perceptions foreigners have of the Soviet Union and its policies.

It is difficult to define Gorbachev's goals and his ability to achieve them. He and those who rule with him share the values and qualities of

Reprinted with permission from *U.S. Policy toward the Soviet Union. A Long-Term Perspective, 1987-2000,* Andrew J. Goodpaster, ed., (Lanham, MD: University Press of America, 1988), 155-170.

those who selected them, embrace and benefit from the communist system, and view the world in much the same way as their predecessors did. However, they entered political life after Stalin's death, they have had different experiences and have acquired different knowledge and ideas, and they have gradually set aside the stable, aged, oligarchy who ruled such a long time. They are more aware of the acute character of Soviet problems and more eager "to get the country going" than their elders have been. Debates among them over particular issues and the rate of change do occur, and those jostling for place and power may advocate particular changes they believe necessary to advance the interests of their bureaucratic or territorial constituencies or simply to increase their personal power. Our knowledge of relations among those in the central circle of power is limited, but the leadership has been fundamentally collective for so long and the general agreement on policy has been so great that we must assume decisions will be reached within the Kremlin walls and that any increases, diminutions, or transfers of authority will be orderly and peaceful.

Gorbachev apparently seeks to create a flexible, dynamic, technologically advanced socialist state capable of competing effectively in political, economic, and military power with the Western democracies. At the same time, he expects to maintain the communist system in which he grew up and in which he has reached the leading position.

He has also given (the correct word) intellectuals and the media more freedom, he has released Sakharov and some other political prisoners, he has "pardoned" some dissenters, and he has emphasized the role of *glasnost'* throughout society. In foreign policy, he has accepted some Western arms control offers he had previously denounced, and the Soviets have made some attractive proposals of their own. But he has not concluded any arms control agreements, or made any significant revisions on Afghanistan, support of Viet Nam in Kampuchea, or his relations with the People's Republic of China, although he has created the impression he seeks changes. In short, in more than two years he has introduced only corrections or modifications, not major modifications in structure or policy. He has promised more than he has delivered, as do most statesmen and politicians.

Moreover, Gorbachev has encountered increasingly visible resistance to his domestic policies, from within the Politburo and the Central Committee and from provincial party officials, planners, managers, workers, intellectuals, subsidized groups, and others who have benefited from the system. He has also collided with the passivity and inertia that the system has long encouraged and that it now seeks somehow to energize. He rules peoples very different from those of China, and even more different from those of Portugal, Spain, or the Republic of Korea. Resistance to change is institutionalized throughout the party, the government, the main institutions, the economy, and the country as a whole. Any leader who seeks to innovate would need several years to consolidate his position, to remove those reluctant to change from their responsibilities, and to create a lasting coalition throughout the party, the government, and the vast country in order to overcome inertia and resistance and to enforce new ideas and approaches.

Somehow observers believe Gorbachev has firm control of power, that the Soviet Union has no alternative or rival leader, and that he is moving slowly because the opposition has deep roots and because the encouraged appearance of opposition increases Western sympathy for him and his policies. Others agree, but conclude that he is not certain of his long-range goals. Others surmise that he has not yet consolidated his authority and that he and those who support him are balancing between groups who oppose change, who seek slow and gradual change, and who seek a thorough restructuring of the economy and even of the political system. Some conclude that this dilemma will lead to the failure of any attempt at modernizing the system and the replacement of Gorbachev by someone less ambitious for change. Still others believe that this will persuade Gorbachev (perhaps already has) to concentrate power in his hands and then force through the changes he seeks, as Peter the Great and Stalin did. In this, he would seek especially the support of the intellectuals and approval of the outside world that Peter and Stalin received.

In short, no foreign observer, and perhaps even Gorbachev himself, can be certain of the extent of Gorbachev's authority, his goals, and the means he will use to achieve those aims. The nature of the system and the number and complexity of the problems suggest that Gorbachev or someone like him will acquire full authority and then seek to make the Soviet Union a technologically modern state. The nature of the scientific and technical revolution and of the shrinking world suggest that no authoritarian system can create the modern economy Gorbachev seeks.

In any case, the basic question is: can Gorbachev and the narrowly constituted elite, comfortable in its achievements and power, aware of the serious problems the USSR faces, but reluctant to face the hazards of change, generate the will to move innovatively to overcome stagnation, decline, and ever more serious future instabilities? Can they persuade the bureaucracy, the factory and farm managers, and the passive population to demonstrate the initiative and entrepreneurship that effective modern industrialization requires? Can they choose between the disagreeable and the intolerable? What will be the consequences of their decisions upon Soviet foreign policy? And what can the United States and its allies do to influence developments within the Soviet Union?

One can conclude with some confidence that the Soviet Union in the next decade or two will remain an authoritarian state controlled by a small group in the Communist Party and a powerful military state with an economy less able to compete with that of other advanced countries than now; that it will confront a set of fundamental, long-term, interrelated, and complicated economic, social and cultural problems even more critical than those its rivals face; and that these issues will require very demanding choices by the leaders, decisions for fundamental structural change that these men will remain reluctant to reach and would find difficult to put into effect. Throughout these years, the USSR is likely to muddle through or muddle down, but will not decline sharply or collapse. Its internal difficulties are such that the leaders, whoever they may be, will almost certainly devote more energy and resources to trying to resolve these problems and less to the empire beyond Eastern Europe, some of which may slip away. The Soviet Union will not become a congenial member of the international community, but will remain a destabilizing element in world politics.

IDEOLOGY

Pragmatists and reasonable men and women find it difficult to understand others who hold fixed ideas or dogmas. Marxism is irrelevant for the great majority of Soviet citizens, including many party members, but some elements of Marxism and of Leninism deeply affect those who rule and their advisers. These ideas create the framework and the atmosphere, or "the political culture," in which these men view the world and the vocabulary in which they think and express themselves. The Soviet leaders believe firmly that Communist Party rule as "the vanguard of the proletariat" is essential within the Soviet Union and that their government must use all resources necessary to sustain rule of those they consider communists elsewhere in the world.

They perceive the world as one in which two rival systems engage in permanent, implacable struggle for domination, a conflict in which they will inevitably triumph, if only after long and cruel conflict. They have successfully blended these Marxist and Leninist doctrines with Russian nationalism in a way that unites most Soviet peoples emotionally behind them. However, they lack the fervor and messianism of Lenin's generation.

THE POLITICAL SYSTEM

The Communist Party will retain control over the Soviet Union, with no likelihood of significant change, especially such as those Spain and Portugal have enjoyed since 1975. The Soviet peoples will remain fundamentally patriotic, loyal, satisfied, and submissive. Dissidences will survive, as will disaffections. In fact, both may increase within a framework the leaders consider manageable, if the current Soviet policy toward openness remains in effect. Disaffections will grow among the workers should living standards remain stagnant, as seems likely.

Debates over policies and disagreements on details will continue among the elites and no doubt among those few who exercise authority, but agreement upon coherent principles and above all on the primary need to maintain control will prevail. These debates occur within a group that combines political, military, economic, and social power. There are no significant institutional rivalries; the Soviet military forces are an inherent and fully enmeshed part of the political system.

Soviet policy will devote special interest to ensuring domestic controls and to maintaining Soviet military power in a world the rulers consider unstable and threatening. The military forces, as the foundation of the system's legitimacy and pride and of the Soviet Union's status as a world power, will retain their high priority in the assignment of economic and intellectual resources. The Soviet Union is an isolated state, supported only by clients, surrounded by hostile peoples and states (some ruled by communists), and facing the likelihood that Japan and China will enlarge and improve their military forces, in part because of fears Soviet policy has helped increase. The armed forces will almost certainly continue to improve in quality and strength, whether or not some arms control agreements on specific categories and numbers of weapons are concluded and whether or not some relaxation of world tensions occurs. They have powerful political and popular support; they represent an unquestioned military-industrial complex; they constitute the principal source of Soviet political influence in the world; and they will continue to reflect the Soviet rulers' fear of Western, especially American, science and technology, as weapons become ever more powerful and accurate.

The system's controls over the Soviet peoples will almost certainly remain complete, whether or not the government relaxes its controls over intellectual life in order to engage the support of Soviet intellectuals and to persuade the outside world the political system is changing drastically, because of the rulers' insistence upon complete authority, especially in uncertain times.

The Soviet rulers, whoever they may be, are likely to direct increased energy and resources inward over this period. This will reflect the acute character of long-neglected domestic problems; the instability of Eastern Europe, which the Soviet leaders consider an essential part of the Soviet empire; and the high costs of empire. The total costs of empire in the early 1980s (excluding defense outlays, but including export credits, military and economic assistance, covert activities, and implicit trade subsidies) was between thirty and forty billion dollars annually, compared to five or eight billion in 1971.[1] Moreover, these ventures abroad have produced deep frustrations and disappointments, beginning of course with China. The likelihood is high that the Angolan and Mozambique Governments, and perhaps that of Ethiopia, will turn against communism and the Soviet Union, strengthening the Soviet tendency to turning inward, continuing the break-up of any international communist organization, and profoundly shaking the faith of communists and noncommunists everywhere in the inevitable triumph of communism.

THE ECONOMY

The Soviet economy, in a splendid burst of growth from the mid-1960s until the early 1980s helped double the standard of living, transform the Soviet Union from a state that had to retreat embarrassingly in 1962 to one that today possesses military strength approximately equal that of the United States, and at the same time greatly expand the Soviet empire in Southeast Asia, the Middle East, Africa, and now Central America.

However, as Gorbachev and many of his associates appreciate, this economy faces acute, fundamental problems so interrelated that resolution appears almost impossible. Paradoxically, some problems are the consequence of the progress achieved and of the means adopted. Above all, they reflect the shortcomings inherent in the Soviet political system as well as the explosion of energy and of new scientific-technical developments in the advanced industrial states, especially the United States.

The central problem is the continuation of a long process of decelerating economic growth: most observers anticipate annual rates of growth of approximately two percent and perhaps basic stagnation. The fundamental cause of this is systemic, over-centralized control, planning, and management of an increasingly complex economic system for which centralization is now counter-productive. The labor supply will increase at only one third the rate at which it grew in the 1970s, and most of the increase will come from Muslim Turks, far removed from the traditional industrial centers, reluctant to move, and likely to become increasingly restive whether or not industrial growth increases greatly in their areas, close to restless fundamentalist Muslim countries. Productivity is only about forty percent that of the United States; the increases in investment goods and consumer supplies necessary to raise this would greatly reduce resources available for the military forces. Agriculture remains a comedy and a tragedy, burdened by the dead hand of the "city boys" and their system, the absence of incentives, and a price system that contributes eight or nine percent of the gross national product to subsidies. These destroy rural initiative and spoil urban residents in the same way as in Poland. The high cost of empire constitutes another essential part of the problem.

The decline of economic growth at a time when most other advanced economies are growing rapidly and changing in character weakens the Soviet Union's attraction as a model and its ability to compete with the United States in international politics. Above all, the resource stringency created by this basically fixed economic pie provides delicate and complicated problems of determining priorities in resource allocation. The international situation and their ideology together persuade the rulers that they must continue to devote thirteen or fourteen percent of the annual product to the military forces, perhaps even a higher percentage, especially of scarce scientific and technical resources. However, the economy can resume growth only if the government can allot increased resources to investment and to consumer goods.

In addition, the West does not stand still. Soviet progress in the old "smoke-stack" industries has slowed just when another wave of the industrial revolution, based on discoveries in science and on improved technology, has created a series of new industries for which the Soviet Union lacks human and material resources. Moreover, the shortened life-cycles of the new technologies that rely heavily on the role of innovative individuals and small firms in the rapid race for new products make it ever more difficult for a centralized economy to catch up. Paradoxically, the pressures of these rapidly-changing advances persuade the Soviets to cling tenaciously to centralized control in order to channel resources to high priority sectors. Finally, a central element of this new wave, called the age of information or telematics, has made knowledge more than ever the world's most important product, one transforming life in the advanced countries and causing a significant change in relations among peoples throughout the world. This revolution rests above all on open access to information, which constitutes a most serious challenge to authoritarian control. In short, the Soviet Union must somehow obtain the resources necessary to enter this new world of international telecommunications or fall behind, as it would have if it had rejected jet engines or nuclear power. But an age in which every microcomputer connected to a printer becomes a potential printing plant is far more hazardous for the system than unjammed radio broadcasts.

The slower rate of economic growth, deferred economic modernization, and the new era in science and technology, its products, and its potential therefore constitute fundamental problems. They are not immediately life-threatening, but they will become ever more acute the longer their resolution is delayed.

Gorbachev's program for the economy, as for Soviet life in general, has thus far provided more encouragement to innovate, promises of a better life under dynamic innovation, and cheer-leading rather than policies. The June 1987 session of the Central Committee may provide a clear description of specific policies, or may instead indicate that Gorbachev's reluctance to announce specific policies or rooted opposition are going to restrict changes to increased social discipline and rhetoric.

A number of Soviet economists for several years have appreciated the problems the economy faces, and their proposals resemble those Western economists have suggested and that Gorbachev publicly proclaims. However, Gorbachev in a feverish national and international publicity campaign first emphasized increased labor discipline and set out to destroy the cancers of corruption and alcoholism. He then transferred his talents to encouraging openness or publicity concerning the shortcomings of the economy, the sterility of cultural life, and the need for dynamism. This was designed to encourage attacks upon the "cake of custom" that encrusts the economy and to win the support of intellectuals for the "restructuring" essential. This has produced some effects that may spill over into the economy: even men such as Sakharov, whom Gorbachev released from exile in Gorki, support him as "the last best hope."

Basically, Gorbachev appears to seek to transform Gosplan and central planning institutions into "think tanks," the ministries into planning organizations, and enterprises into relatively independent concerns. Selected enterprises are allowed to decide the use of their earnings. However, he remains opposed to "market socialism," and the ability of "independent" enterprises to innovate effectively when they lack direct access to raw materials and markets and when prices remain fixed seems low. He has encouraged small family business in service industries, where rapid improvements are likely and popular approval sure to follow. Perhaps his most sensational decision was that to end the vast and expensive river diversion project, the planned investment in which he can now divert to more productive uses. If the draft decree now under consideration for allowing "joint ventures" in the Soviet Union with foreign enterprises should become law and should be sufficiently attractive to foreign corporations, that too might have a dramatic effect, especially upon foreign opinion.

In agriculture, where the People's Republic of China began its remarkable economic advance ten years ago, Gorbachev has increased state procurement prices and encouraged contract brigades, which decentralize authority and introduce incentives through piece work and a bonus system.

In Kursk, an experiment plows profits back into a cooperative and ties earnings directly to productivity. Above all, Gorbachev has been discussing *Prodnalog,* a tax in kind for collective and state farms. This might have the same effect as a similar tax with which Lenin introduced the NEP. Indeed, many foreign observers remain surprised that Gorbachev has not adopted the NEP policies, retaining control of "the commanding heights" of the political and economic system and allowing the released energies to resolve the economic issues. Gorbachev could also weaken opposition to such economic policies by wrapping the mantle of the Great Lenin around himself and this approach.

Thus far, Gorbachev has retained the political and economic system without significant change and has only introduced more discipline, enthusiasm, and efficiencies. These small changes may have significant temporary influence upon production and may even lead Gorbachev further toward restructuring than he plans to go. However, the Central Committee meeting in June 1987 on economic reform and the special party conference in 1988 on democratizing the party, but only the party and only up to the regional level, are critical for Gorbachev and significant progress toward "restructuring."

SOCIAL AND DEMOGRAPHIC ISSUES

The loyal and passive Soviet peoples have always rallied to their government and state when these have been in hazard, and they have demonstrated enormous recuperative abilities in the most grueling circumstances. They will continue to show these qualities. However, they are increasingly dissatisfied. This is because Soviet achievements have created a differentiated social structure and rising expectations, because of increased knowledge of the benefits people in the advanced industrial states enjoy and of the special advantages their privileged exploiters possess, and because of the increasing strains and shortages of recent years. As a great historian wrote of an earlier critical period, the Soviet Union is "a swollen state, a spent society." It must now replenish the strengths of society or face drastic decline.

Thus social and demographic issues are becoming increasingly obvious and grave. The state in its obsession with economic and military growth has paid inadequate attention to the visible and invisible infrastructures which underlay all modern societies, so that neglected housing, transportation, and health care have created serious social problems and undermine the bases of Soviet power. Alcoholism is a social disease in both sexes and even among the young, one against which even a forceful and dramatic campaign will make little progress.

Demographic trends show a very low rate of population growth among the Russians and the others who live in European Russia, but a rate two and a half times higher among the Muslim Turkic peoples of Central Asia. Indeed, the Soviet Union is already the largest Muslim power in the world, and one of every five Soviet citizens will be a Muslim in the year

2000. The rise of dissident nationalisms and the revival of Islam and other religions create very delicate issues, especially because the national and religious minorities tend to live along sensitive boundaries and have excitable and interested friends abroad. These problems are manageable for the next ten or fifteen years, but constitute a visible strain and will become ever more crucial and complicated. The rising rate of infant mortality and the declining rate of male longevity foreshadow basic issues the deferral of which will raise ever more grave consequences.

Lethargy and passivity among the workers and peasants constitute another serious issue. The unsatisfied thirst for consumer goods hampers efforts to increase productivity, and the pessimism and nostalgia evident throughout Soviet life sap the confidence supposedly characteristic of communism. In short, a corrosive crisis of morale is becoming ever more dangerous. This is especially visible among "the heroes' children," unappreciative of their elders' achievements, deeply infected by Western culture, and cynical because of the gap between what they see and what they are taught.

CULTURAL AND INTELLECTUAL LIFE

The "silence in Russian culture" that Sir Isaiah Berlin noted three decades ago and that Gorbachev has identified more recently has become more pronounced.

Basically, the Soviet Union is a formal, rigid, intolerant, and cynical society. Marxism-Leninism has little impact upon most Soviet citizens, in spite of the constant hammering and perhaps in part because of it. Evidence abounds, especially in the relentless drives against religion, that many, perhaps most, reject official values and that old and new faiths are growing, especially among the young. Signs of intellectual vigor stir beneath the surface, particularly among scientists, other intellectuals, and the media, but these flowers rarely break through the cracks. The current campaign of openness in the arts has led to a kind of flowering of literature and the theater in particular and has won Gorbachev enthusiastic support of most Soviet intellectuals, even Sakharov and some dissidents, and many foreign observers. However, Soviet, East European, and Chinese experience all suggest that the government may find the surge of ideas it has unleashed difficult to manage and that it will again restrict this thaw or blooming.

Dissidents are few - perhaps 500,000 in a population of 275,000,000 - but Lunacharsky noted that the harder one hits a nail on the head, the deeper it goes into the wood. The disaffected may represent the tip of an iceberg that is growing beneath the surface and that will become increasingly visible as time passes and as *Glasnost'* spreads.

Western culture, high and low, has swamped Soviet urban society, and seeps throughout the country. This and the character of Soviet intellectual resources indicate that the USSR is not well equipped to compete in an international competition in which culture at every level plays an increasingly important political role.

EASTERN EUROPE

The Soviet leaders consider control over Eastern Europe vital to Soviet survival. The six states and their peoples add military bases and great human and economic strengths to the Soviet Union and to communism. Their leaders, military and security as well as political, are loyal to the Soviet Union. They share most Soviet goals and policies and realize that their existence and survival depend upon the Soviet Union. These states' economies are substantially bound to that of the Soviet Union. The rulers and their people also appreciate that the Soviet leaders will not hesitate to use "raw force" to ensure control.

However, while the Soviet Union exercises hegemony in Eastern Europe, it cannot ensure security or stability. Eastern Europe resembles "the sick man of Europe" of the nineteenth century or an organism trying to reject an alien system grafted upon it in time of weakness. Eruptions of one kind or another similar to those that have broken out on occasion since 1953 are quite likely. Indeed, the NATO states should prepare policies now for the kinds of crises likely to arise in the unstable area in the next two decades.

Poland, led by a military junta, is a cancer, at the moment in remission. The Polish people have simply rejected communism, root and branch: no regime in the world faces a people and their church so united in rejection.

All these countries' rulers are handicapped by a double illegitimacy: they are communists, and they are considered agents of an alien government. Nationalisms as they have revived have turned from hostility to Germans to antagonism against the Soviets. The economic problems, except in Hungary and Eastern Germany, are like those of the Soviet Union, but are more grave, as are their social and cultural tensions and popular awareness of political incompetence and corruption.

The East European states at one time contributed economically to the Soviet Union, but they are an increasingly expensive economic liability, draining perhaps as much as twenty billion dollars a year from their Soviet neighbor. They desperately require access to Western science, technology, and energy to renovate their economies. The magnet of the West, from jazz and jeans and colas to information and computer technology, attracts them as powerfully as the sun does a sunflower.

The transfer of authority and the changes in policy and style under Gorbachev are introducing disruptions into Soviet policy for Eastern Europe, as it has every time since 1953. Finally, of course, each ruling party in each East European country must transfer authority from one set of aged leaders to another generation, an issue even more delicate than in the Soviet Union because of the nature of the economic and social strains, Western influence, the role the Soviet Union plays, and above all, the absence of the kind of collective agreement among the ruling group that prevails within the Soviet Union.

Thus, Eastern Europe constitutes an intractable problem, one which paradoxically has grown more serious as the fruits of the economic and social changes the communists have produced have grown. The Soviet

Union has no attractive options: allowing the Polish Government to honor the 1980 agreements, for example, would lead to changes unacceptable to the Soviet Government, even if those changes could be controlled within Poland and could somehow be restricted to Poland. Increasing the subsidies is difficult, if not impossible. So tighter controls, ideally unobtrusive, seem increasingly likely as do efforts to strengthen CEMA and the Warsaw Pact and to make them somehow reliable Soviet instruments.

THE WORLD OUTSIDE

The Soviet Union is becoming ever more an integral part of a shrinking world community, in spite of its rulers' efforts to isolate their peoples. The elite's level of knowledge and understanding of the world, and that of the ordinary Soviet citizen, both continue to grow. Diplomatic relations bring states together at the top, infecting all those who travel or deal with foreigners. Foreign trade, the acquisition of Western science and technologies, cultural exchanges, communists from other lands, radio broadcasts, even and perhaps especially *glasnost'* - all contacts sap the control over access to information central to the system. The Soviet rulers recognize that ignorance loses wars, but that education foments revolution - but expanded education is central for survival and progress in the twentieth century.

At another level, international politics centers upon competition between two great powers for influence and power. In this test, the Soviet's main strength, indeed almost its only resource, is military power. This has won respect and created a fear useful for Soviet political purposes, and it has helped establish communist states controlled by or loyal to the Soviet Union. However, Soviet inability to compete in economic power, cultural and intellectual vitality, and scientific and technical advance handicaps the Soviet Union in the basic competition with Western states. The poor performance of communist states in the past decade or two has reduced the attractions of that faith almost everywhere, especially in the power centers of the world. The end of the Soviet myth and the declining attractiveness of the model have affected performance and faith within the Soviet Union as well. If the People's Republic of China should prove able to maintain successfully its efforts "to achieve socialism with capitalist methods," it would produce a number of significant consequences for the Soviet Union. Thus, it would not only create a sparkling rival communist model, weakening Soviet influence throughout the world, but it would also transform this vast backward neighbor into one more prosperous, advanced, and powerful.

Of course, sudden successes abroad - in the Philippines, Central America, or South Africa, would revive Soviet power and enthusiasm. But the renewed education the expansion of Soviet power since 1975 has provided the world, especially the invasion of Afghanistan, suggest that opportunities abroad will continue to decline and will provide Soviet leaders another reason to turn inward.

CONCLUSIONS

All societies at all times face problems or challenges. Indeed, the United States at home and abroad faces a set of issues that in some ways resemble those of the Soviet Union and that may be as grave. American difficulties do not constitute an emergency nor threaten overthrow of the system, nor do those of the Soviet Union, but the Soviet dilemmas are so numerous and complicated that they may reflect a systemic crisis. The Soviet situation is as acute as in the 1920s. Then a great leader defined an inspired reversal of policy called the New Economic Policy, instilled dedication and enthusiasm, and obtained some foreign assistance in order to reconstruct the economy and create the foundations for a "new society."

The problems of the last part of this century are just as grave, but they are also cumulative, interrelated, and intricate, and they involve the Soviet Union's role in international politics. The system established in the decade before the Second World War may have outlived itself. In any case its heroic age ended some time ago. However, it is not going to collapse or change greatly. It retains great reserves of power and resources, uncontested control over society, powerful traditions of patriotism and loyalty, a sense of discipline many societies lack, and a "cake of custom" as powerful as in other established systems.

The likelihood of significant political change seems low, even under Gorbachev, and sharp economic innovations remain unlikely because drastic economic shifts would so directly affect the political system, which seems incapable of readjusting to new problems.

One of the most forceful impediments to transformation is the primacy Soviet leaders grant the military forces and foreign policy. These together provide the system its legitimacy and constitute the main instrument of Soviet power and prestige. Ideological restrictions are also important. Soviet leaders are convinced that the party alone has the right and capacity to define policy and to direct society. A third limitation is the character of the issues the system faces and the way in which they are so interrelated, as they are in all complex societies, that any action to affect one would deeply influence the others and reverberate throughout the entire system. The Soviet Union in effect resembles a delicate mobile more than a monolithic bloc.

Another limitation is the character of Soviet society, ironically one of the principal goals and achievements of more than sixty years of communist rule. No authoritarian government can expect to overcome years of encouraged inertia and passive acceptance of authority when it urges its people to respond quickly to permission or even to an order to innovate. In fact, encouraging initiative and enterprise in an authoritarian system is a contradiction in terms. Moreover, the Soviet Government could hardly expect its thousands of officials suddenly to abandon their beloved authority.

But the principal supporter of present arrangements and the abiding opponent of innovation is the system itself. The party bureaucrats and the economic managers see innovation as a challenge to ideology and control, and *control* remains the basic word in the communist vocabulary, for the leaders as well as for the "grey barons" throughout the country. Those in authority are committed by their concern for personal security and power, their ideology, and their view of the world to defend their preceptorial role and to resist any change that might challenge their position. In addition, all the other millions who benefit from communist rule are not only reluctant to accept new policies but are positioned to hamper even the most skilled and resolute rulers who seek change.

Increased Soviet participation in the world economy, welcome though that might be to all who see fruitful consequences from such an action, could not provide much assistance toward resolving the deep-seated troubles, and would in fact raise the temperature of political issues. The reluctance of the advanced industrial states to advance large credits will remain great, unless Soviet behavior is quite different from that since 1975 and unless a depression strikes the Western world. Even so, the rigidity of the Soviet planning system, its price structure, the quality of its manufactured products, and Soviet inability to produce goods other than oil and gold, both of which have internal and external limitations, to pay for imports, reduce the likelihood that greater participation in the world economy could be a *deus ex machina.*

The likelihood is therefore great that the Soviet leaders will continue to talk a great deal about change, but will emphasize labor discipline, law and order, Soviet and Russian nationalism, small economic relaxations and efficiencies, patching, tinkering, and increasing Soviet military power. They will probably reduce their costly overseas commitments, and at the same time acquire whatever foreign economic-technical assistance they can, without the infections that accompany. Small changes can of course lead gradually to large ones, but the high likelihood on domestic problems is muddling through and a slow decline or erosion of Soviet power, rather than any dramatic transformation.

Soviet foreign policy will depend as much upon the policies of the United States and its allies and upon the appearance of opportunities as it will upon the domestic sources of Soviet strengths and weaknesses. In any case, Soviet leaders will surely be as alert as they will be prudent. The Soviet Union, like most societies in apparent decline, is also likely to sharpen and improve its diplomatic and political warfare skills. Soviet sophistication in traditional political warfare, as well as in disinformation, aid to "liberation" groups, the use of proxies, and terrorism, is likely to improve as some of its other more fundamental strengths decline.

Gorbachev and those around him no doubt recognize the gravity of the Soviet plight and may reiterate Lenin's policy of the 1920s, which maintained political controls and ideological purity, allowed some freedoms in the arts, and encouraged some innovations (that proved temporary) in the economy, especially in agriculture. Such a policy, which seems sensible and even absolutely necessary to Western observers, would win the support of intellectuals and wrap the mantle of Lenin around the changes. They might weaken the barriers throughout the Soviet system that thwart innovation and release energies that would enliven the Soviet economy. Such a program would promise enormous benefits, but would also put the established system, and those who rule and benefit, at risk.

Under such a program, the party would retain full control of the commanding heights of political monopoly, the military and security forces, information, heavy industry, and foreign trade. It would also encourage family units and the expansion of private plots in agriculture, with some freedom in trade for those peasants; broadened autonomy for industrial units; some small-scale enterprise or genuine cooperatives in the production and distribution of consumer goods; increased importation of foreign capital and technology through some of the devices Lenin adopted or that the People's Republic of China encourages; and a stance and slogans in foreign policy that appear peaceable. Under such a program, the willingness to believe the Soviet Union a pacific state would burgeon in Western Europe and among credulous and fearful people throughout the world. Foreign businessmen would rush to assist, and some governments would provide easy credits. The Soviets could play with increasing skill upon the varieties of anti-Americanism that flourish around the world, launch new "peace" offensives, encourage the drift of Western Europe and the United States away from each other as their interests and policies in much of the world collide, and capitalize upon the opportunities for meddling and scavenging that will inevitably arise.

But all this is unlikely, sensible and necessary though it may seem to outsiders and perhaps even to Gorbachev himself.

Throughout the next ten or fifteen years, whatever the Soviet leaders choose to do, the principal policies upon which the United States should concentrate upon include:

1. Strengthening the American economy and resolving its basic social problems.
2. Maintaining strong and resolute military forces, including revitalized mobile conventional forces, based upon a national service act.
3. Working closely with its European, Japanese and other allies to reach an agreed definition of Soviet policies and consistent allied goals, concepts, strategies, and policies. The United States should coordinate allied defense, trade, cultural, and human rights actions toward the Soviet Union and Eastern Europe. The absence of mutual confidence, general understanding, and agreement constitutes one of the West's major handicaps.
4. Encouraging the West European states to become self-confident, to move toward further political, economic, and military unity, and to increase their ability to defend themselves.
5. Widening the Atlantic community area and encouraging other countries to benefit from increased trade with the advanced industrialized countries and the free flow of men, information, and goods in conditions that encourage them to develop and control their own economic resources.
6. Cooperating with the Soviet Union and all other states in efforts to reduce the basic problems that affect all the world, such as pollution.

7. Encouraging the Soviet Union to reform its political and economic system and to participate actively in the world economy.
8. Defining carefully with its allies that information and those technologies and equipment that all should deny to the Soviet Union because they would directly increase Soviet military capabilities, which is clearly not in the West's best interest.
9. Devising joint actions to respond to outrageous Soviet domestic and foreign policies, other than trade restrictions, which are inefficient and divisive.
10. Encouraging slow, gradual change in Eastern Europe, differentiating among the six countries and making economic assistance conditional upon continued progress toward greater independence and more open and pluralistic political, economic, and social arrangements.
11. Raising the quantity and quality of the flow of information into Eastern Europe and the Soviet Union by expanding cultural and educational exchange and broadcasts from satellites, and pressing for fulfillment of the Helsinki Agreement. Raising the level of knowledge and understanding and intensifying the Western orientation are among the most important and least expensive actions we can undertake to assist these peoples, and ourselves.
12. Recognizing that the contest with the Soviet Union will be a long one, that it will remain at heart a political struggle, that American capacity to change the Soviet system or to reduce its authority is very limited, and that no quick or early answers are likely.
13. Increasing greatly popular knowledge and understanding of the Soviet Union and of the world. In a democratic society, policy necessarily and properly requires public support: the most sensible policies will be effective only when the public understands and endorses them.

NOTE

1. Charles Wolf, Jr., K.C. Yeh, Edmund Brunner, Jr., Aaron Gurwitz, and Marilee Lawrence, *The Costs of the Soviet Empire* (Santa Monica, 1983).

Conclusion: Looking Ahead

Trying to identify and describe what has happened, particularly in the recent past, tests the knowledge and understanding of the scholar, who can never be certain that even the main elements of his analysis will prove correct. Estimating with any confidence what is likely to occur in the future, and recommending actions that even the most powerful government should undertake to affect the course of events, are even more difficult, especially in an age of such rapid change. Thus, those who looked into the future in 1945 did not anticipate or even mention computers. No one in 1985, even Mr. Gorbachev, judged that he would adopt the policies that in 1989 have stirred Soviet life and surprised Soviet citizens and even the most astute observers. Moreover, no one can anticipate coups, assassinations, natural disasters, successive poor harvests, or trade wars. In short, we "see through a glass darkly" whenever we try to determine even the basic outlines of the future.

Nevertheless, some developments within the Soviet Union and Eastern Europe have such deep and strong roots and have grown at such an increasing rate of speed over a long period that specialists everywhere agree that these states constitute "the sick man of Europe." The problems that affect these countries are so multiple, so interrelated, so structural, and so much a part of the system that they will almost certainly constitute the Soviet leaders' highest priority for at least the next decade.

The Soviet Union will remain a powerful military state and perhaps a destabilizing force in the world. However, whoever the leaders and whatever their particular policies, the Soviet Government will almost certainly continue the recent emphasis upon turning energies and ambitions away from the world. The Brezhnev era, in which the party maintained an ineffective command economy and authoritative political system, ignored the fundamental economic and social weaknesses. The Gorbachev years, in which the leaders launched a restructuring program, have brought into vivid light these shortcomings and the horrors and crimes of the past. Together, this quarter of a century under different rulers has helped bring on the present crisis, which has its foundations in the system established seventy years ago. They have shaken faith throughout Soviet society and created such political and economic turmoil that the Soviet Government must concentrate upon drastic domestic changes and trimming its international commitments.

The likelihood is high that the Soviet Union for economic reasons will reduce its military forces and expenditures dramatically, no doubt in such a way that it will obtain maximum strategic and political benefits. It will direct deliberately dramatic foreign policy excursions mainly toward Western Germany and Japan, who have recovered from 1945 far more impressively than has the USSR. Thus, it will seek to transform its retreat into a victory, to swing these crucial states away from their allies, and to obtain access to their capital, science, and technology.

On the western fringes of the Soviet empire, Poland and Hungary in particular have moved slowly and fitfully through appalling domestic failures and hazards toward increasing independence, more pluralistic forms of government, and market-oriented economies. The other states in this part of Europe, except Eastern Germany, suffer problems of the same nature, and will ultimately follow the same tortuous paths as a new generation assumes leadership, or will stumble further into economic deterioration and political desperation. The unbinding of Soviet rule over this part of Europe has quickened as the weakness of the Soviet Union has become more apparent, and the likelihood for continued drift away from Soviet rule is high. If the Soviet Government should try to block or reverse this flow, the internal and external penalties it would suffer would be staggering.

The United States should realize from the experience of the last fifty years that its capability to affect the politics, policies, and conduct of the Soviet Union, and even of Panama, are limited. Accepting these restrictions should constitute the first principle: the United States and its allies should see themselves as gardeners, not mechanics.

Americans should also appreciate that the most important American instruments are the character of its political, economic, and social system and the way it conducts itself at home and abroad. The United States should therefore concentrate upon improving its political structures and society and resolving or at least reducing the problems that fester and the others that will surely succeed them. Maintaining strong economic growth without high inflation, reducing the twin deficits, and avoiding an economic recession are parts of the same crucial foundation for American policies.

The American Government and its allies should also concentrate upon maintaining the cohesion and vitality of their alliances, which have survived many stresses, strains, and predictions of collapse. They will now encounter skillful and dramatic ploys aimed at increasing the significance of pacifism and neutralism, doubts about the need for nuclear forces in Western Europe, and conflicts over trade policies. They must maintain a credible and resolute defense, not only against military pressure but also against terrorist attacks, because the sense of security essential for peaceful progress rests upon the freedom from fear that the United States and the alliances have provided for forty years. A flexible and imaginative policy that assures security and at the same time helps arrange the mutual reduction of Soviet and Western armed forces therefore occupies a high priority.

The third basic assignment should be managing or helping organize a smooth shift in national responsibilities, as Japan and Western Europe in particular, but other states and areas as well, acquire additional economic power and political authority. The advances of these states represent substantial achievements, not a defeat. Successfully modifying the new division of responsibilities will reduce in a blessed fashion the heavy share of responsibilities that the United States has borne for forty years.

The good sense and grace with which the United States acts toward less advantaged states, particularly its near neighbors in Central and Latin America, will greatly affect its relations with its allies and the communist states as well. The United States should continue to defend its national interest and help ensure that no foreign state acquires a military base in the Americas, but accept generously the decisions these peoples make. It should encourage these states, including Cuba, to work toward genuine independence, open and pluralistic governments, and steady economic progress.

Political realities within the United States and the Soviet Union as well make rapid and vast changes in their policies and their relationships with each other unlikely and even hazardous. The ideological and strategic issues that separate East and West will not yield to grand plans or large agreements. The West should first of all encourage the Soviet Union to engage in a deliberate process of moving toward an open, pluralistic society that cooperates with others in trying to resolve the many universal problems the world faces. The Soviet leaders should know that only actions that increase Western trust will acquire them access to the treasures they need to create a modern economy. Relaxing controls and allowing ever more political, economic, and cultural freedoms, withdrawing their troops and those of their surrogates from other states, reducing the military threat they pose to the world, and ending support for aggressive dictatorships, terrorist movements, and other disruptive forces will achieve gradually increased access to the imagination and riches of the Western world.

The existence, vitality, and conduct of the Western states and their insistence that the communist states advance toward more open and pluralistic societies constitute the most important instrument Western states and peoples can provide to the peoples of Eastern Europe. They must win independence and freedoms by themselves from communist governments now willing to share some power only because they have no alternative. The West should of course recognize Soviet concerns about another form of invasion from or through its Western neighbors. It should not strengthen these governments, or the Soviet Government, by providing easy economic aid. It should refuse even to consider any agreements, under either benign or threatening auspices, that would restrict these peoples' right to self-determination by requiring they remain "within a socialist framework" or a "Commonwealth of Socialist States."

Instead, the Western states should use their diplomatic, economic, and cultural resources and skills to help these peoples quietly and gradually move along the narrow lane opening before them.

The Western states should maintain the national and international programs that have assisted these peoples first to survive and then to advance: firm military defenses, frank criticisms of violations of agreements and human rights, honest information through Western radio broadcasts and other avenues of communication, and generous responses to the dismantling of controls and restrictions.

The United States and its allies should establish a task force, joint policy planning center, or clearing house to stimulate ideas that will put Western resources to effective use at a time when opportunities multiply for non-threatening progress. The West should utilize the Soviet and East European thirst for increased access to the West by pressing for abolition of restrictions on the free flow of men, information, and goods and for opening cultural centers, libraries, bookstores, and programs for teaching Western languages and industrial, agricultural, and commercial skills. It should encourage increased voluntary participation by universities, private foundations, churches, trade unions, organizations of scientists and other scholars, and other such groups in increasing knowledge and in expanding communications. It should also encourage and support the efforts of private businesses and banks to assist non-party and non-government businessmen and farmers through cooperative research and production projects, managerial training, export promotion, opening access to Western markets, and joint ventures. Western governments should assist these states to resolve their foreign debt problems by encouraging debt-equity exchange, refinancing, conversion to long-term bonds, and emergency assistance.

In every instance, Western governments, private organizations, and individuals should identify and strengthen those private individuals and organizations most capable of improving the quality of life in their communities and of moving their states toward an open market and political pluralism. The progress these peoples make toward increased power-sharing and respect for human rights should help define the character and quality of assistance they receive.

In a way, the decades since 1949 have educated Western states and peoples to meet the opportunities the failures of communism now provide. The most visible Western institution equipped to attract and assist those who wish to make their societies more open and free is the European Economic Community. Those who guide this mechanism, one of a number of West European political, economic, and cultural institutions that attract and can assist the peoples in the East, should use skills acquired in creating the Common Market and in assisting Portugal, Spain, and Greece. The same policies and the same measured awards for meeting specific conditions that helped these three states achieve political democracy, sustained economic progress, and increased participation in the community's activities should guide and support the community in its policies toward the peoples of Eastern Europe. In short, the West European states should encourage these governments to undertake the same journey these other European states have made and to create and build upon new relationships with Europe and the world.

In this way, the West and the East together can, and should bring about the "break-up or gradual mellowing" of the Soviet system that was the hope and vision of 1947 and that has guided Western policy since then.

Index

Academic exchange programs, 4, 150–153, 155–156
Adenauer, Konrad, 141, 145
Afghanistan, 88, 90, 93, 104, 185, 188, 196
Agriculture, 22, 200
Albania, 9, 37, 41, 54, 58, 63, 66–67, 72, 74, 90–91, 96, 98, 104
Algeria, 26
Amalrik, Andrei, 56, 179
American Council of Learned Societies, 151
American Friends Service Committee, 151
Amnesty International, 175
Angola, 178, 199
Anti-Americanism, 6, 19, 26, 71
Antisemitism, 57
Atomic Energy Commission, 151, 158
Australia, 6
Austria, 87, 90, 137, 139–140
Austrian State Treaty, 31, 134, 140–141

Bahro, Rudolf, 101
Barghoorn, Frederick, 121–122, 124
Bay of Pigs, 6
Belgium, 137
Beria, Lavrentii, 32
Berlin, 43
Berlin, Isaiah, 56, 100, 203
Berlin airlift, 3
Berlin Conference, 140, 143
Berlin Wall, 5, 54, 62, 84, 101, 176
Beveridge, Albert, 115
Bidault, Jacques, 143
Biermann, Wolf, 101, 175
Bismarck, Otto von, 115
Blanc, Louis, 114
Bled Agreement, 31
Bohlen, Charles, 2
Bompard, Maurice, 115
Brandt, Willy, 62
Brezhnev, Leonid, 91, 104, 163, 189, 211
Brezhnev Doctrine, 53
British Broadcasting Corporation (BBC), 3, 78, 174
Building bridges, 69
Bukharin, Nikolai, 123, 125–126
Bukovsky, Vladimir, 119
Bulganin, Nikolai, 134

Bulgaria, 37, 41, 53–54, 68, 73, 81, 87, 93–94, 96–97, 101, 103
Burma, 43

Cambodia, 67, 71
Canada, 135, 137
Carlyle, Thomas, 114
Carter, Jimmy, 179, 181
Catherine the Great, 117
Catholic Church, 19, 23, 68, 72, 89–90, 93, 102, 113, 116, 118, 182
Central America, 6, 8, 199, 213
Central Intelligence Agency (CIA), 6, 158–159, 164, 178
Ceylon, 43
Chaadaev, Peter, 114, 129
Charter, 10, 77, 89, 102, 176
Chernyshevskii, Nikolai, 113
Chicherin, Georgii, 123
China. *See* People's Republic of China
Chou En-lai, 45
Cominform, 16, 31, 33, 40, 46, 58, 67, 88, 121
Commission on Security and Cooperation, 175, 179, 182
Common Market, 10, 26, 60–62, 70, 95, 99, 105, 139
Concert of Europe, 117
Congo, 27
Containment, 15–16
Convergence, 22
Cooper, James Fenimore, 115
Council for Mutual Economic Assistance (COMECON or CEMA), 41, 45, 55, 59–60, 87, 94, 205
Crimean War, 116–118
Cuba, 25, 27, 67, 178, 188
Cultural exchanges, 11, 22, 77–79, 85, 150–153, 155, 169–171, 176, 180–181, 183
  French-Soviet, 115
  German-Soviet, 115–116
  West European-Soviet, 76, 203
Cyprus, 27
Czechoslovakia, 17, 21, 45, 53–56, 59–60, 62, 68, 70, 72, 80, 83, 87–89, 92–100, 103, 143, 152, 171, 173

Danilevskii, N. Ia., 119–120

215

Darwin, Charles, 115
Department of State, 157–158, 165
　Bureau of Educational and Cultural Affairs, 151, 155
De-Stalinization, 19, 32
Detente, 62, 79, 88, 178
Deutsche Welle, 3, 78
Disengagement, 21
Dissidents, Soviet, 174–175, 177, 180, 196, 203
Djilas, Milovan, 35, 40, 93
Dostoevskii, Fedor, 112–113, 115–116, 119
Dubcek, Alexander, 54
Duclos, Jacques, 139
Dudintsev, Vladimir, 43
Dulles, John Foster, 18, 65, 69

East Berlin, 62, 68, 108
Eastern Germany. *See* German Democratic Republic
Economic Commission for Europe, 138
Egypt, 6, 43
Eisenhower, Dwight, 18, 20, 69
Embargoes, 191
Emerson, Ralph Waldo, 115
England. *See* United Kingdom
Ethiopia, 43, 199
European Defense Community (EDC), 32, 129, 138–139, 141–143, 146
European Political Community, 135

Fadeev, R. A., 119
Federal Bureau of Investigation (FBI), 158, 178
Federal Republic of Germany, 21, 25, 28, 63, 70, 75, 82–83, 94, 96, 134, 142, 145–146, 212
Federation of American Scientists, 178
Finland, 137, 145
Ford, Gerald, 65
Ford Foundation, 4, 151
Fourier, Charles, 114
France, 10, 26, 55, 90, 116, 137–138, 142–143, 147, 190
Franco-Soviet Treaty, 143
French Communist Party, 139
Fulbright Fellowship, 183
Furtseva, Ekaterina, 38

Gaulle, Charles de, 23, 26, 104
Geneva Conference, 31, 65–66, 79, 134, 143, 146
German Democratic Republic, 5, 17, 21, 35, 45, 53–54, 57, 59, 62, 65, 70, 75–76, 83–84, 87, 89, 92–94, 98, 101–104, 141–143
German refugees, 142
Germany, 10, 17, 26, 59, 116, 141–144, 147, 190
Gierek, Edward, 68, 96, 102
Ginsburg, Alexander, 175
Gladstone, William Ewart, 114–115
Glasnost', 205
Gomulka, Wladyslaw, 49, 55, 59, 68, 73–74, 89, 102

Gorbachev, Mikhail, 4, 6, 8–9, 11, 195–197, 199, 201–202, 204, 207, 211
Greece, 3, 10, 17, 26, 63, 87, 137, 177

Havermann, Robert, 101, 175
Hawthorne, Nathaniel, 115
Helsinki Final Act (Agreement), 3, 65–66, 101, 169, 172, 174, 176–180, 184
Herzen, Alexander, 119
Hitler, Adolf, 6, 15, 19
Honecker, Erich, 55
Hoxha, Enver, 41, 91
Hua Guofeng, 91
Human rights, 185
Hungarian Revolution, 35, 93
Hungarians, 10, 20
Hungary, 5, 19, 21, 23, 26, 36, 38, 41, 44–46, 50, 53–54, 58, 60, 68–69, 72, 74–75, 81, 83, 87–88, 90, 94, 96–97, 99–100, 171, 212
Husak, Gustav, 73, 96, 100

Ibsen, Henrik, 115
Ignatiev, P. N., 119
India, 24, 43, 51, 64, 197
Indonesia, 43, 51
Inflation, 99
Information Media Guarantee Program, 183
International Copyright Convention, 173, 175
International Labor Organization, 139
International Monetary Fund, 81
International Research and Exchanges Board, 151, 159
International Telecommunications Union, 175
Inter-Parliamentary Union, 187
Inter-University Committee, 151, 159–160
Iran, 90, 105
Islam, 203
Israel, 6, 137
Italian Communist Party, 177
Italy, 26, 63, 70, 90, 113, 137–138

Jamming, 174, 182
Japan, 3, 60, 64, 105, 137, 212
Jefferson, Thomas, 180
Jews, 117, 175
John Paul II, Pope, 89–90, 102, 104
Johnson, Lyndon, 28

Kadar, Janos, 54, 60, 68, 73, 89, 93, 96, 100
Kampuchea (Cambodia), 196
Karamzin, Nikolai, 111
Kardelj, Edvard, 33, 37, 43
Kennan, George, 2, 15, 16, 20–21, 50, 69, 88, 106
Kennedy, John F., 27–28
KGB, 158, 162–163
Khomiakov, Alexei, 115
Khrushchev, Nikita, 19, 21, 25, 32–38, 40–44, 50–51, 54, 71, 75, 97, 110, 113, 121–122, 134
Kol Israel, 174
Korea, Republic of (South Korea), 8, 96, 133, 196

Korean War, 18, 31, 69
Kosygin, Alexei, 163
Krimsky, George, 175
Kuusinen, Otto, 37

Lacy, William S. B., 172
Laos, 67, 71
Latin America, 213
Lebanon, 43
Lenin, V. I., 17, 42, 92, 116, 120, 122-123, 137, 180, 202, 207-208
Liberman Reforms, 60
Lippmann, Walter, 48, 66, 92, 106
Lithuania, 83
Litvinov, Maxim, 123
Ljubljana Program, 38-39, 45, 50
Lowell, James Russell, 115

McCarthy, Joseph, 19
McCarthyism, 6
Macaulay, Thomas B., 116
Maine, Henry, 115
Malenkov, Georgii, 133-134, 137
Mao Tse-tung, 44-45, 190
Marshall, George C., 16
Marshall Plan, 5, 59
Marxism-Leninism, 2, 7-8, 11, 23, 39, 43, 47, 56-57, 91, 100, 111, 115, 120-122, 133, 155, 198, 203
Medvedev, Roy, 57, 76
Mexico, 64, 96
Middle East, 8
Mikoyan, Anastas, 33, 37-38
Mill, John Stuart, 114, 130
Mindszenty, Jozsef Cardinal, 83
Molotov, Viacheslav, 32-33, 123, 140-141, 143-144
Monnet, Jean, 104
Morley, John, 114
Moscow Conference, 140
Moscow University, 111
Mozambique, 199

Nagy, Imre, 36, 40-41, 69, 88
Nasser, Gamal, 43
National Academy of Sciences, 84, 151, 158, 178
National Institute of Health, 150
Nationalism, 26-27, 55, 72, 74, 76, 104, 153, 182, 203-204
New Course, 31, 68, 93, 136
New Economic Mechanism, 72, 74, 90, 96
New Economic Policy (NEP), 202
Nixon, Richard, 6
Nordau, Max, 115
North Atlantic Treaty Organization (NATO), 10, 15-16, 20, 26, 48, 53, 61, 65, 70, 76, 105, 123, 129, 134, 141, 144-146, 204
North Korea. *See* Republic of Korea
Nuclear issues, 24-25, 28

Oder-Neisse boundary, 75, 83
Oil, 94-95, 188
Old Bolsheviks, 122-125

Olympic Games, 185
Orlov, Iurii, 175
Orthodox Church. *See* Russian Orthodox Church

Panslavs, 113, 115, 119
Pasternak, Boris, 43, 129, 179
Peace Corps, 157
Peaceful coexistence, 22, 36, 46
People's Republic of China, 2, 3, 6, 23-27, 36, 42-44, 48, 54-55, 64, 67, 70-71, 74-75, 77, 90, 93, 96, 98, 152, 164, 196, 201, 205, 208
Peter the Great, 11, 125, 180, 189
Pius IX, Pope, 115, 118
Pobedonostsev, Konstantin P., 110-114, 116, 118-119, 129
Pogodin, Mikhail, 111
Poland, 5, 9, 18, 21, 23, 44-45, 49-50, 53-56, 59-60, 62, 65, 68, 70, 72, 74-75, 81, 87-89, 92-93, 97-99, 102-103, 127, 143, 171, 204, 212
Polish Revolt, 19, 35, 54
Polycentrism, 24, 74, 91
Portugal, 10, 177, 179, 190, 196
Poznan, 19, 88
Prague, 5
Protestantism, 113
Public Health Service, 151
Pugwash, 178

Quemoy, 45

Radio Free Europe, 3, 78, 175
Radio Liberty, 3, 78, 174-175
Radio Peking, 174
Rakovskii, Mieczyslaw, 123
Rankovich, Aleksandar, 37, 39
Revisionism, 47
Republic of Korea (North Korea), 8, 96
Riasanovsky, Nicholas, 118
Rockefeller Foundation, 4
Rokossovsky, Konstantin, 19, 93
Roosevelt, Franklin D., 6, 15, 67, 82
Rumania, 4, 23, 53-55, 58, 60, 63, 66, 68, 72, 74-75, 81, 87, 90-92, 94, 99, 173
Russian Orthodox Church, 111-112

Sakharov, Andrei, 56, 76, 102, 179, 201, 203
SALT. *See* Strategic Arms Limitations Agreement
Samarin, Iurii, 115-116
Schuyler, Eugene, 115
Schweinitz, Hans von, 115
Seeley, John, 114
Self-determination, 27
Sino-Soviet relations, 3, 23, 25, 43, 91, 93
Slavophiles, 111, 113-114, 118
Solidarity, 10
Solzhenitsyn, Alexander, 76, 84, 179
Sontag, Raymond J., 7
South Korea. *See* Korea, Republic of
Soviet Union
  Dissidents, 174-175, 177, 180, 196, 203

Economic difficulties, 186, 189
Emigration, 175
Friendship societies, 136
Military power, 135, 186, 198–199, 204–205
Ministry of Higher and Specialized Education, 161–162
"Peace" campaign, 138–143
Population growth, 202
Propaganda, 110, 160, 164
Supreme Soviet, 110, 137
Spain, 10, 113, 122, 177, 179, 190, 196
Spencer, Herbert, 115
Sputniks, 21, 129
Stalin, Joseph V., 6, 9–11, 19, 31, 34, 39, 43, 54–55, 59, 67, 88, 90, 121, 123, 135, 146, 172, 189, 196
Stevenson, Adlai, 2
Strategic Arms Limitations Agreement (SALT), 172, 177
Strategic Arms Limitations Agreement II (SALT II), 82, 181
Sudan, 43
Sumner, B. H., 110, 115, 125
Sweden, 90, 137
Syria, 137

Terrorism, 8
Thorez, Maurice, 139
Tito, 16–17, 19, 32–33, 35–38, 40–49, 54, 63, 66–67, 74, 88, 92
Tocqueville, Alexis de, 1, 5, 9, 61, 93, 115, 153
Togliatti, Palmiro, 35
Tolstoi, Leo, 111, 115, 119, 129
Trade, 22, 60–61, 74, 81–82, 92, 94, 138, 185, 190–192, 205
Trotsky, Leon, 123
Truman, Harry, 67
Truman Plan, 5, 16
Turgenev, Ivan, 115
Turkey, 3, 10, 17, 26
Tvordoklebov, Andrei, 175
Twentieth Congress of the Soviet Communist Party, 19, 32–34
Twenty-first Congress of the Soviet Communist Party, 41

Twenty-fourth Congress of the Soviet Communist Party, 55, 60, 64

U-2, 42
Ulbricht, Walter, 54
United Kingdom, 26, 70, 135, 137
United Nations, 3, 15, 27, 36, 38, 43, 67, 69, 82, 139
  Charter, 84
  Children's Fund, 139
  General Assembly, 41, 90
  Security Council, 2
  United Nations Economic and Social Organization (UNESCO), 138

Vatican, 3, 83
Venturi, Franco, 119
Viet Nam, 6, 27, 69, 71, 105, 178, 188, 196
Voice of America, 78, 174
Voroshilov, Kliment, 40

Warsaw Pact, 20, 54
Watergate, 105, 178
West Berlin, 25, 53, 61, 63, 82–83, 175
West European Union, 134, 143–146
West Germany. *See* Federal Republic of Germany
White, Andrew, 115
Witte, Sergei, 116–117, 189
Workers' Councils, 34
Worker self-management, 39
World Bank, 81
World Federation of Trade Unions, 136
World Health Organization, 139
World Peace Council, 136
Wyszinski, Cardinal Stefan, 19

Yugoslavia, 3, 6, 16–17, 24, 31–44, 47–49, 54–55, 58, 63, 67–72, 74, 81, 88, 90–91, 94, 134, 137

Zarubin, Georgii, 172–173
Zemskii sobor, 118
Zhdanov, Andrei, 110, 121, 123
Zola, Emile, 115